Business Advantage

Teacher's Book
Advanced

Jonathan Birkin

CAMBRIDGE
UNIVERSITY PRESS

CAMBRIDGE UNIVERSITY PRESS
Cambridge, New York, Melbourne, Madrid, Cape Town,
Singapore, São Paulo, Delhi, Mexico City

Cambridge University Press

The Edinburgh Building, Cambridge CB2 8RU, UK

www.cambridge.org
Information on this title: www.cambridge.org/9780521179324

First published 2012

Printed in the United Kingdom at the University Press, Cambridge

A catalogue record for this publication is available from the British Library

ISBN 978-0521181846 Student's Book with DVD
ISBN 978-052-1179324 Teacher's Book
ISBN 978-1107637832 Personal Study Book with Audio CD
ISBN 978-1107666344 Audio CDs

Development of this publication has made use of the Cambridge English Corpus (CEC). The CEC is a computer database of contemporary spoken and written English, which currently stands at over one billion words. It includes British English, American English and other varieties of English. It also includes the Cambridge Learner Corpus, developed in collaboration with the University of Cambridge ESOL Examinations. Cambridge University Press has built up the CEC to provide evidence about language use that helps to produce better language teaching materials.

The *Cambridge Advanced Learner's Dictionary* is the world's most widely used dictionary for learners of English. Including all the words and phrases that learners are likely to come across, it also has easy-to-understand definitions and example sentences to show how the word is used in context. The *Cambridge Advanced Learner's Dictionary* is available online at dictionary.cambridge.org. © Cambridge University Press, Third Edition 2008, reproduced with permission.

DVD Worksheets by Jeremy Day

Acknowledgements

Author's thanks
I would sincerely like to thank Chris Capper and Neil Holloway, in particular, at Cambridge University Press for their help in supporting and suggesting ideas. I am also extremely grateful for the diligent editorial work of Helen Forrest and Jeremy Day.
Jonathan Birkin

Contents

Introduction to the course

Who is the course for?

Business Advantage is a three-level course: Intermediate (B1), Upper-intermediate (B2) and Advanced (C1).

The series as a whole is aimed at learners who wish to progress their knowledge of both English and business. It is suitable for students studying business studies and business English in higher education and for professionals in the workplace.

How is the course structured?

There are 14 units in each Student's Book. Each unit is divided into three lessons that are designed to last for 90 minutes each. The unit topics have been carefully researched and chosen to provide your learners with a comprehensive foundation in the main areas of business you would expect to find on an academic business studies course or on a general management training course.

The lessons in each unit are divided as follows:

Theory

These lessons will help your learners gain a new understanding of key business principles and ideas. You will find interviews with professors and lecturers as well as carefully researched texts by leaders in the field of business.

Practice

Here you will find case studies of real companies based on texts and interviews with business people. They will help your learners to apply the theories to the business world. We have included a wide variety of different businesses from different countries.

Skills

The skills lessons are based on real recorded communications in companies and provide learners with key skills for work. We have included skills traditionally covered in coursebooks like presentation and negotiation skills, as well as other vital skills that are often ignored by ELT books like relationship-building and decision making.

The lessons in each unit are designed so that they can be followed consecutively by the teacher or taught discretely.

After every second unit you will also find a **Writing** lesson. Each writing lesson is based around authentic materials and enables your learners to produce a variety of effective written business communications. Each lesson is designed so that learners learn about the process of writing as well as the functions; this means they can tailor each topic to their own everyday needs.

How is each lesson structured?

In each lesson you will find the following:

Introduction

This is where learners are introduced to the main content in a user-friendly format. Learners start to engage with the materials in the lesson by discussing their opinions on the topic, by interacting with visual information and completing personalisation exercises and quizzes.

Language focus

This is designed to improve and broaden vocabulary and grammatical range. The language syllabus covers the main tenses appropriate for the level plus an innovative lexical syllabus drawn extensively from research and actual examples of English used in business taken from the Cambridge English Corpus – one of the world's largest databases of language used for linguistic research. The database has been exploited to identify typical word combinations found in the data, and to inform the grammar and vocabulary focused on and used in the exercises.

Reading or Listening

Each lesson contains either a reading or a listening text. The reading and listening texts in Lessons 1 and 2 are about real business theories and practices from the point of view of experts in the field. Your learners will find the material interesting and motivating from both a linguistic and business perspective.

In Lesson 3 learners hear recordings based on real meetings from the Cambridge and Nottingham Spoken Business English Corpus (CANBEC) and other authentic materials. The language presented is the real language used in business and will help your learners improve a wide variety of business skills in a number of different situations.

Output

Each lesson builds progressively to a final output section. This is a group task where learners use the language and ideas presented to solve a problem or deal with a dilemma or issue in a business setting.

What else is there in each unit to help learners?

In each unit you will also find the following:

Critical analysis

This helps learners develop critical thinking skills by interacting with texts, theories and ideas to explore different points of view and develop their own opinions.

Intercultural analysis

Learners are encouraged to look at the material presented from the cultural point of view of the author or speaker and compare it with their own ideas and experiences. By raising intercultural awareness learners will start to develop a knowledge and understanding of where and why cultural differences occur.

Transferable skills

Learners obtain skills that can be applied to their everyday work and study outside of the English language classroom.

How was the language in the Student's Book chosen?

We have combined the language that you would usually expect on an Advanced (C1–C2) business English course with a language syllabus informed by corpus research. Every skills lesson is based on real recordings of business conversations, which means you can be confident that your students are learning real business English. Real presentations, real conversations and real negotiations – they are presented with minor editing to give your learners exposure to how business people really speak.

How flexible is *Business Advantage* for my learners' needs?

The books have a modular approach, which means that your learners don't have to study all the units from start to finish in the order they appear, although you may choose to do this.

You may decide to divide the book into different sections. One teacher may teach all the Theory sections, another the Practice lessons. Or your needs might be better met by having a dedicated writing course using the seven Writing lessons or a course focused specifically on communication skills using the 14 Skills sections. Alternatively, you may wish to pick and choose from the topics and units that are most relevant to your learners' needs.

What other material is there to support the course?

The Teacher's Book

- The Teacher's Book has been written with monolingual and multilingual class profiles in mind and includes ideas on how to use the Student's Book effectively according to whether the class is one-to-one or contains a large or small number of students. You will find detailed instructions on how to make the course work for you.
- All the units have an accompanying Worksheet that is designed to extend the work done in the Student's Book and give students support.
- There are also three Progress tests included in the Teacher's Book to further help your learners consolidate their knowledge.
- For more information on what to find in the Teacher's Book and how to get the most out of it, see below.

The Personal Study Book

- After completing each unit of the Student's Book there are exercises in the Personal Study Book that relate directly to the materials learners have studied in class.
- Learners are encouraged to become more autonomous by analysing the *can do* statements in each unit and deciding how they can improve for themselves.
- After every two units there is an extra reading based on a guru, a theory or a company. Each reading is accompanied by a set of exercises that will help learners to recycle and expand their vocabulary and business knowledge in connection with the topics they have studied in the Student's Book.
- After every two units there is also a Writing section which consolidates and extends the writing topics covered in the Student's Book.
- The Personal Study Book also comes with all of the audio from the Skills lessons in the Student's Book, with exercises to reinforce the material and extra recordings to aid with pronunciation.

DVD

There is a DVD with the Student's Book that can be used in class or at home by the students, with accompanying photocopiable Worksheets (see pages 145–160). After every second unit, you can use the DVD to offer your learners extra content on the target topic. You will find case studies, interviews and opinions on a variety of important business features. Use the material to complete the exercises and to stimulate conversation in the classroom. The video scripts are on the website: www.cambridge.org/elt/businessadvantage.

Professional English Online

On the Professional English Online website (www.cambridge.org/elt/pro) you will find regularly updated activities to use in class: a jargon-buster that looks at words in the news; a blog that keeps you up-to-date with ELT matters; articles and interviews with ELT and business experts. You will also find reviews of other books published by Cambridge University Press and competitions where you can win prizes.

Further information about getting the most out of the Teacher's Book

The Teacher's Book has been carefully written to make sure that you get the most out of the content in the Student's Book. If you are teaching one-to-one or large groups, monolingual or multilingual groups you will find it a valuable resource. In the Teacher's Book you will also find the following:

Help with business knowledge

Each unit starts off with an overview of the unit to give you more information on the theories, case studies and skills that are going to be covered. In the Student's Book you will find real business theories and real companies presented through texts based on authentic documents and re-recorded interviews with business experts. We offer extra support in the Teacher's Book, but you might also find it useful to do more online research, either in preparation for the class or with your students.

Classroom management

In the Teacher's Book there are extra suggestions for one-to-one classes, small groups and large groups, as well as procedures for monolingual and multilingual groups. You can choose to follow the instructions that best support your group of learners or use them flexibly to suit your needs as a teacher.

There is quite a lot of pair work and group work within the course, because speaking the language for only a little of the lesson is not good value for the time spent in the classroom. Learners can increase their speaking and listening time substantially if they do pair or group activities.

When forming pairs or groups, you could: make a list of pairs you want before the lesson starts or just tell them when the time comes; have an introductory mingle before learners sit down where they find themselves at a given signal; put learners together who have birthdays in the same month, have the same interests and hobbies, have the same favourite TV programme or football team, or have the same favourite food; simply move the desks around, etc.

You should monitor learners during all pair and group work exercises, as this gives them the chance to ask any questions and you the chance to correct any fundamental breakdowns in communication. If there is an odd number of students, make a group of three rather than making a pair yourself, as you will be effectively ignoring the others. Reorganise them later in the lesson and pair them with someone else so they get more chance to speak.

Error correction can be done in a variety of ways including: correcting on the spot; noting down errors and writing a worksheet to be used later; writing errors on the board and eliciting corrections; recording learners, who can then listen for and correct their own errors. You should also encourage learners to give feedback to their peers after longer pieces of dialogue.

Further ideas for the teacher and the learner

You will find extra ideas to supplement the activities in the Student's Book, such as brainstorming activities and alternative ways of setting up activities. Brainstorming can be used effectively through the use of spidergrams, mind maps and general discussions at the start of a topic or activity. It is important to remember that during the brainstorming stage all ideas have equal value, so do not reject any of your learners' ideas during this stage.

In both the Student's Book and the Teacher's Book you will find a number of activities where learners are asked to personalise and speak about their own experiences around a given subject. This is important as it promotes fluency and gets learners to think about the topic from their own point of view. In the Teacher's Book you will find ideas for how to do this and in the Student's Book learners are encouraged to personalise frequently before looking at the opinions of others through the Intercultural analysis and Critical analysis sections. Nevertheless, think about how the topic relates to your specific learners and their cultural backgrounds and life experiences to make sure that they get the most out of the materials.

Some of the concepts taught in *Business Advantage Advanced* will be completely new to some learners, so it is important that you check that your learners have understood what has been taught from a topical and linguistic point of view. In the Student's Book and Teacher's Book you will find concept-checking questions, but you may also feel the need to ask your own questions or to elicit information before starting an activity. You might like to try the 'traffic-light method' with your students, where they hold up a green card if they fully understand the information, orange if they are unsure and red if they need further in-depth help.

Every lesson in *Business Advantage* leads up to an output activity, which is designed to allow learners to demonstrate what they have learned in the lesson and to consolidate their knowledge; this allows learners to have a freer practice and to develop fluency. You should try to set up groups for this activity in a way that allows all members to contribute. Where an individual has a longer piece of dialogue you might like to ask other learners in the group to make notes and offer feedback. You could record or video the output sessions to use as feedback or to show progress over the course. In the Teacher's Book you will also find notes on how to exploit the material at each stage of the output.

Using the audio

You will find ideas on how to exploit the audio in both the Student's Book and the Teacher's Book, and the instructions given provide for a variety of texts and ensure that learners are orientated towards the text before they listen. In general, learners are given the opportunity to listen to each recording twice.

You may like to alternate tasks and exploit the recordings in different ways. You might like to try jigsaw listening, predicting content before listening or further exploiting the recordings for pronunciation practice and identification of linguistic features. It is important that learners are exposed to as much listening as possible. You will find extra listening practice in the Personal Study Book and on the DVD that accompanies the Student's Book that your learners can use for extra practice at home. You may also wish to guide your students to business podcasts and interviews that are available on the Internet to study in their own free time.

Additional materials

You will find photocopiable Worksheets in the Teacher's Book that will help your learners to further consolidate their knowledge of the topics, grammar and vocabulary on offer in the Student's Book (see pages 127–144). There are also three Progress tests for you to use in class (see pages 126–126). In the Personal Study Book learners will find three more tests, additional exercises, and reading and listening practice for use in their free time.

For regularly updated activities, vocabulary that's in the news and for your own professional development, visit www.cambridge.org/elt/pro for all of your business English needs. We also advise you to use *Grammar for Business* as a valuable reference guide and the *Cambridge Advanced Learner's Dictionary* for the exercises that require further vocabulary work.

1 Market entry strategies

Overview of the unit

1.1 Theory: An overview of market entry strategies

'The most important single fact about a free market is that no exchange takes place unless both parties benefit.'

Milton Friedman

Market entry is when a company or individual sells a new or existing product to a group of consumers not previously targeted in any geographical region. It can be achieved through a variety of means including acquisition, cooperation, expansion of distribution channels or innovation. The option a seller takes when deciding how to enter a market depends on the country and the product or service that is being sold. Furthermore, each option has its own legal and financial implications.

Common market entry options include direct exporting, where the seller contacts potential customers overseas and sells to them directly, or uses an agent who takes a percentage for their efforts. Indirect exporting involves the seller selling to a distributor who then resells directly. Other market entry strategies include a partnership or joint venture, where a local company is set up and is authorised to sell, represent or manufacture the seller's product. There is also licensing and franchising, whereby the seller authorises another individual or company to use their intellectual property. This gives the licensee or franchisee the right to manufacture the product using the seller's technology and/or the ability to operate the seller's business model and brand. Royalties are given as a percentage of sales from licensed intellectual property.

Finally, there is Greenfield development, where manufacturing facilities in the target market are established and built up at the beginning.

1.2 Practice: Entering the global market

Profile: Quintessentially

Quintessentially is a British company founded in 2000 by Ben Elliot, Aaron Simpson and Paul Drummond. It is headquartered in London and has over 60 offices worldwide, a portfolio of 32 sister businesses and a staff of almost 700 covering its market. Developing an idea based on exclusive hotel 'concierge' services, the company describes itself as a 'luxury lifestyle company' providing a tailor-made, individual and specialist service which is available round the clock, every day of the year. Its ethos is to provide specialist advice, insider access and exclusive benefits in the areas of property, art, fashion, dining, luxury travel, event production and publishing.
As the world's leading private members' club it provides unlimited access to privileges, preferential rates and bespoke services to clients seeking travel bookings, restaurant recommendations and access to exclusive events such as award ceremonies and film premieres.

1.3 Skills: Brainstorming

Brainstorming is synonymous with idea generation and is quite often a face-to-face group task, where the group combine their thought processes in a creative atmosphere to find solutions to a problem. In addition to the face-to-face group context, brainstorming can also use new electronic media such as video conferencing. It can also happen on a one-to-one basis, which some commentators think is more focused.

Overall, the effectiveness of brainstorming techniques is measured in terms of the quality and quantity of the ideas generated in relation to the amount of time and effort put in. It is influenced by participants welcoming outlandish ideas, postponing judgement and generating as many ideas as possible within an atmosphere where the ideas generated can be combined and improved upon without loss of face.

1.1 Theory: An overview of market entry strategies

Introduction

1 Group learners to discuss products they use and their origin and to fill in the table. Alternatively, in small groups, brainstorm brands and their nationality on the board.

2 Learners discuss the questions in their groups or hold a class discussion.

> ***Suggested answers***
> Possible risks: not knowing the market, not understanding the customers' needs and habits, paying too much for services and supplies, foreign currency devaluations, political risks, war.
> Possible opportunities: sales growth in new markets, economies of scale with potentially lower unit costs, understanding new ways of doing things, i.e. gaining expertise and know-how.

Listening: Defining different types of market entry strategies 1.02

1 Learners work alone to complete the task then check in pairs.

2 Play 1.02 and elicit the answers.

> ***Answers***
> 1 e 2 a 3 b 4 f 5 c 6 d

3 Play the track again for learners to take notes. Elicit the advantages and disadvantages.

> ***Answers***
> 1 Indirect exporting – Advantages: Export houses are easy for foreign companies to use. Useful as a first entry step to get a feeling for a new market.

2 Direct exporting – Advantages: Using a company that already produces other complementary products allows you to access their client base.
3 Acquisition – Advantages: You acquire a presence in the country with a ready list of customers. Disadvantages: Problems integrating your acquisition into your own existing business. Acquisition will require some restructuring. Problem of valuation – difficult to know how much the company is really worth.
4 Greenfield development – Advantages: You can design everything afresh. You don't have difficulties of integration associated with acquisition. Disadvantages: No customer base and no distribution and sales structure and network.
5 Joint venture – Disadvantages: 80% failure rate in first five years. Local company will eventually grab your know-how and technology and then end the partnership.
6 Franchising – Advantages: Gives franchisor a lot of control – for example, you can stipulate the price and the way the product is sold.

Audio script
Dr Dennis De
Indirect exporting
Small and medium-sized companies can use export agents based in the exporter's home country, or use export houses to enter international markets. They buy from the supplier and sell to their customers in a different country. If most of the companies or the customers you want to address, let's say in Japan, don't know you, they don't know how reliable you are as a supplier. Or how good and reliable your products are. So if an export house already has good relationships with customers, it's very easy for foreign companies to use them. Companies use the service of export houses and export agents as a first entry step to get a feeling for the market.
Direct exporting
At some point, after testing the market through indirect exporting, you might look for a corporate partner in the target market you're exporting to. That could be a distributor or could also be another company; it's usually not a competitor, but a company that sells a certain variety of products and can nicely complement its product portfolio with your product. So they have their customers in the country already and you're basically surfing that.
Acquisition
Acquisition can be a very interesting way of entering a country because you're acquiring a presence in a country and a list of customers this company happens to have already. So that makes life easier for you. You might even have some production within the country; all of that is very helpful. The problem often is integrating your acquisition. You'll have some restructuring to do, and some integrating of this new business with your business. The other problem is one of paying the right price. What is the company really worth?
Greenfield development
If you do a Greenfield it's like planting a new garden; you can design everything afresh according to your plans. Completely new production facilities. There's a lot of freedom – you don't have all the difficulties and integration that you have with acquisition. So these are huge advantages. The disadvantage is that you don't have a customer base you start off with. So you're not buying into a given distribution or sales structure.
Joint venture
A joint venture involves two companies setting up a third together that they jointly own – the new joint venture company. In my experience it's not a useful strategy for companies to pursue, as roughly eighty percent of all joint ventures actually fail within the first five years. That's because the motivation behind setting up the JV is different for the two companies involved. Basically the local company, in China for example, wants to gain know-how and technology and offers access to its customers in China to the international company through a fifty-fifty joint venture. Eventually the local company will have understood and grabbed the know-how and doesn't need you any longer, because it has the access to its customers anyway.
Franchising
Franchising is a sales model – a distribution model. So you have a particular product, or a way to serve a product, like coffee for instance. Take Starbucks. This is the right to serve coffee in a certain way with certain mugs and a certain logo and in a certain fashion – a system. And you. as the franchisor, can rent out this right, and charge the franchisee a percentage of their turnover for the right to run the franchise. The franchise model is going to give you a lot of control because when you rent out the right to sell your products using your brand you do so under certain conditions. You may want to stipulate the way the product is sold for instance, the way it's presented. You might even define the price at which it is sold.

Critical analysis

Pair learners to discuss the questions before eliciting a few of their ideas.

Suggested answers
The main advantage of a joint venture is that it doesn't require a vast amount of funds to set up. It therefore gives the company the possibility to access new markets, resources and specialised staff while also sharing the risks and costs with a partner.

Language focus: Market entry terms and concepts

1 Pair learners to complete the descriptions then check with the class. Alternatively, ask learners to write a brief description of the terms before matching them and checking.

Answers
1 electronic distribution
2 overseas production
3 risk exposure
4 exit strategy
5 profit opportunity
6 control
7 commitment

2 Briefly discuss the question with the class as a whole.

Answers
Overseas production would be included in: joint ventures, acquisition, franchising (each franchisee is a service delivery centre in that new market), Greenfield site development (new production facilities abroad).

Reading: Entry strategy overview

1 Learners work in pairs to predict if the statements are true or false. They read the text to check and feed back to the class.

> ***Answers***
> 1 False (in indirect exporting there is no direct contact with customers)
> 2 False (there is no sequential process and each strategy involves differing levels of risk)
> 3 False (smaller companies have fewer options)
> 4 True
> 5 True
> 6 False (it is often hard to change without substantial risk)
> 7 False (success depends on the ability to configure the need for profit with exposure to risk)
> 8 True

2 Learners discuss the question in pairs before feeding back to the class.

Output: Select an appropriate market entry strategy

Stage 1

Put learners into three groups of roughly equal size and direct each group to the relevant pages. Allow a few minutes for reading, and then check their understanding of the roles, e.g. *What advantages and disadvantages do you have to discuss?*

Stage 2

Regroup learners to include at least one member of the groups in stage 1 to retell what they have read and decide on the best market entry. You may wish to take a whole class vote on the best market entry strategy.

1.2 Practice: Market entry strategies

Profile: Quintessentially

Introduction

1 Write *concierge* on the board and elicit what it could mean, e.g. doorman, advisor, porter. Ask learners to read the definition and discuss possible services as a whole class.

> ***Suggested answer***
> Guests could use a concierge service to help them organise bookings for theatres, events and trips and to book taxis.

2 Pair learners in larger classes to discuss similarities and differences and elicit a few of their ideas.

> ***Suggested answer***
> The concierge service in a hotel and the service that Quintessentially provides are similar in that they can both organise bookings and tickets for places and events in the local area you are staying. However, Quintessentially go beyond the normal service offered by a hotel in that they can also help with investments, deal with more unusual requests and offer assistance in different geographical locations. You are not dependent on staying in the hotel.

Listening 1: Quintessentially client profile (1.03)

Learners predict the answers then listen to the recording to check. Play 1.03 again if necessary then check as a class.

> ***Answers***
> 1 60% male: 40% female
> 2 35–55 (but can be younger)
> 3 business people and entrepreneurs, also celebrities and models
> 4 travel a lot, like the finer things in life, do exciting and interesting things
> 5 closed Sydney Harbour Bridge for a marriage proposal

> ***Audio script***
> **Interviewer:** Can you tell us something about who the typical Quintessentially member is?
> **Paul Drummond:** The typical profile is sixty percent male, forty percent female and between thirty-five and fifty-five, but obviously can be younger or older. They tend to be business people or entrepreneurs, and successful in their own right. Obviously we have celebrities in the entertainment business, models and so on, but typically it is your high net worth business traveller, or business executive.
> **Interviewer:** And in terms of personality, lifestyle and aspirations?
> **Paul Drummond:** The key determining factor is that members travel a lot. They are typically people who like the finer things in life and are sophisticated in that way, and like to do exciting and interesting things. They won't be reclusive millionaires.
> **Interviewer:** What kind of unusual requests do members make?
> **Paul Drummond:** The first thing I want to say is that the majority of what we do is very practical – assisting members when they are going from A to B to C to D. But in terms of unusual requests there have been many: for example, we closed the Sydney Harbour Bridge so a member could propose to his partner at the top of it.

Intercultural analysis

Pair learners to discuss the questions then elicit a few of their ideas.

> ***Suggested answer***
> Wealthy people are more internationally mobile than other sections of the population; they may well have studied overseas and have friends, contacts and interests abroad. As such there is a high probability that the lifestyle, aspirations and tastes of the rich in one country will be internationalised. This means in practice that luxury lifestyle companies such as Quintessentially can offer more standardised services. Cultural differences will still be apparent, but there will be less need for high levels of differentiation of products and services.

Listening 2: Characteristics of new country markets and local partners 1.04

1 Ask learners to predict possible answers in pairs.

2 Play 1.04 before re-pairing learners to check answers. Elicit what Quintessentially does when it looks for a new market, what it assumes and what the main aim is.

> ***Answers***
> 1 high net worth individuals
> 2 vibrant restaurant scene
> 3 existing membership network
> 4 very important
> 5 think again
> 6 well positioned
> 7 entrepreneurial
> 8 the brand's sake

> ***Audio script***
> **Interviewer:** What are some of the issues you consider when deciding on entering a new country market?
> **Paul Drummond:** We look to see whether there's a good base of high net worth individuals who could potentially be members. Is there a vibrant restaurant scene, a nightclub scene, events party scene?
> **Interviewer:** How do you choose a local partner?
> **Paul Drummond:** Typically we're approached through our existing membership network. Somebody has joined up, really liked the service and then gone 'Well, you're in New York and you're in London–why aren't you in Kuwait, or Saudi Arabia?' And then we have gone and met with them, got to know more about them and then worked out if there is a business opportunity for them and for us in their city.
> **Interviewer:** How important are first impressions when you actually meet that potential partner for the first time?
> **Paul Drummond:** Oh, I think they're very, very important, because it is fundamentally a people business. So if your first impressions aren't spot on, or aren't positive anyway, then you need to think again. I mean, it's not a hundred percent as I'm sure you know, but this business is driven by the dynamism of the individuals in it. And so we take it as read that potential partners are well connected, sophisticated and well positioned within, you know, whatever country it is. What I'm always looking for is people who are entrepreneurial. People who have lots of energy and are driven to succeed. What we don't really want are people who are attracted by the brand for the brand's sake.

3 Pair learners into different nationalities if possible to discuss the questions. Re-pair them to report on their discussions. You could extend the activity using a game of word association with 'first impressions', 'high net worth individual' 'attractive market' etc.

> ***Suggested answer***
> 1 Having liquid assets generally means they have money to spend on enjoying the type of lifestyle that companies such as Quintessentially promote. Wealthy people with property assets but minimal cash are unlikely to sell their assets to finance a lifestyle of spending on services promoted by Quintessentially.

Listening 3: Quintessentially's market entry strategy 1.05

1 Focus on the diagrams. Elicit how learners would describe them, e.g. *hub*, *spoke*, *wheel*, *hierarchical*, then discuss the question as a whole class.

> ***Suggested answer***
> Diagram A shows a company with branches that are answerable to the head office, but there is less hierarchy and we can assume more autonomy to make decisions locally. Diagram B shows a company with a line of hierarchy where everything is controlled by the head office.

2 Learners predict their answers, listen to the recording, and then check their answers.

> ***Answers***
> 1 franchise model
> 2 Diagram A
> 3 The partner pays the capital costs to set up the office, which also allows for fast expansion; a local partner knows and understands the local culture and market.
> 4 It allows the company to provide a consistent high standard of service.

> ***Audio script***
> **Interviewer:** What is Quintessentially's preferred method of entry into a new international market?
> **Paul Drummond:** Our preferred one is through a franchise model. We've got our own offices which we own a hundred percent of, and we operate a kind of hub and spokes structure. So in each of the regions of the world we have a wholly owned office. So America is New York, London is Europe, Dubai is Middle East and Africa, and Hong Kong is the Far East. And then off that we typically run franchises which are managed by the hub office. There are a number of reasons for that – one is, obviously, the partner takes the capital costs involved in setting up the office. And I don't think we would have expanded as quickly as we have without that. But it's not just about the cost side of things. It's actually very important for the cultural side too. What do I know about the local society and contacts in, for example, South Korea and Seoul? Well, now it's a lot more, but before it was very little.
> **Interviewer:** What kind of control of your international operations does Quintessentially head office feel is desirable?
> **Paul Drummond:** We are a brand and service business, so it's important that the brand is projected in a consistent way across the world. And it's important that when a member goes to Athens or São Paulo, that they are treated the same, at the same high level. And so control is a key factor – I mean, it's a cliché, but 'you are only as strong as your weakest link', and if a member has a horrific experience in, er, Seoul or Tokyo, even if they mostly spend their time in London or New York, then they're going to remember that experience.

Transferable skill: Using a diagram to take notes

1 Replay 1.05 for learners to label the correct diagram before feedback.

> ***Answer***
> The wheels in Diagram A are the regional markets: America, Europe, Middle East and Africa, Far East. The hubs (centres) of the wheels are the four hub cities for these markets: New York, London, Dubai, Hong Kong.

2 Learners discuss the questions in pairs before comparing their answers in groups.

> ***Answers***
> 1 The ends of the spokes represent the franchise offices. The hub cities are wholly owned branches of Quintessentially. These wholly owned offices manage the franchises for that particular region.
> 2 'Hub and spokes' is both a metaphor and a visual representation of an international organisational structure. It refers to a wheel where the hub is clearly the centre of operations, to which the individual spokes are attached.

Language focus: Adding emphasis to explanations

1 Focus learners' attention on the sentences and elicit how they are constructed. You could draw attention to the term 'introductory phrases' and their construction.

> ***Answers***
> These sentences begin with the word *What* or a noun phrase such as *The key determining factor is …* , *The first thing I want to say is …* The first part of the sentence finishes with a form of the verb *to be*. Both parts of the sentence contain a verb. These types of constructions are known as *cleft sentences*.

2 Learners work in pairs to think of more examples. Then elicit ideas from the class, e.g. *the main advantage is*, *the big disadvantage is*, *our biggest concern is*.

> ***Suggested answers***
> the main advantage is … , the big disadvantage is … , our biggest concern is … , the biggest task facing us is … , the main reason is … , the thing is … , What is important here is … , What we need is …

3 Write the sentences on the board and elicit learners' ideas on how to make them stronger.

> ***Suggested answers***
> 1 What is important to remember is (that) joint ventures often fail.
> 2 The benefit of the franchise model is (that) it allows Quintessentially to standardise quality.

4 Learners complete the sentences individually. Then pair them to compare their ideas. Ask them to agree or disagree with each other's views. Alternatively, in smaller classes, ask a learner to read out a sentence and ask the others to agree or disagree with the statement.

> ***Suggested answers***
> 1 … to decide if you can do business with this person.
> 2 … recruiting senior managers with strategic vision.
> 3 … that they understand the local market.
> 4 … to get good PR coverage in local markets.
> 5 … failing to find the right local partner.

Output: Selecting a franchise partner in a new country market

Stage 1

Group learners appropriately and refer them to page 137 to read the profiles. Ask them to come to agreement about which partner they would sign a contract with and why.

Stage 2

Ask learners to complete the sentences about their choice individually. Then make larger groups for them to come to a consensus agreement about where to open an office.

Alternatively, in smaller classes you could assign one market to each learner and ask them to defend their choice to the rest of the group using the summary sentences.

1.3 Skills: Brainstorming

Introduction

1 Pair learners to organise the stages of brainstorming, then form new pairs to compare their ideas and feed back to the whole class briefly.

> ***Answer***
> 4, 2, 5, 1, 3

2 Group learners and ask them to think of as many different uses for an everyday object as they can. You may wish to use pictures instead of objects. You could do this by setting a target, at least ten different uses. Re-group them to report back on their discussions.

Listening 1: Principles of running a classic brainstorming session 1.06

1 Learners predict the guidelines they think will be mentioned and then listen. As feedback, discuss the importance of the non-mentioned points as well as those that are mentioned.

> ***Answer***
> Guidelines mentioned: 1, 4, 5, 7, 8, 10, 11

> ***Audio script***
> **Manager:** One of the best ways of generating ideas is brainstorming. Everybody used to brainstorming? It's really easy, very easy. What you do, you have your group together, and you have a facilitator, somebody that presents the problem, and you also have somebody that's going to be the scribe. Their job is just writing – on a whiteboard or a flipchart. You sit round and you tell them that they can say anything they like, no holds barred, and nobody's going to criticise anything they say. The problem is presented, and they think about it for a minute, and then they say anything that comes into their head. And I mean anything. And the scribe just writes it up, as fast as he can.The idea is that it's quantity that breeds quality. Because the more ideas you get, the better your problem-solving is likely to be. If you only get a few ideas, you've only got a few things to look at. Whereas the more ideas you get, the more chances you've got of getting something that's really good. But you don't at any stage say, 'What did you say that for?' – you know, something like that, you just don't do that sort of thing. You allow people to say what they like, write it down. Also you have to set a time limit because people get tired, it takes a lot of energy to do this, and concentrate on it. So you set your time limit, right we'll have say twenty minutes, half an hour at the most, then you stop and look at it, and say 'Anybody want to add anything else?' When you've finished, you just tear off all your flipcharts, and put them up round the room so people can read them. You then move on to the selective phase where you start to narrow …

2 Group learners to discuss the questions before briefly discussing them as a whole class.

> ***Answers***
> 1 Guideline 8
> 2 In the selective phase, people select information that best solves the problem posed at the beginning of the brainstorming session. Whilst the emphasis in the first phase is on generating a large quantity of ideas, the emphasis in the second, selective phase is on quality. The selective phase is more controlled, and creative and lateral thinking tend not to be used.

Listening 2: A problematic brainstorming session 1.07

1 Write *aim* on the board and elicit possible meanings, e.g. *point*, *purpose*, *reason*, *target*, before instructing them to listen for the aim of the session and elicit the answer.

> ***Answer***
> The aim is to list the reasons why they need to be consistent when dealing with customer enquiries.

> ***Audio script***
> **Manager:** ... that's the situation. Erm, what I'd like to do is now if maybe ... if you can kind of work in groups or perhaps two or three of you on the ... on the flipchart. List down reasons why you think that we need to be consistent with the way we deal with customer enquiries. Anything that goes through your head, such as the need to follow a company standard. Also, remember the customer feedback was that we are inconsistent in answering calls. That was particularly ...

2 Pair learners to discuss the questions before re-pairing them to report their discussions.

> ***Answer***
> There is no problem posed which the participants need to solve. Instead, they are given the solution and told to come up with reasons to support it. In addition the manager 'leads' participants to the answer that he wants – the reference to following the company standard and customer feedback. Classic brainstorming sessions allow for creative thinking.

Language focus: Using fluent pronunciation features to move discussions forward 1.08–1.10

1 Learners predict possible links. Then listen to mark them before comparing in pairs and giving class feedback.

> ***Answers***
> 2 Mandy, what do‿you think‿about that?
> 3 That's‿a great‿idea!
> 4 What‿about building‿on Paul's‿idea to ...

> ***Audio script***
> 1 Anyone else got anything to add here?
> 2 Mandy, what do you think about that?
> 3 That's a great idea!
> 4 What about building on Paul's idea to ...

2 Pair learners to practise saying the sentences. Discuss why the words are linked.

> ***Answers***
> The rule is that we link two words together when the end of the first word finishes with a consonant or consonant cluster (e.g. /ŋk/ in *think*) and the start of the second word begins with a vowel (e.g. /ə/ in *about*).

3 & 4 Ask learners to say the sentences aloud before they write them. Elicit their ideas on the board. Then play 1.09 before asking learners to repeat the sentences. You could also ask learners to write down what they hear, and then say them. Elicit the standard spelling on the board.

> ***Answers and audio script***
> 1 We're going to start by looking at ...
> 2 How about going with Ian's idea to ...
> 3 Let's go with this idea of ...
> 4 Maybe we should go with Dave's idea of ...

5 Play 1.10 and elicit which slogan matches which company.

> ***Answers***
> 1 McDonald's
> 2 L'Oréal
> 3 Nike

> ***Audio script***
> 1 I'm lovin' it
> 2 Because you're worth it
> 3 Just do it

6 Replay 1.10 , asking learners to write the slogans in full. They could say the slogans individually or you could say them as a whole class.

> ***Answers***
> 1 McDonald's: I'm lovin' it (aymlovinit)
> 2 L'Oréal cosmetics: Because you're worth it (becuzyaworthit)
> 3 Nike: Just do it (jusdoit)

Critical analysis

Pair learners to discuss the questions before brief whole-class feedback.

Output: Brainstorming a new brand slogan

Stage 1

Elicit some brands that the learners are familiar with. Decide on one to focus on.

Stage 2

Group learners, ask them to choose a facilitator and refer them to the relevant pages. Ask the facilitators to prepare for their brainstorming session and ask the others to review ways of adding emphasis to explanations from the unit. Tell them they have six minutes to conduct their brainstorming session in their groups.

In smaller classes you could always use only one of the types of brainstorming, or discuss the best one before using it.

Stage 3

Make two groups and ask them to compare results and create an advertising slogan in a time limit of 10 minutes.

Worksheet 1 (see page 127)

Improve your knowledge of aspects of pronunciation

Level **C1 +**

Time **55–60 minutes**

1 Lead-in (10 minutes)

Pair learners to discuss the questions.

Suggested answers
1 Depends on learner's opinion – sometimes natives don't realise that their audience is using a second language.
2 Defined as the relative prominence of a syllable within a word.
3 Defined as how we say things. It is classed as falling, rising, rise-fall or fall-rise.
4 Depends on learners' L1. Examples could include expressing disapproval, expressing surprise, formation of questions, etc.
5 If learners are unfamiliar with the phonemic chart, explain that the symbols represent the phonemes, or sounds, used in the pronunciation of English. You could give examples of words using some of the sounds.
In pairs, learners discuss those they find difficult – this will vary according to their L1. Write the sounds on the board and elicit words including those sounds. You could extend this by doing a minimal pairs exercise, e.g.
/ʃ/ and /tʃ/, /iː/ and /ɪ/ , /æ/ and /ʌ/, /θ/ and /ð/, etc.

	Monophthongs				**Diphthongs**			
Vowels	iː	ɪ	ʊ	uː	ɪə	eɪ	**voiced** unvoiced	
	e	ə	ɜː	ɔː	ʊə	ɔɪ	əʊ	
	æ	ʌ	ɑː	ɒ	eə	aɪ	aʊ	
Consonants	p	b	t	d	tʃ	dʒ	k	g
	f	v	θ	ð	s	z	ʃ	ʒ
	m	n	ŋ	h	l	r	w	j

2 Odd word out (10 minutes)

Learners work in pairs to find the odd sound out. You could pronounce the example to help them.

Answers

/ʌ/ company	budget, ~~bullet~~, substitute, judge, production
/tʃ/ launch	pitch, switch, structure, ~~characteristic~~, chain
/æ/ shadow	~~horizontal~~, massive, analyse, tablet, lack
/ə/ dependant	entrant, conspicuous, rival, ferocious, ~~franchising~~
/iː/ team	boutique, technique, bean, ~~resort~~, piece

3 Connected speech (15 minutes)

1 Write the sentences on the board and drill them by saying them very slowly to start off with, gradually building up speed. Elicit where learners think the words are linked. Focus on final constant, initial vowel links. You could elicit other links, e.g. consonant–consonant, or discuss weak forms and contractions in more advanced groups.

Answers
1 Let's start with‿a quick‿ice-breaker and then generate some‿ideas‿in three groups.
2 What‿a brilliant‿idea! We should‿implement‿it‿immediately!
3 I believe that‿it‿is quantity that breeds quality.
4 We tend‿to think‿our target profile group‿are successful‿in their‿own right.
5 What‿about franchising‿as‿an‿option?

2 Changing word stress in sentences affects tone of voice. As an extra activity, ask individual learners to say the sentences in different ways, e.g. *boring*, *exciting*, *offensive*. Elicit how the others would react if somebody spoke to them this way. You could extend the activity and ask them to write the sentences as if sent by text message and whether it is similar to the way they hear them. For example, a bored speaker would not emphasise any words while an excited speaker would emphasise the words that carry meaning, as below.

Answers
1 Let's **start** with a quick **ice breaker** and then **generate** some **ideas** in **three groups.**
2 What a **brilliant** idea! We should **implement** it **immediately!**
3 **I believe** that it's **quantity** that breeds **quality.**
4 We **tend** to think our **target profile** group are **successful** in their own **right.**
5 **What** about **franchising** as an **option?**

4 Setting up a website role play (25 minutes)

1 Group learners to brainstorm ideas for the *Pronunciation help!* website. You could use some of these ideas to stimulate discussion:
- Individual sounds pronunciation app
- Pronunciation bingo with the phonetic script
- Phoneme dominoes with individual sounds and words
- Marking individual word stress exercises
- Writing the script for a clip of Mr Bean
- Minimal pairs with problem sounds
- Transcribing exercises

2 Learners present their ideas to the class. Elicit which website would be most successful, and why.

2 Standardisation and differentiation

Overview of the unit

2.1 Theory: Different approaches to international marketing

> 'National markets are held together by shared values and confidence in certain minimum standards. But in the new global market, people do not yet have that confidence.'
>
> *Kofi Annan*

International marketing is an attempt by multinational companies to find a common brand platform for their products and services across international borders. This platform should have the ability to be developed centrally and implemented locally. It is the use of techniques that are often used in domestic markets, including market identification and consumer targeting across national boundaries. Some commentators suggest that international marketing is simply the 4 Ps of the marketing mix adapted to take into account the differences in consumer preference in different countries.

An important marketing decision can often be whether to standardise or adapt a product or service to the target market. For many commentators, it is impossible to attempt complete homogenisation of the marketing mix across the globe except in the case of a limited number of goods such as medical equipment.

However, for many, the global market has become homogenised to the extent that some multinational companies that sell such products as hair care products and toothpaste can market their products in the same way across the world.

2.2 Practice: Piaggio Vietnam

Profile: The Piaggio Group

The roots of the Piaggio Group go as far back as 1882 when Enrico Piaggio bought some land near Genoa to start a wood-working plant with his son Rinaldo.

In the 1920s and 1930s, Piaggio started producing engines and vehicles based on its own patents and manufactured products like cable cars, funicular railways, trams and trolley buses. In 1938 Rinaldo Piaggio's two sons took over as CEOs of the company. One of the sons focused on the aviation and railway industry, while the other pursued a dream of making mobility accessible and affordable for Italians. In 1946 the first Vespa was produced.

By the 1960s the company had been split into aviation/railways and scooters and this latter part was taken over by Gilera, a motorcycle company, in 1969. The company went through various management changes in the 1970s and the first scooter with plastic bodywork was launched in the 1980s. A 50th anniversary edition of the Vespa was launched and, in 1999, a boutique in Los Angeles was opened for the scooter. In 2004 it signed an agreement with Zongshen for the manufacture and sales of Italian technology in Asia.

When Moto-Guzzi was acquired, Piaggio became the largest group in the Italian two-wheeler market with 35% market share selling 600,000 vehicles a year and 8 plants operating in over 50 countries worldwide.

2.3 Skills: Managing time

Time management is the organisation of information well enough to register it without spending too much time procrastinating. It is often seen as an essential skill in today's workplace which has to be learned rather than taught.

Tips to help the management of time include managing inboxes effectively by using different folders, prioritising tasks, bookmarking most visited sites, recognising the limits of multi-tasking, setting goals by using a to-do list and managing unwanted interruptions.

2.1 Theory: Different approaches to international marketing

Introduction

1 Pair learners to discuss why they think the promotions failed, before referring them to page 167–168 to check their answers.

Answers

1 Unlike in Italy, in the USA both children and adults generally eat cereal and toast for breakfast. Biscuits would be considered an unhealthy option for breakfast; they are acceptable for a mid-morning or afternoon snack.
2 Nearly 100% of all washing machines sold in the UK are front-opening models, as they are generally located in the kitchen under a worktop/counter.
3 The company thought that the word *embarazar* ('to make pregnant') meant 'to embarrass', so the ad read: 'It won't leak in your pocket and make you pregnant.'
4 For many Asians, white flowers represent bad luck and even death.

2 Briefly discuss as a whole class what lessons can be learned from the mistakes. Alternatively, group learners to discuss the question before feedback.

> ***Suggested answer***
> Companies need to do research on their local market before acting. As well as issues such as language, there will be customs, habits, tastes and sensitivities are that are culturally determined. In short, often the way people do things is different in different countries and that has implications for the way you do business in those places.

Language focus 1: International marketing terminology

Ask learners to work individually to match the definitions before comparing in pairs and checking answers.

> ***Answers***
> 1 g 2 h 3 d 4 f 5 c 6 a 7 b 8 e

Reading: Two perspectives on international marketing strategies

1 Write *skim* and *scan* on the board and elicit what the words mean in terms of reading skills: *skim* is to get a general understanding and *scan* is to find specific information. Learners work individually to match each text to the author's opinion before feeding back.

> ***Answers***
> 1 Text B
> 2 Text A

2 & 3 Pair learners to read a text each and answer the questions. Ask them to compare answers with a learner who read the same text before exchanging information with their original pair. Then find out who agrees with which text and discuss the reasons for their opinions.

> ***Answers***
> **Text A**
> 1 competitive capabilities and competitive position in the marketplace
> 2 They don't sell any beef products such as hamburgers or Big Macs. (Note that the word *hamburger* comes from the city of Hamburg where the hamburger was first made, so a hamburger can be made from any meat.)
> 3 globalisation strategy and differentiation strategy
> 4 companies whose products are not culturally specific and whose promotions are easily understood
> 5 very uncommon
>
> **Text B**
> 1 to achieve the benefits of economies of scale, e.g. lower production costs per unit
> 2 They think that these are universal, i.e. they communicate across cultures.
> 3 They are not universal: they reflect the value system of the home country.
> 4 Speak to consumers in each country in a way they understand.
> 5 cultural segmentation, i.e. different promotions for different segments according to differences in the customers' culture

Language focus 2: International marketing word formations and word partnerships

1 Learners work individually to complete the table before checking in pairs and feedback.

> ***Answers***
> a standardise
> b standardised/standard
> c differentiate
> d different/differentiated
> e adapt
> f adaptable
> g environmental
> h globalise
> i global
> j segment
> k segmented
> l minimise
> m minimal

2 Learners complete the sentences individually before brief class feedback.

> ***Answers***
> 1 standardised/differentiated
> 2 minimise
> 3 global
> 4 environment
> 5 segment/segmentation
> 6 adaptation/differentiation

3 Learners complete the sentences before discussing and comparing them in pairs.

> ***Suggested answers***
> 1 … product adaptation to the needs of local markets.
> 2 … then it makes more and more sense to plan strategy around global market segments across countries, not simple market segments within countries.
> 3 … how influential the socio-cultural environment is on customers' buying behaviour.
> 4 … ensure that their tax obligations are minimised.
> 5 … promote closer integration between member states, then companies are more likely to take a standardised approach to their regional marketing strategy.

Output: Adapting advertising to fit different cultures

Stage 1

Group learners of the same nationality if possible and refer them to the extra material and exercises on pages 138 and 142.

Stage 2

Groups design and present an advertisement for the same product/service they read about.

Stage 3

Groups present their advertisement, explaining what changes they made. You could record and play back this advertisement using audio software.

2.2 Practice: Piaggio Vietnam

Profile: The Piaggio Group and Piaggio Vietnam

Introduction

1 Group learners to read the profile and discuss how Vespas built for the Asian and European markets may differ. Take brief feedback.

2 Brainstorm what learners know about Italy on the board as a class, before discussing how the ideas and stereotypes learners come up with connect with the Vespa brand.

Language focus 1: Describing brands and products

1 Learners work individually to choose the correct option. You could either elicit or ask them to compare their answers before feedback.

> ***Answers***
> 1 historical importance
> 2 identity
> 3 representative
> 4 comfortable and efficient
> 5 functional
> 6 brands and products

2 Discuss how these words could be used to describe the Piaggio and Vespa brand, as in the example.

Listening 1: Brand strategy 1.11

1 Focus learners' attention on the questions and ask them to predict possible answers before playing 1.11, checking in pairs and taking feedback.

> ***Answers***
> 1 The values are (Italian) heritage, design and glamour; customers are 'buying an Italian dream'.
> 2 in exactly the same way
> 3 They will introduce the Piaggio brand.
> 4 It will be 10–20% higher.
> 5 top end of the mass market
> 6 They're not a low-quality brand. It's not in their core DNA.

> ***Audio script***
> **Interviewer:** How can you take a brand which is so closely related to Italian culture and internationalise it, or make it relevant to Vietnamese consumers?
> **Costantino Sambuy:** We're entering the Vietnamese market with the Vespa brand which is an extremely strong brand, that remains the same all over the world. Our values are linked with heritage, with design, with Italy, with glamour. Whoever buys a Vespa is buying an Italian dream. So we're positioning this brand in exactly the same way as we would do in England, or in America. The second phase of the penetration of the Vietnamese market is going to be different, because in that phase we are going to enter with another brand: the Piaggio brand with a series of plastic scooters, the Vespa on the other hand is made of metal. So with Vespa we are entering the local market at three times the price of a typical competitor scooter. With Piaggio the price will be ten to twenty percent higher than the local market.
> So at the moment the first entry is very much at the top of the pyramid ... actually, we are creating the top of the pyramid because the market doesn't exist, and then the second phase we are going to go closer to the mass market but still at the top end of this.
> With the Piaggio brand, our product will need to be incredibly adapted to the local market. The basic concept though remains the same in Vietnam. We are not going to go to the bottom end of the mass market with a product that we may be technically able to make but is a product that we have never made before. It's not that we don't know how to make it, but it is not really our core market. We're not a low-quality brand. It's not in our core DNA.

2 Briefly discuss how their own ideas differ from Costantino Sambuy's.

Listening 2: Promotion strategy 1.12

1 Learners listen and make notes in the table.

2 Learners compare notes in pairs. Play 1.12 again for them to add more detail before re-pairing them to compare again.

> ***Answers***
> **Promotion:** In Vietnam the strategy is to emphasise the connection to Italy (obvious and irrelevant to Italians), plus more extreme positioning as a glamorous, fashionable brand in Vietnam.
> **Dealer network:** In Vietnam, there is more standardised branding and service and it is more professionally organised. In Europe, the network is not standardised apart from at flagship stores.
> **Celebrities:** Hollywood stars such as DiCaprio are used across global markets, but local celebrities are very important. Local Vietnamese celebrities need to be seen on Vespas in Vietnam.

> ***Audio script***
> **Interviewer:** How is the promotion and advertising strategy for Vespa different in Vietnam compared to your home market in Italy?
> **Costantino Sambuy:** It's similar, but in Vietnam there is much more emphasis on Italy. An Italian icon. In Italy you don't say it's an Italian icon, it's obvious, it's irrelevant. So here in Vietnam we very much underline the Italian heritage. And secondly we make the positioning a bit more extreme. So we make it, in this case, much more glamorous, much more fashionable than it is in Italy. Our dealer network in Vietnam has this standardised branding too. It's very professionally organised. In Europe, whenever we go to our motorcycle dealer, to a scooter dealer, you will see them with different methods, different colours, different branding. Here, in Vietnam, dealers are all the same, in uniforms, following the same instructions. You find a similar concept in Europe, but only in flagship stores. So today we have seventy points of sale around the country which are all exactly the same, always the premium image that we require, always the product displayed how we require it.
> **Interviewer:** Right. What about celebrities? Who do you use to promote the brand image?
> **Costantino Sambuy:** Historically, Vespa has positioned itself strongly in the cinema business, starting with 'Roman Holiday' onwards. And so there is some activity happening on a global scale. But we tend to use local celebrities, because they are more relevant to the everyday people who buy our product. Even though we do use the big Hollywood stars such as DiCaprio. But we still try to associate with the local market.

Listening 3: Product strategy 1.13

Ask learners to predict if the statements are true or false, play 1.13 and pair them to check their answers.

Answers
1 True
2 False (seat is lower and handbrakes are closer to the handlebar)
3 True
4 False (it was a failure because people could see online that it was not originally from Italy)
5 False (innovating locally does not work)

Audio script
Interviewer: If I've got an Italian Vespa LX, made in your factory in Italy, and the Vietnamese Vespa LX made in your factory in Vietnam, are they identical?
Costantino Sambuy: The two Vespas are exactly the same for ... I would say ninety-eight percent of the components. There are only two modifications we make for the ergonomics of the Asian customer. The seat is slightly lower, and the handbrakes are slightly closer to the handlebar because the hands are slightly smaller. So we just had to adapt to the local customer. From a product standpoint it is the same, the engine is the same, the suspension is the same because the customer usage of the product is the same. This is not a workhorse, this is something you want to be seen with around town with your friends. It's something you want to be brightly coloured, you want a fantastic colour on it, and the same thing would happen in Italy. So the positioning is the same, the product is the same. And actually, if we changed something, we would not sell it! To give an example: we added a very fashionable colour, a fuchsia, a strong pink, thinking that that would be a great colour, and widely appreciated. People went online and saw that this product was not distributed in Italy, therefore it was not originally from Italy, and therefore they didn't buy it. This was a huge failure. So as soon as we start innovating locally, we force it locally, it doesn't work. So that really taught us a lesson.

Critical analysis

1 Briefly discuss as a whole class the advantages of having Vespas in movies.

Suggested answer
It associates Vespa with the glamour of Hollywood and its star actors. As the film is also set in Rome, it reinforces the connection between Italy and the brand for a non-Italian audience.

2 Group learners to brainstorm as many product placement examples as possible before holding a class discussion on the benefits.

Suggested answer
In general, product placement works by connecting a company's products and brands to the association the public has of that particular movie or actor.

Language focus 2: Describing products, brands and markets

1 Learners work individually to find the word that doesn't collate before comparing in pairs and feedback.

Answers
1 branded
2 mass (you can say *mass market brand* but not *mass brand*)
3 emerging
4 competition (but you can say *competitive market*)
5 innovation (you can say *brand innovation* but not *innovation brand*)
6 retailer (but you can say *retail product*)

2 Focus learners' attention on the example and elicit one or two other examples from their experience. Direct them to the four lists to write an example for one of the compound adjectives in each list for a product or brand they know about. Pair them to compare their ideas and find out more.

3 Learners work individually to fill in the gaps before comparing in pairs. Take feedback.

Answers
1 core product
2 niche market
3 premium-priced
4 fastest-growing segments
5 well-known brand

Transferable skill: Using repetition for persuasive effect 1.14

1 Play 1.14 and elicit which words were repeated. Ask learners to practise or briefly drill the sentences.

Audio script
1 Our values are linked with heritage, with design, with Italy, with glamour.
2 So we make it, in this case, much more glamorous, much more fashionable than it is in Italy.
3 From a product standpoint it is the same, the engine is the same, the suspension is the same because the customer usage of the product is the same.

2 Ask learners to write an introductory sentence for introducing the Piaggio brand individually, using the examples. Put them in small groups to practise before deciding which of their ideas are best, and why.

Suggested answers
a The Piaggio scooter will be far superior to the competition; in terms of product quality, in terms of service levels, and in terms of reliability.
b The Piaggio brand will be very different from the Vespa brand; it will have a different image, a different price and be aimed at a very different target market.

Output: Brand positioning

Stage 1

Put learners into groups of around three and refer Group A to page 138 and Group B to page 142.

Stage 2

Ask for pairs of volunteers to give the A and B presentations to the management board. While the managers are listening to the presentations, they should plan questions to ask. After asking their questions, they choose the best strategy.

2.3 Skills: Managing time

Introduction

1 Write *procrastinate* on the board. Elicit learners' ideas on meaning before reading the dictionary definition and discussing the question briefly in pairs.

2 Pair learners to complete the table, before re-pairing them to compare their answers and taking feedback.

> ***Suggested answers***
> 1 deal with crises
> deal with pressing problems
> 2 build relationships
> prepare for meetings
> take time out to relax
> creative thinking
> 3 respond to needless interruptions
> deal with boss's bad moods
> 4 surf the net
> chat with colleagues

3 Give learners a little time to add an activity to each of the boxes if possible, before eliciting a few of their ideas.

4 & 5 Hold a class discussion or group learners to discuss the questions before feeding back.

> ***Suggested answer***
> A good time manager will prioritise and put tasks in all four boxes; a bad time manager will probably group all tasks in box 1.

Language focus: Time management language

1 Learners work in pairs to complete the collocations before forming new pairs to check answers.

> ***Answers***
> 1 f 2 a 3 g 4 c 5 i 6 j 7 h 8 d 9 e 10 b

2 Elicit the collocations on the board and which are good or bad for time management.

> ***Answers***
> Failing to keep track of time, suffering from procrastination and missing a deadline are all bad for time management.

3 Pair learners to discuss how to advise someone who procrastinates a lot.

> ***Suggested answer***
> If you suffer from procrastination you will probably find that you are always trying to catch up on your work. It might help you to make a 'to-do' list and prioritise the most important task. This should help you to decide on objectives and help you to avoid missing deadlines.

4 Discuss the proverb either in small groups or as a whole class.

> ***Suggested answer***
> It means if you don't plan properly, you will not achieve your goals. Planning can be inappropriate when it may hinder spontaneous thought or action, and lead to inflexibility.

Listening 1: Lecture on time management 1.15

1 Focus learners' attention on the topics and elicit their predictions on what the speaker may say.

2 Instruct the learners to make notes before playing 1.15.

> ***Suggested answers***
> **Goals, priorities and planning**
> Ask why you are doing this.
> Ask what will happen if I don't do it.
> **Experience**
> Experience teaches us how to do things better – we learn from our mistakes.
> **Planning**
> Plan at multiple levels: day, week, semester, etc.
> Build flexibility into your plan.
> **'to-do' lists**
> Do the most difficult / least attractive thing first.

> ***Audio script***
> **Randy Pausch:** Let's talk first about goals, priority and planning. Any time anything crosses your life you've got to ask, this thing I'm thinking about doing – why am I doing it? Almost no one that I know starts with the core principle of 'There is this thing on my "to-do" list, why is it there? What is the goal? Why will I succeed at doing it?' And here's my favourite. 'What will happen if I don't do it?'
> The other thing to remember is that experience comes with time and it's really, really valuable and there are no short cuts to getting it. So good judgement comes from experience, and experience comes from bad judgement. So if things aren't going well, that probably means you're learning a lot and it'll go better later.
> Planning is very important: one of the time management clichés is 'Failing to plan is planning to fail'. And planning has to be done at multiple levels. I have a plan every morning when I wake up and I say what do I need to get done today, what I need to get done this week, what do I need to get done each semester. And that doesn't mean you are locked into it. People say 'Yeah, but things are so fluid, you know I am going to have to change the plan', and I'm like 'Yes. You are going to have to change the plan'. But you can't change it unless you have it. So have a plan, acknowledge that you are going to change it, but have it so you have the basis to start with.
> The last thing about 'to-do' lists, or getting yourself going, is if you've got a bunch of things to do, do the ugliest thing first.

3 Group learners to compare their notes and to discuss the usefulness of the advice. You could build up a list of the most useful ideas mentioned on the board.

Intercultural analysis

1 & 2 Group learners into different nationalities if possible to discuss the questions. Alternatively, in smaller classes, you may wish to brainstorm cultural stereotypes regarding punctuality and what could happen if people from two types of cultures meet.

> ***Suggested answer***
> Person X (from the punctual culture) will probably arrive on time for the meeting and expect Person Y (the person from the more flexible culture) to also be there. If Person Y isn't there, Person X may become angry or frustrated at having to wait, and see this as a lack of respect. Person Y, arriving late, will perhaps find Person X's attitude as inflexible and even shocking.

Listening 2: IT company team meeting 1.16

Ask learners to predict possible answers before playing 1.16 and taking feedback.

> ***Answers***
> 1 False (she says her own deadlines change if no one is checking up on her)
> 2 True (Jennifer and William do)
> 3 True (they can work out a new deadline if there is a problem with the existing one)

> ***Audio script***
> **Jennifer:** I'm not sure how popular this is going to be, I was thinking of, and this will include myself, well, being more strict with deadlines.
> **William:** It would have helped me quite a lot because that last project took me ages.
> **Jennifer:** Well, that's what I was thinking.
> **William:** But I do set my own deadlines, but then they just change.
> **Jennifer:** Yeah. Well, that's what I was thinking 'cause I do the same. When nobody's actually checking up on you it's very easy just to move a few weeks.
> **William:** You just move it. And I do the same with revision. I've got really lazy on that. It depends how good people think they are at giving themselves their own deadlines. But I mean it might help me. I think it might help me to do exams, for instance.
> **Steve:** There is a slight problem with that, because, say it was happening in June and you set yourself a deadline, in the preceding weeks there happened to be like a lot of maybe illnesses or holidays coming up.
> **William:** Yeah. That's the other thing.
> **Steve:** If you're on your own you can't always predict how busy you are.
> **Jennifer:** No, absolutely. But what I'm saying is, we have deadlines and then if you say, you came to the week before you knew your deadline was up and then you said to me that I'm not going to meet this deadline because, you know, last week three people were off sick or I've been on my own all week or something. Then we could sit down and work out a … a new deadline so that, you know, that we could agree on. 'Cause at the minute we're just sort of going indefinitely on and on and on. Without any cut-off point.

Critical analysis

1 & 2 Group or pair learners to discuss the questions before brief feedback.

> ***Suggested answers***
> 1 Generally, yes. The team seem to be fairly open and honest about the need to have stricter deadlines, but also about the realities of their workplace and the need for some flexibility.
> 2 She does not seem very strict, but she obviously thinks this is important. She seems to be trying to involve the team members in the improvement process.

Output: Advising an employee on better time management

Stage 1

Put learners into groups of four to discuss how the employee could best use her time. You could also ask them to discuss how a manager could approach such a discussion appropriately.

Stage 2

Pair learners to role play a meeting between the employee and her manager about her time management performance.

Stage 3

Re-group the learners to report back. In smaller groups, they could report back as a class.

> You may want to watch Sequence 1 on the DVD to find out more about International marketing in class or ask learners to watch it for homework. There is an accompanying worksheet on page 147.

Worksheet 2 (See page 128)

Improve your knowledge of brand strategy

Level **C1 +**

Time **55–60 minutes**

1 Lead-in (10 minutes)

Pair learners to discuss the questions.

Suggested answers

1 *Brand positioning* refers to target consumers' reason to buy your brand in preference to other available substitutes. *Brand strategy* is defined as a long-term plan for the brand in terms of who is the audience and their likely experience of the brand.
2 Depends on learner's own preferences.
3 Own brands are products which have the trademark or label of the shop which sells them, especially a supermarket chain. They are normally cheaper, so are aimed at the price-conscious consumer.
4 Probably Apple: it has captured the market's imagination with its products.
5 Notably packaging, sports and celebrity endorsement, product placement.

2 Describing types of brands (15 minutes)

1 Pair learners to discuss which adjectives match. Encourage them to give reasons why.

Suggested answers

Premium brand – authentic, confident, mysterious, rare, sensual
Well-known brand – comfortable, famous, recognisable, reliable, reputable
Leading brand – chief, foremost, primary, principal, superior
Own brand – affordable, economical, inexpensive, inferior, thrifty

2 Group learners in different nationalities if possible to discuss adjectives associated with brands in their countries of origin. If you have a monolingual class, you could ask them to think of adjectives they typically associate with different countries.

3 Building brand loyalty and awareness (15 minutes)

1 Pair learners to match the branding concepts and definitions before feedback.

Answers

1 brand extension
2 brand management
3 dominant brand
4 brand experience
5 iconic brand
6 brand recognition
7 brand recall
8 first-thought-of brand

2 Re-pair learners to ask and answer questions about their consumer attitudes to different branded products.

4 Brand strategy for 'QT cola' role play (20 minutes)

1 Pair learners to decide on the best strategy for QT. Encourage them to discuss why they think their ideas are better and to take notes on the final agreement

2 In pairs, learners design a slide representing their brand strategy to present to the rest of the class. Take a vote on the best strategy.

Writing 1: Writing notes for presentations

Overview of the unit

Writing notes for presentations takes the pressure off having to remember every fact. It can help with the order and flow of the presentation whereas memorised delivery can often take the spontaneity out of delivery as it can limit inflection and tone of voice. Notes can also serve as a safety net if the presenter loses their place or forgets what to say next.

Notes are there to remind and should not be written out fully. They are only there as a tool in the effective delivery of a presentation and they should not be the focus. Generally, they should be easy to read, they can be written on index cards, sheets of paper or in the notes field in presentation software, and they should not hinder the presenter from focusing on the audience.

Introduction

1 Pair or group learners to discuss the questions before brief feedback.

2 Focus learners' attention on the ways of raising money and elicit in a tally chart on the board which is the most popular. Discuss as a class or in small groups the effectiveness of each.

3 Re-pair learners or discuss as a group images used by charities to raise money.

Language focus: Preparing slide presentation notes 1.17

1 Elicit what 'DRTV' means, before pairing learners to practise presenting the slides.

2 Play 1.17 and re-pair learners to discuss the differences before class feedback.

Audio script
Slide 1 – Creating DRTV
Andrew Guy: Thank you for inviting me along to talk about using TV adverts to further the aims of your organisation. I'm going to start by telling you a bit about the background to creating a TV advert.
Slide 2 – Principles of DRTV
Andrew Guy: So, let's talk a little bit about the basic principles of DRTV. There are two key parts to DRTV. One is an emotional connection with the subject matter. You have to get people to care before they start thinking about your cause and before they will start donating money. The first thing you have to do is appeal to people's emotions and then you give them the reasons to support you.

3 Check understanding of key words such as *emphasise, abbreviations, acronyms,* etc. before eliciting which guidelines were used. You could use these words to create a vocabulary match.

Answers
All the guidelines are used except 2 and 9.
1 15 secs, 30 secs
3 aim of talk, 2 key parts to DRTV, etc.
4 (*secs* = seconds)
5 (acronyms: DRTV, TV; symbols: – = + / ...)
6 (Thank you for inviting me ...)
7 (Aim of [the] talk, Get people connected to [the] subject), first [talk about] emotion)
8 (■)
10 see audio script on page 149

Writing skill: Creating bullet points on slides and adding notes 1.18

1 Learners work in pairs to complete slides 3 and 4, then form new pairs to check answers and feed back to the class.

Suggested answers
Slide 3:
1 Simple, compelling proposition
2 Reason to respond now
3 Persuasive engaging words
4 Clever, demanding ideas rarely work
Slide 4:
1 Length of advert critical
2 Include lots of captions and voice-overs
3 Show needs and solutions
4 Make it clear you need response from beginning

2 Play 1.18 and elicit which points are expanded.

Suggested answers
Slide 3: fourth bullet point
Slide 4: first and fourth bullet points

Audio script
Slide 3 – Reasons
Andrew Guy: So what reasons do you need to give people to get them to respond? The first thing to say is that in your TV advert you have to give someone a very, very simple idea of why they should respond. And it has to be compelling. It has to be immediate. There has to be a reason why people should want to care now, and involved in there should be persuasive, engaging words. Be very, very wary of the clever idea that some agencies might pitch. DRTV is not a sophisticated format, it doesn't lend itself to clever, creative ideas that some of the big agencies might like to pitch. It has to be very simple. It has to be based around something that everyone can understand in a short space of time. It has to be simple.

Slide 4 – Reasons
Andrew Guy: The length of the advert is absolutely critical, and in some ways the more you say, the more you sell, and so we tend to recommend that ninety seconds is ideal. Sixty seconds is possible, but a thirty-second advert is far too short. Within that ninety seconds you should include lots of captions, lots of voiceover. We want to see the telephone number and we want to see it big at the bottom of the screen. And we want to hear as much as possible about the need and the solution that your organisation's providing. And as I said in the previous slide, don't be clever. Keep it simple. And most important of all, make it clear from the very beginning of the advert that you are expecting a response – you want them to give you their money.

3 Learners write a brief summary note. Pair learners to check answers and elicit a few examples.

Suggested answers
Slide 3, fourth bullet point: big advertising agencies
Slide 4, first bullet point: 90/60/30 secs
Slide 4, fourth bullet point: telephone number bottom of screen

Critical analysis

Pair learners to discuss the question before eliciting advantages and disadvantages on the board. In larger classes, you could group learners to discuss a bullet point before reporting back.

Answers
Text-only presentation
Advantage: quick to prepare and especially appropriate for regular weekly internal presentations within the company or organisation.
Disadvantage: having no visual images means that slides are less engaging and consequently it is more difficult to maintain an audience's interest.

Image-only slides
Advantage: the right image can easily inspire an audience.
Disadvantage: for inexperienced presenters there are no text prompts to help them talk through the slide.

Combination of text and image
Advantage: clear explicit linking of words and images helps the audience to absorb information yet still provides text prompts to help more inexperienced speakers.
Disadvantage: slides can get crowded with too much information on them, which can make them difficult to see properly.

Output: Prepare and deliver a welcome presentation

Stage 1

Group learners, ask them to decide on the type of welcome presentation and then tell them to design four slides on blank sheets of paper.

Stage 2

Learners write notes on the slides using the guidelines before passing them to another group.

Stage 3

With their new notes, groups highlight stressed words before practising the presentation and giving it to the group who gave it to them. Allow time for them to discuss possible improvements.

You could record the presentations and play them back for learners to discuss improvements.

3 Competition within industries

Overview of the unit

3.1 Theory: Five Forces Theory of Competition

> 'Markets are constantly in a state of uncertainty and flux and money is made by discounting the obvious and betting on the unexpected.'
>
> *George Soros*

The Five Forces Theory of Competition is accredited to Michael Porter and was set out in a book published in 1980 called *Competitive Strategy: Techniques for Analysing Industries and Competitors*. In this book, Porter applied microeconomic principles to business strategy and he analysed the strategic requirements of industrial sectors, not just of specific companies. The theory is often used for an analysis of competitive position and when making investment decisions within an organisation. For Porter, the five forces are:

- existing competitive rivalry between suppliers (e.g. advertising, product range, pricing)
- the threat from new market entrants (e.g. economies of scale, brand identity and loyalty)
- the bargaining power of buyers (e.g. volumes, just-in-time schedules, changes in cost)
- the bargaining power of suppliers (e.g. geographical coverage, number of companies)
- the threat from substitute products and technological change (e.g. trends, legislation).

Porter argued that the strength of each force can vary from industry to industry, but when considered together, their changing dynamics could determine the long-term profitability within each industrial sector.

3.2 Practice: The UK budget hotel industry

Profile: The UK budget hotel industry

The UK branded budget hotel sector is expected to more than double in size in the next few years and will account for over a quarter of the total hotel market. It has been seen as the 'engine room' of the hotel industry as poor-quality mid-market and independent hotels no longer satisfy consumer requirements. The industry has become increasingly branded and consolidated as consumer tastes have changed to demand low-priced accommodation with consistent standards coupled with brands they can rely on and trust. The market is dominated by Travelodge, Premier Inn and Holiday Inn Express, who have opened new hotels through acquisition, development and conversions of former mid-range hotels and independents. Overall, the UK continues to be a growing market for branded budget accommodation, but it remains behind more mature markets such as the USA and France in terms of supply.

3.3 Skills: Making a sales pitch

Selling is one of the oldest professions, because doing business typically involves a relationship between someone offering a good or service and someone bargaining a price for it.

The impact of a sales pitch depends not only on what is said, but how it is said. Notes and visual aids can help in a good sales pitch, but they should not detract from the overall message.

Many people are put off by a salesperson's incompetence and lack of knowledge about the product they are presenting. A good sales pitch is where the presenter is educated, believes in the product, builds a relationship with and is willing to answer questions from the audience. A sales person should also remember that they are selling more than the actual physical product and they may be offering unquantifiable concepts such as excitement, freedom and social relationships.

3.1 Theory: Five Forces Theory of Competition

Introduction

1 Pair learners to discuss one of the situations.

2 Briefly elicit their ideas for each of the scenarios.

Listening 1: General description of the 'Five Forces' diagram (1.19)

1 Focus learners' attention on the diagram and elicit predictions for the missing word, before playing 1.19 and getting feedback.

Answers

1 new entrants
2 competitive rivalry
3 substitute
4 buyers/suppliers
5 suppliers/buyers

Audio script

Interviewer: Porter's Five Forces model explains a firm's competitiveness. He's saying that the state of competition in an industry depends upon five basic competitive forces. Can you talk us through the model?

Alex Muresan: The five forces that we have are three which Porter considers to be from horizontal competition – the threat of new entrants, competitive rivalry among existing competitors and the threat of substitute products or services. And the other two forces are what Porter calls vertical competitions. These are the bargaining power of suppliers and bargaining power of buyers. All these ...

Interviewer: Can I just interrupt you a second? What does he mean by 'horizontal competition' and 'vertical competition'?
Alex Muresan: Well, when you think of the supply chain if you visualise it vertically from suppliers all the way to buyers, you've got the suppliers, which would be your manufacturers. You've got some intermediates there, like wholesalers. Then you'll have potentially the retailers in your supply chain–and then the customers, the buyers. So if you position it vertically, this is your vertical chain. The horizontal level is those people who compete on the same level with you; they're supplying the same or substitute products to the market that you target. So it would be similar businesses to yours, competitors of yours, but on the same level in the supply chain.
Interviewer: Right.
Alex Muresan: Now any change in these forces normally requires the business to reassess the market place, given the overall change in industry information. So the arrows show there is an influence on the part of these factors onto your organisation.

2 Play 1.19 again. Let learners check their answers in pairs before a class check.

Answers

1 Horizontal competition is competition from firms at the same level; vertical competition is competition from the buyers and suppliers in the supply chain. Note that while the diagram shows buyers and suppliers on a horizontal axis, they are said to be in vertical competition as they are not on the same level.
2 Horizontal competition: new entrants, substitutes, competitive rivalry amongst existing competitors
Vertical competition: buyers and suppliers
3 Firms should reassess the market place.

Transferable skill: Using a diagram to express ideas

Check learners' understanding of the diagram by asking a few concept questions, e.g. *Who is the producer? Can you think of other competitors? Who are the consumers?*

Learners work in pairs to draw a diagram for one of the example products, then form new pairs to describe and draw. In larger groups, you could group them to describe and draw their diagrams for the different products to each other.

Listening 2: Analysis of competitive rivalry 1.20

1 Learners work individually to complete the sentences before listening.

2 Play 1.20 and elicit their answers.

Answers

1 more
2 less
3 more
4 less
5 more
6 less
7 more

Audio script

Alex Muresan: For most industries, the intensity of competitive rivalry is the major determinant of competitiveness and this depends on a number of factors as well. One of them is the concentration of the industry. What Porter means by this is that, for example, an industry with many competitors of equal size will lead to more intense rivalry – the pressure on companies to compete will be higher, as they are more likely to have similar strengths and weaknesses. Another factor is the rate of market growth. If you have slow growth you will have greater rivalry. High-growth markets, less rivalry.
Interviewer: Because in low-growth markets, they'll be competing ...
Alex Muresan: For the same customers. Yes. And usually in slow-growth markets, for example, you'll be struggling to target the same customers as everybody else. Another factor would be the structure of costs and this is to do with the costs incurred by organisations, in that particular industry or sector. When an organisation incurs high fixed costs, for example, the pressure will be price cutting to fill capacity which will increase competitive pressures. Then there is another factor called a degree of differentiation and it's ...
Interviewer: This is still competitive rivalry?
Alex Muresan: Yes. It's another factor that influences competitive rivalry. There are a number of them. Some products cannot be copied easily; they are highly differentiated and some are strongly branded, which differentiates them even more. In this kind of case, customers see the difference between different products, and so have a reason for buying a particular product. This kind of environment is associated with less intense rivalry. The opposite is true where more intense competitive pressures in an industry occur and customers see products from different companies as very similar. In this situation, they tend to buy the product with the lowest price.
Interviewer: Right.
Alex Muresan: Then we have switching costs. When switching costs are high – because the product is specialised and the customer has invested a lot of resources in learning how to use it – rivalry is reduced. So customers tend to stick with the product that they have invested the most money, effort and time in.
Finally, you have exit barriers. When exit barriers to leaving a market are high, the rivalry will be more intense than when they are low. So companies won't quickly or easily exit industries if they don't see opportunities elsewhere.

3 Elicit possible endings for the sentences, then allow learners to listen again to check answers.

Suggested answers

1 ... they have similar strengths and weaknesses.
2 ... the same customers.
3 ... fill capacity.
4 ... tend to buy the product with the lowest price.
5 ... a lot of resources in learning how to use it.
6 ... they don't see opportunities elsewhere / exit barriers are high.

4 Group learners to discuss the factors.

Language focus 1: Changing comparisons

1 Elicit the differences in structure and meaning in the examples.

> ***Answer***
> The first sentence shows a standard comparison for specific, fixed circumstances. The second sentence moves the emphasis to *more competitors* to highlight the important information.

2 Pair learners to complete the sentences, before re-pairing them to compare answers. You may wish to elicit an idea or two for each of the sentences.

> ***Suggested answers***
> 2 ... the more likely they will buy on quality considerations and therefore the less competitive the industry will be.
> 3 ... the more new companies will enter into the industry and consequently the more competitive the industry will be.
> 4 ... the more likely customers will switch to substitutes and as a result the higher the competition in the industry is likely to be.

Language focus 2: Phrases of competition with dependent prepositions

1 Learners predict possible answers to the questions.

> ***Answers***
> 1 on, with (*as* would also be correct)
> 2 of, of
> 3 on
> 4 of, in, upon (*on* would also be correct)
> 5 of, in

2 Elicit the prepositions from the diagram on the board

> ***Answers***
> threat **of** new entrants/substitutes
> rivalry **among** existing competitors
> bargaining power **of** suppliers/buyers

3 Pair learners to discuss the question. Re-pair them to report to another partner.

> ***Suggested answer***
> There would be a cost in terms of time and effort: learning how the new operating system works. There would also be a financial cost as most operating systems cost money. Some peripherals, such as printers and mobile phones, might only work with the old operating system and so would also need to be replaced.

Output: Analysis and presentation of an industry's competitive forces

Stage 1

Briefly discuss and decide on an industry sector and geographical focus as a class, before putting learners into three groups to brainstorm competitors in the sector. Elicit these on the board.

Stage 2

Refer group A to page 138, and group B to page 142. Group C should read their information on page 30. Clear up any vocabulary problems.

Stage 3

Re-group learners to report on the information they read about, agree on and create a five forces diagram for the industry from stage one. You could re-group learners again to present their diagram to each other.

3.2 Practice: The UK budget hotel industry

Profile: The UK budget hotel industry

Introduction

1 As a class, discuss what is the most important factor in choosing a hotel.

2 Learners form pairs to brainstorm differences around the different considerations, and then form new pairs to compare. You may wish to elicit their ideas on the board.

Language focus 1: Effectively conveying information with noun phrases

1 Learners work individually to make the noun phrases.

> ***Answers***
> 1 the no-frills airlines
> 2 one thing the recession has taught businesses
> 3 a major beneficiary of any decisions
> 4 confident predictions about the coming year
> 5 the UK budget hotel chains
> 6 conspicuous value for money

2 In pairs, learners put the noun phrases into the text. You may wish to check answers after the first question with weaker groups.

> ***Answers***
> a 2 b 6 c 1 d 4 e 5 f 3

3 Learners work in pairs to decide on a title before feeding back.

> ***Suggested answers***
> Main idea: Companies that offer great value for money, like cheap airlines and budget hotels, can do well even in difficult financial times.
> Suggested title: Low prices push up profits

Transferable skill: Effective reading using skimming and scanning

1 Briefly check understanding of skim and scan reading, then ask learners to discuss which skills are used in the situations.

> ***Answers***
> 1 skimming
> 2 skimming
> 3 neither (you need to read this carefully)
> 4 scanning
> 5 scanning

2 Elicit the appropriate reading technique. Then learners answer the questions before feedback.

> ***Answers***
> 1 scanning (answer: Frank Barrett)
> 2 skimming (answer: A journalistic style)
> 2 skimming (answer: Budget hotels)
> 4 scanning (answer: Yes – the UK)

3 Discuss the question as a whole, or in larger classes, group learners before eliciting their ideas.

> ***Answers***
> They both save time, but there is a danger that you may miss key information or get the wrong overall impression.

Reading: Newspaper article on budget hotels

1 Elicit learners' ideas after they skim read.

> ***Answer***
> a promotional

2 Learners skim the article individually. Elicit their answers.

> ***Answer***
> Statement 2

3 Learners predict answers, before scanning the article and checking answers in pairs.

Answers

	cheap airlines	budget hotels	supermarkets
'no frills' style	Yes	Yes	Not stated
invite early booking	Yes	Yes	
self check-in	Yes	Yes	
monitor prices of rival chains	Not stated	Yes	Yes
offer budget and luxury ranges	Not stated	Not stated	Not stated
conduct price-cutting	Not stated	Yes	Yes
offer a 'price check' programme	Not stated	Yes	Not stated

4 Ask learners to skim read for any other interesting information. Elicit a few examples.

Language focus 2: Recognising persuasive language

1 Focus learners' attention on the sentences and elicit possible examples of emotional language.

> ***Answer***
> 1, 2 and 4

2 Ask learners to underline examples. Then check their answers.

> ***Answers***
> 1 In the budget hotel war, it seems everyone's a winner.
> 2 They love the value we offer, our clean and comfortable rooms and the warm welcome they receive from our team members.
> 4 The ferocious competition can only mean ever more attractive prices.

3 Pair learners to discuss the questions before feeding back.

> ***Answers***
> 1 1 b 2 c 3 d 4 a
> 2 Catch our smile: happiness (and humour in the meaning of *catch* – usually the collocation is *catch a plane*)
> Motion and emotion: a feeling of attachment to the car
> Save today, save tomorrow: caring about money but also about the environment
> Stay smart: stay in a stylish hotel / make a clever choice about accommodation

4 Group learners in different nationalities if possible, to discuss the questions before brief feedback.

Output: Presenting a hotel chain

Stage 1

Group learners. Refer Group A to page 138 and Group B to their information on page 33. Each group should prepare a short presentation.

Stage 2

Each group makes their presentation. Record them if possible. Make notes on their use of body language and take a vote on the best one. You could ask the listening learners to take notes on the emotional language used, and then elicit their ideas.

3.3 Skills: Making a sales pitch

Introduction

1 & 2 Group learners to discuss the questions before eliciting advantages and disadvantages on the board.

> ***Suggested answers***
> **Advantages:**
> - advert in newspaper/magazine: reach a large group of people; possible to select target group based on readership profile of the newspaper or magazine
> - trade fair: best way to provide tailored information, responding personally to prospective customers' questions; opportunity to listen as well as provide information
> - stand-up sales presentation: possible to engage a group of people, answer questions and build relationships better being physically at a client's premises
> - brochure: provides reference 'summary' of product/service features and benefits that a salesperson can leave with the client

Disadvantages:
- e-presentation on the company website: difficult to interact with customers through a web presentation, although possible to use chat forums in certain circumstances
- advert in newspaper/magazine: allows virtually no interaction with the client; can be very expensive
- trade fair: limited time to go into much detail with each person who visits the stand; may also be time-wasters to deal with
- stand-up sales presentation: costly compared to e-presentation – takes time and money to visit an individual client's premises
- brochure: compared to providing information on website, information in a brochure will date quickly and can't be updated without costly reprinting

Listening: Sales presentation 1.21

1 Focus learners' attention on the questions and elicit synonyms and examples for key words, e.g. *big business = large corporations*, *small business = start-up*, *IT consultancy = computer solutions*, *positive side of business = growth*, *about the company = history*, *business problem = lack of time*.

Play 1.21 and elicit learners' answers and why.

Answers
1 B
2 C

Audio script
Speaker: Imagine the scenario … You've got a great business. Things are moving forward. You're generating more income. Employing more people. The only thing is, all of these good things lead to more administrative tasks, more paperwork, more communication channels and more people to share information with – giving you an ever-increasing need to organise and tie together strands of expanding information before they fly out of control.
All of this takes your precious time away from doing what you do best – making your business flourish. And you don't want to stop that whilst it's in full flight.
So you put things off – 'it's on my "to-do" list'. But the longer you leave it, the more chaotic things get as you struggle to keep on top of it all – information might not be on-hand when you need it, and sales leads could start slipping through the net.
Sound familiar?
It's the growing pains of any successful business. But Bizantra means it doesn't have to be this way. Bizantra offers you a complete, low-cost suite of all the essential applications you need to organise and grow your business efficiently.
Bizantra means you don't have to rely on clunky, expensive and complicated software aimed at big corporations. Bizantra is a simple, intuitive and cost-effective alternative. And when you come to look back at this exciting stage of your company's growth, you'll recognise it as a time when you really started to step up your business game.

2 Ask learners to predict possible answers before playing 1.22 to check answers and feedback.

Answers
1 great
2 paperwork, communication
3 familiar
4 doesn't have to be
5 intuitive, cost-effective

Audio script
1 You've got a great business.
2 … more administrative tasks, more paperwork, more communication channels.
3 Sound familiar?
4 It's the growing pains of any successful business. But Bizantra means it doesn't have to be this way.
5 Bizantra is a simple, intuitive and cost-effective alternative.

3 Learners match the language to presentation techniques before comparing in pairs and feeding back.

Answers
1 b 2 d 3 e 4 a 5 c

4 Learners work individually to write a descriptive sentence. Pair learners to compare in larger groups or elicit their ideas on the board.

Language focus 1: Presentation techniques of persuasion 1.23

1 In pairs, learners predict the persuasion technique, then work in groups to discuss ideas.

2 Play 1.23 for learners to check their answers.

Answers
1 smaller
2 wherever
3 prioritise
4 to help make
5 gives you
6 Bizantra won't
7 simple
8 great-value
9 see for yourself

Audio script
Bizantra is an integrated suite of all the essential, latest-technology business tools for the smarter, smaller business.
It gives you everything a growing business needs, all in one place and for just a small subscription fee. Bizantra makes collaborating easy. Use as many of Bizantra's Shared Spaces as you need to connect with your team, whether they're across the office or on the other side of the world. Share documents, discussions, tasks and contacts with whomever you want, wherever they are.
Whether you're on or offline, at your PC or on the web, with Bizantra you'll have access to your whole business, whenever you need it.
Create opportunities and strengthen customer relationships with our powerful Contact Management and Email Marketing. Store contacts, track discussions and prioritise your sales efforts in one place, then set up email marketing campaigns in minutes.
Stay on top of increasing staff demands with Bizantra HR.

Easily manages record keeping, absence tracking and compliance to help make informed staffing decisions, fast. Designed for smaller businesses, our easy-to-use Finance application gives you an at-a-glance summary of all your finances so you can manage them easily. Giving you more time to focus on what makes your business tick. Bizantra does all that and much more. And it comes with rock-solid security, so you know that, even if your PC fails you, Bizantra won't. Bizantra is integrated, efficient and simple. You don't need technical expertise; you just sign up, download and away you go. And with a no-commitment, great-value price, you'll wonder how you did business without it. Why not see for yourself? Sign up for a free 60-day trial now.

3 Discuss the question as a whole class or pair learners in larger groups.

Suggested answer
The presentation describes Bizantra's product service features and benefits. Unlike the first presentation, it is not divided into two clearly identifiable parts; the structure moves between features and benefits throughout the presentation.

4 Learners identify examples in the highlighted sentences of the first four techniques in question 3 of the Listening.

Answers
Contrast a problem with a solution:
... even if your PC fails you, Bizantra won't.
Use a positive adjective to show enthusiasm:
great-value
Group three adjectives together to give a higher impact:
Bizantra is integrated, efficient and simple.
Repeat the same language structure to make a powerful impact:
... whomever you want, wherever they are.
Store contacts, track discussions and store your sales effort in one place.

5 Learners match the remaining highlighted sentences with the other presentation techniques before checking in pairs and feeding back.

Answers
1 Why not see for yourself?
2 ... the smarter, smaller business
3 Easily manages record keeping, absence tracking and compliance to help make informed staffing decisions, fast. ... our easy-to-use Finance application gives you an at-a-glance summary of all your finances ...

6 Learners extend their product descriptions and either read them to each other in pairs or you could elicit their ideas individually in smaller groups.

Language focus 2: Pausing and stressing words in presentations 1.24

1 Focus learners' attention on the presentation excerpt. Ask them to predict where the speaker pauses before playing the first two sentences of 1.24 again and getting class feedback.

Answers
1 Bizantra | is an integrated suite | of all the essential | latest-technology | business tools | for the smarter | smaller business.| It gives you everything | a growing business needs, | all in one place | and for just a small | subscription fee.

2 Elicit and discuss their ideas about which words are stressed and the position of pauses.

Answers
The pauses are located immediately after the stressed words. The exception is for common word partnerships, such as *latest-technology*, *business tools* and *small(er) business*. These partnerships generally have both words stressed, but there is no pause after the first word as this would split the partnership down the middle.

3 Play 1.24 and elicit the style of delivery in each version of the same short presentation. Ask learners to give reasons for their answers. These could include speaker's intonation, speed of delivery, etc.

Answers
1 A 2 C

Audio script
1 ... You've got a great business. Things are moving forward. You're generating more income. Employing more people.
2 ... You've got a great business. Things are moving forward. You're generating more income. Employing more people.

Output: Make a persuasive e-presentation of a product or service

Pair learners and ask them to write a presentation using the knowledge gained in the unit. Learners can practise in pairs and you could re-pair them to listen to other presentations. Elicit the types of presentation techniques used.

Worksheet 3 (See page 129)

Improve your knowledge of prepositions

Level **C1 +**

Time **55–60 minutes**

1 Lead-in (10 minutes)

Pair learners to discuss the questions.

Answers

1 before a pronoun, noun or gerund
2 This links a noun or pronoun to a particular moment, e.g. *on Wednesday, in winter, at 11 o'clock*
3 This shows a change in place of a noun or pronoun, e.g. *along the road, to France, from Russia, into the door, onto the roof, towards town.*
4 Two or three words together to form a single preposition, e.g. *as of, because of, in front of, in charge of, as well as, on top of.*
5 Most learners of English find prepositions difficult, as direct translation is often impossible.
Ways of learning prepositions include: looking them up in a dictionary, reading authentic English texts and learning high frequency phrases off by heart.

2 Visualising prepositions of place (15 minutes)

1 Learners individually illustrate the prepositions using brackets, dots and dashes. Discuss as a whole class whether visualisation makes it easier to remember prepositions.

Suggested answers

IN [.]	BETWEEN / . /	ACROSS ≠
AT [.	ABOVE ·–	BELOW –·
THROUGH ≠	ON	BEHIND ∧·
NEAR [.	AMONG ⁘	AGAINST /|
OUTSIDE ·C	INSIDE C·	OPPOSITE ⁒

2 In pairs, learners make business-related sentences using the prepositions.

Suggested answers

The company was **in** trouble.
It was **at** the point of collapse.
It was going **through** a difficult time
The boss was **near** the edge.
The company was **between** audits.
The loss was **above** expectations.
The shareholders were **on** his back.
He was **among** enemies.
The company **across** the road were doing well.
The competition was **below** standard.
He was **behind** schedule.
He was **against** the wall.
He was thinking **outside** the box.
They were **inside** the time limit.

Alternatively, pair learners to create a story using the prepositions. They could nominate the preposition to be used to continue the story.

3 Prepositions that collate with *time* (10 minutes)

Pair learners to fill in the gaps, before checking as a whole class or in groups.

Answers

1 in 2 until 3 for 4 By 5 at

4 Dependent prepositions (10 minutes)

1 Pair learners to match the list of verbs to their associated prepositions. Make sure learners understand that this exercise is verb + preposition + (something).

Answers

TO	consent, contribute, introduce, refer, respond
FOR	aim, apologise, apply, ask, prepare
FROM	prevent, protect, recover, suffer, save
IN	believe, invest, specialise, succeed
OF	accuse, approve, consist, know, think
ON	concentrate, depend, focus, rely, insist
WITH	agree, argue, deal, interfere, provide

2 Pair learners to find the verbs that may take other prepositions. Encourage use of dictionaries if necessary.

Suggested answers

approve **for**, argue **about**, think **about**, invest **for**, interfere in

5 Dependent prepositions dialogue (15 minutes)

Pair learners and give them a set time to write a dialogue to include five of the verbs in exercise 4. After they are finished, ask them to read out their dialogue replacing the preposition with a noise such as a tap on the table. Their classmates can then guess the missing preposition.

4 Entrepreneurship

Overview of the unit

4.1 Theory: Fostering entrepreneurship

> 'Entrepreneurs are simply those who understand that there is little difference between obstacle and opportunity and are able to turn both to their advantage'.
>
> *Niccoló Machiavelli*

Fostering entrepreneurship means channelling the flair and drive that encourages people to take the risk of establishing commercial enterprises. Economic growth is assisted when entrepreneurs seek to exploit business opportunities by allocating resources optimally or by seeking completely new ways of using the same resources.

International comparisons show that entrepreneurial success comes from the synergy between a conducive institutional environment, targeted government programmes and cultural factors which promote risk-taking. Generally, entrepreneurship requires efficient domestic and foreign financial markets, a flexible labour market, a transparent corporate taxation system and bankruptcy laws.

Self-employment is often seen as an indicator of the strength of entrepreneurship, although this is not always true. There are many constantly changing ways of being entrepreneurial and no one set of characteristics can describe what it takes to be an entrepreneur. However, studies show that most exhibit self-confidence, diligence, a willingness to take risks, optimism, creativity and foresight.

There is also no real link between entrepreneurship and employment. A start-up business can lead to growth and a subsequent rise in the level of employment, but this same business can also force less efficient firms to exit the market.

4.2 Practice: Jack Ma and Alibaba

Profile: Jack Ma and Alibaba.com

Jack Ma, a former English and International trade instructor at Hangzhou Dianzi University, is chairman and CEO of the Alibaba group and a board member at Japan's Softbank and the Huayi Brothers Media Corporation. Alibaba was established by its eighteen founders, led by Mr Ma, in 1999 and it now has offices across China, India, Japan, Korea, Europe and the USA. The group is the holding group of a number of subsidiaries of Internet-based businesses that facilitate domestic and international trade with and within China. Alibaba.com is the flagship member of the group and it uses marketplaces for buyers and suppliers to do business online effectively.
Alibaba Cloud Computing was established in 2009 and provides the holding group with e-commerce data. Alipay.com, which is an affiliate of the group, provides a secure way for individuals and businesses to make and receive payments on the Internet. China Yahoo! Is part of the Alibaba group and a strategic partnership with Yahoo! Inc. It is the leading Chinese language portal for news, email and search.

4.3 Skills: Collaborative and aggressive negotiation strategies

Negotiations occur in business, non-profit organisations and government, among nations and in personal situations. The aim is for negotiations to be viewed entrepreneurially and collaboratively to develop synergies that benefit both sides.

Negotiation approaches and styles are often described as competing, collaborating, compromising, avoiding and conceding. In game theory, the competing style can be classified as 'I win, you lose', collaborating as I win, you win, compromising as 'we both win', avoiding as 'I lose, you lose' and conceding as 'I lose, you win'.

As position is everything in a negotiation, it is wise to have the knowledge to use all these approaches depending on who you are negotiating with, their perceived style and the context.

4.1 Theory: Fostering entrepreneurship

Introduction

1 Books closed, write *entrepreneur* on the board and brainstorm associated adjectives. Draw learners' attention to the definition and the list of characteristics, before working alone to select which ones describe an entrepreneur, then comparing in pairs and feedback.

2 Re-pair learners to discuss the questions. You could extend the exercise by holding a debate on the possibility of being born an entrepreneur.

Language focus 1: The language of risk

1 Learners choose the correct options to complete questions 1–3. They then work in pairs to answer the questions and the follow-on question before whole-class feedback.

> *Answers*
> 1 for 2 of 3 to/towards

2 Learners categorise the collocations and work in pairs to decide which applies to their own attitude to risk.

> *Answers*
> 1 mitigate risk, spread risk, minimise risk
> 2 take risks
> 3 understand risk, tolerate risk, calculate risk, control risk

3 Learners categorise the actions, before justifying their answers in pairs.

> ***Answers***
> 1 reputational risk
> 2 operational risk (and possible financial risk)
> 3 reputational risk (and possible financial risk)
> 4 financial risk

Listening 1: New research on risk (1.25)

1 Focus learners' attention on the definition. Elicit any possible synonyms for *impulsive*, e.g. *hasty*, *rash*, *impetuous*. Briefly discuss the question as a class.

2 Ask learners to predict possible answers, before playing 1.25 and taking feedback.

> ***Answers***
> 1 B 2 A 3 C

> ***Audio script***
> **Interviewer:** Can you tell us a little bit about what the new risk research tells us? And why it is important for the business community?
> **Dr Shai Vyakarnam:** We saw this as an opportunity, between the Centre for Entrepreneurial Learning and the Department of Psychiatry, to look at entrepreneurship in a slightly different way. We thought it would be fun to apply some of the tests that the psychiatrists normally do to our entrepreneurs, and compare them with so-called successful normal managers.
> **Interviewer:** And were the results very different?
> **Dr Shai Vyakarnam:** The tests were conducted between hot and cold decision-making. The cold parts are the calculating parts – the mitigating of risk, and analysing situations. And in those cases there's no difference actually between entrepreneurs and other successful people. But the difference arose really in the so-called hot decision-making. The impulsivity tests. The test of gambling. The test of taking risks. And the differences are really stark.
> **Interviewer:** So entrepreneurs are risk-takers. Does that mean they don't quite fit into management models of today?
> **Dr Shai Vyakarnam:** Well, that's quite possible. There's certainly this group of serial entrepreneurs, the risk-takers. They've started more than two companies. Some over fifty. And I guess if we're looking at their approach to impulsive behaviours, it goes contrary to the flow of management generally, which is all about business planning, budgeting and so on. And so the impulsiveness of the entrepreneur combined with the planning skills traditionally connected with management roles would be the ideal combination. Entrepreneurs, if they are impulsive, wouldn't fit ideally into the management role.

3 Learners work in pairs to discuss the questions. You may like to elicit what hot and cold decision making is, i.e. risk-taking behaviour and analysing situations.

Transferable skill: Conveying meaning visually

1 Elicit what each of the pictures could represent, e.g. bright idea, growth, risk, and discuss which one best illustrates entrepreneurship.

> ***Suggested answer***
> The image of the light bulb shows an entrepreneur as idea generator.
> The image of the hands holding flowers shows an entrepreneur as someone who grows, nurtures, creates and produces.
> The image of the rodeo shows an entrepreneur as risk-taker.

2 Elicit learners' ideas or ask them to draw an image for display.

Listening 2: Young entrepreneurs (1.26)

1 Discuss the question as a whole class. Alternatively, in mixed age groups hold a debate on whether youth is a factor in entrepreneurship or not.

2 Play 1.26 and elicit the answer onto the board.

> ***Answer***
> Dr Shai Vyakarnam agrees with the statement. His reasoning is that young people have a similar risk profile to serial entrepreneurs.

> ***Audio script***
> **Interviewer:** Young people take more risks so if you want to be an entrepreneur, you ought to start your business when young?
> **Dr Shai Vyakarnam:** Yes. That's a really interesting point because the data is showing us that a 51-year-old entrepreneur, serial entrepreneur, has a very similar risk profile to most 17- to 27-year-olds. Whereas managers have a similar risk profile to people of their same age across the population as a whole. So certainly if the younger people are more open to taking risk – have a higher appetite for it, then we should give advice which goes contrary to what they normally get. We normally tell graduates 'Go get a proper job. Get some experience. Earn some money. Learn the skills. And then go start a company if you want to.' Whereas what we should be saying is 'Have a go to begin with when you are young, when the risks don't seem so great. Learn about entrepreneurship. Maybe learn your own attitude towards risk. Go and find somebody who has done it before and try to learn from them.' A bit like an apprentice. Go and learn from many of them. Get networking. Stretch your boundaries. Do things that are new and different, away from your routines. Try to get a feeling for what it is to take a risk – not just the scholarly view of risk, but actually deep down in your gut, what it feels like.

Language focus 2: Giving friendly advice (1.26)

1 Pair learners to predict possible answers.

2 Play 1.26 again for them to check and take feedback.

> ***Answers***
> 1 get 2 Get 3 Earn 4 go 5 Learn 6 Go 7 Go
> 8 Get 9 Stretch 10 Do

3 Elicit what word stress is and if changing it can affect meaning (i.e. how words are said and how it can affect meaning; this is often known as *tone of voice*). Play 1.27 and ask learners to mark the stress. Elicit their ideas on the board. You could also drill the sentences.

Answers
1 The phrases are said as commands or orders. The word stress is as follows: Go and learn from many of them. Get networking.
2 The phrases are said as a form of friendly advice. The word stress is as follows: Go and learn from many of them. Get networking.

Audio script
1 Go and learn from many of them. Get networking.
2 Go and learn from many of them. Get networking.

4 In pairs, learners discuss the question. Elicit and discuss the most valuable piece of advice.

Output: Propose a project to foster entrepreneurship in schools

Stage 1

Group learners to discuss the situation using the ideas given for 5–10 minutes. With older learners you could discuss what learners think would *engage* teenagers *fully* before you group them.

Stage 2

As a group, learners give a presentation, while the others evaluate it using the criteria given. You could take a vote on the idea that would appeal most to teenagers.

4.2 Practice: Jack Ma and Alibaba

Profile: Jack Ma and Alibaba

Introduction

Pair learners to discuss questions 1–3 before brief feedback. You could re-pair learners to report on their previous discussions.

Suggested answer
Alibaba provides an opportunity for Chinese and foreign businesses to reach a global market for their products without using intermediaries. It is useful for small companies as it can put them in touch with partners that they otherwise may not have contact with. In particular it opens up opportunities for foreign buyers wanting to access Chinese suppliers and for Chinese suppliers wanting to access a global marketplace. As trade is direct without intermediaries, the cost of doing business is reduced.

Reading: The rise of Jack Ma

1 Learners match the summaries to the paragraphs and give whole-class feedback.

Answers
Paragraph 1: The achievements of Jack Ma
Paragraph 2: The philosophy of Jack Ma
Paragraph 3: Different companies connected to Alibaba.com
Paragraph 4: How the Internet has grown in China
Paragraph 5: How the Internet is used in China

2 Learners complete the sentences before comparing answers in pairs and feeding back to the whole class.

Answers
1 primary business tool
2 mental discipline
3 Yahoo! and Softbank
4 the Chinese government
5 competitive and profitable

3 Learners work in pairs to find the words and phrases. Elicit their ideas on the board. Alternatively, group learners into fives or sixes and give each group member a paragraph. Ask them to underline two or three words from their paragraph and think of an example sentence with a word or phrase that means the same. Their group-mates then scan the paragraph to find the word. Allow them to use dictionaries as required.

Answers
1 weighting
2 world('s) stage
3 counter-intuitive
4 conventional wisdom
5 formulate
6 an online payment platform
7 a steep curve
8 government backed
9 overturned
10 internet filtering technologies

Critical analysis

1 & 2 Briefly discuss synonyms for *pros and cons*, e.g. *advantages and disadvantages*, *benefits and drawbacks*. In pairs, learners discuss the questions.

Answer
Doing things differently from the general view of what is the 'right thing to do' is perhaps a higher-risk strategy. However, it also ensures that thinking is original and creative, which leads to radical innovation.

Language focus: Quantifying data

1 Focus learners' attention on the three sentences. Elicit how they could be said differently.

Suggested answers
1 a huge number of
2 over 50% of
3 80% of

2 In pairs, learners discuss what the expressions can describe before feedback. You may wish to brainstorm common countable and uncountable nouns that learners find difficult before they do this exercise, e.g. *data*, *accommodation*, *information*.

> ***Answers***
> Internet users: 1, 2, 3, 4, 6, 7, 9, 10
> Internet traffic: 1, 4, 5, 6, 8, 10

3 Learners individually identify and correct the errors before comparing in pairs. You could ask learners to write the answers on the board to check.

> ***Answers***
> 1 The population of those countries varies from around 30 million to 225 million. / The number of people of those countries varies from around 30 million to 225 million.
> 2 Global Ports Inc. only handles a small quantity of freight in Europe.
> 3 Only a small number of people work over 12 hours a day. / Only a small fraction of the workforce works over 12 hours a day.
> 4 The great majority of UK tourists go to France, but a significant number also go to Spain.
> 5 With the new booking system, the number of visitors is now controllable.

Output: Starting a business in China

Stage 1

Put learners into four groups of roughly equal size and refer them to the relevant pages to read. If you have a small class you could concentrate only on Groups A and C.

Stage 2

Learners work together in their groups to make notes on the business partner they require and any other information they think necessary before the meeting.

Stage 3

Groups A and C/B and D meet to discuss their business needs and offers. After about 10 minutes regroup so that Groups A and D/B and C work together.

Stage 4

In their groups from stage 1, learners decide who to do business with and why. After a few minutes, elicit their decisions as feedback.

4.3 Skills: Collaborative and aggressive negotiating strategies

Introduction

1 Focus learners' attention on the quote. Elicit their ideas on what it might mean and whether or not it is good advice, e.g. *Yes, it is best to maintain relationships in initial negotiations, rather than always go for the maximum benefit for yourself or your company, if you want to do business again.*

2 In pairs, learners consider the offers and the issues before deciding which to take. They then form new pairs to report back on their discussions.

Language focus 1: Negotiating strategies

1 Ask learners to match the definitions individually and elicit their answers. Pair them to think of any examples, and then elicit one or two. Alternatively, write *collaborative* and *aggressive* on the board and elicit possible related words, e.g. *joint effort*, *work together*, *side with* and *offensive*, *pushy*, *self-assertive*.

> ***Answers***
> a collaborative, e.g. compromising
> b aggressive, e.g. threatening

2 Learners work in pairs to match the strategies to the categories.

> ***Answers***
> Collaborative: commitments, open information exchanges, promises, recommendations, shared secrets
> Aggressive: blank refusals, commands, threats, warnings

3 Learners form new pairs to match the ways of expressing negotiating strategies with similar meaning, before whole class feedback.

> ***Answers***
> 1 d 2 g 3 c 4 a 5 e 6 f 7 b

4 Elicit which expressions are said more frequently.

> ***Answer***
> In the corpus, the examples in the left-hand column are extremely rare or non-existent. This is because they can sound very aggressive. In every case, expressions in the right-hand column are far more typical.

5 Discuss as a class the advantage of each approach or pair learners in larger classes.

> ***Suggested answer***
> This relates to the quote at the top of the page. If you want to maintain a long-term relationship, then probably a collaborative approach will mean the relationship is better. However, if the situation is extremely serious then a more aggressive approach may achieve your goal.

Listening 1: Discussing effective negotiating 1.28

1 Ask learners to predict the correct option, before playing 1.28 and checking answers.

> ***Answers***
> 1 b 2 b 3 a

> ***Audio script***
> **Salesperson:** But I love it when it gets to negotiation stage, 'cause you know they want to buy. If they start to negotiate, they want you.
> **Sales manager:** Absolutely.

Salesperson: If it really comes down to it and someone says 'Look we want to deal with your company. We want you to be our supplier but you're five thousand higher than the competition and I can't justify it to my group financial director.'
Sales manager: Yeah.
Salesperson: What I tend to do when people start mentioning the word 'discount', the way I tend to do it is I tend to throw it back at them: 'Well, fine. We can probably do something but, you know, what are you going to do for me? Because it's a two-way street. I can't go back to my manager and say 'I've given them a ten percent discount because I felt like it.' And then they say 'Oh, what we'll do is we'll upgrade the lease from level 2 to level 4.'
Sales manager: Uh-huh.
Salesperson: And then I'd say 'Well, okay. If you can commit this level of business to me, this is what you're going to pay now ... and I'll shift this cost to the back end of the deal and you don't have to pay it till the end of the year.' So that's the way I tend to work.
Sales manager: Yeah.
Salesperson: I suppose with more junior salespeople they're afraid – you know, they think 'Oh, I've got to give a discount, you know, because otherwise I won't get the deal.'
Sales manager: Hmm.
Salesperson: And I think if you hold your own as a quality supplier, people have respect for it.
Sales manager: Absolutely. If you need to offer some discount then go for the win–win. You know you want something back. We'll give discounts on two-, three-, five-year contracts. Get someone to take the contract out for two years, we'll give a five percent discount. Fine. You've tied them in for two years.

2 Learners discuss the question in pairs before brief feedback.

Answer
They prefer a collaborative approach, as they use win/win strategies that have a benefit for both sides.

Listening 2: A price negotiation 1.29

Ask learners to predict possible answers before playing 1.29 and checking.

Answers
1 d 2 a 3 b 4 c

Audio script
Manufacturer: Would you bend a little and leave it at the same price? James? Just say yes or no.
Supplier: I'm hesitant to do it as we've held our prices for a long time and we try to be competitive. I know we have a laugh and a joke and we do try and be competitive and it's ...
Manufacturer: I tell you where you can give us something, James.
Supplier: Yeah?
Manufacturer: You know where the service contract was a hundred and twenty? And you've made it a hundred and twenty-six?
Supplier: Yeah.
Manufacturer: It would look nice as a round figure. A hundred and twenty-five.
Supplier: Yes. I can definitely work that one.
Manufacturer: To be fair, it would look even better at a hundred and fifteen.
Supplier: But it's a round figure. We're happy with a hundred and twenty-five.

Language focus 2: Collaborative negotiating language

1 Learners match the collaborative language to the examples before checking in pairs. You could refer learners to the underlined phrases in the audio script for listening 1 and 2 if they require a context.

Answers
1 g 2 f 3 c 4 a 5 b 6 e 7 d 8 h

2 Pair learners to match the answers with the functions before grouping them to check answers and feedback. You could ask them to brainstorm other examples of language that match the functions in exercise 1, e.g.:

1 *In reality I think a longer time scale is necessary.*
2 *We could probably accommodate if we ...*
3 *I am not saying that's right, but ...*
4 *That's par for the course.*
5 *I am not in a position to make a decision presently.*
6 *If you agree, then I'll be able to ...*
7 *How could we make that more equitable?*
8 *It would be a comedy of errors if ...*

Answers
1 8h 2 3c 3 4a 4 7d 5 6e 6 2f 7 5b 8 1g

Intercultural analysis

Books closed. Elicit any examples of corporate hospitality learners may know of. Group learners in threes or fours to discuss the question before brief feedback. You could also ask them to rank the ways in order of acceptability.

Output: Negotiating on cost

Stage 1

Refer learners to question 2 of the Introduction to this section and group them according to the size of your class to discuss what strategies would be best in a cost negotiation for 5–10 minutes.

Stage 2

In their groups, one person takes the role of the seller and the others take different roles to role play the negotiations set out in the Introduction. You could design four other role cards for variety, e.g. replace *car* with *holiday home*, *computer* or *record collection*; replace *garage* with *property agency*, *computer recycling shop* or *record collector*.

Stage 3

Write *debrief* on the board and elicit possible synonyms, e.g. *report back*, *share information*. In their groups learners debrief themselves on their negotiation strategies.

You may want to watch Sequence 2 on the DVD to find out more about Competition and entrepreneurship in class or ask learners to watch it for homework. There is an accompanying worksheet on page 149.

Worksheet 4 (See page 130)

Improve your knowledge of risk-taking behaviour

Level **C1 +**

Time **55–60 minutes**

1 Lead-in (10 minutes)

Pair learners to discuss the questions.

Suggested answers

1 You must take risks to make money.
2 Giving birth, buying a house/car, accidental death, extreme weather events. You can take out insurance policies to cover most events, e.g. life insurance, house and car insurance.
3 Recession, over-supply in the market, disruptions in supply, etc. Offering consumer credit or loyalty programmes, monitoring footfall in competitors, bulk buying of stock, etc.
4 Have confidence in your actions, weigh up the pros and cons, be optimistic, etc.
5 They may be out of date, faulty or damaged in some way.

2 Risky behaviour (15 minutes)

Pair learners to mark the characteristics of a successful and unsuccessful entrepreneur appropriately. Encourage them to discuss the reasons for their choice.

Successful:

- thinks and acts on their feet
- can think 'outside the box'
- has a highly competitive spirit
- has a strong work ethic
- can deal with failure

Unsuccessful:

- ignores their own intuition
- feels embarrassed to 'sing their own praises'
- is motivated by fear rather than optimism
- stands their ground with aggressive behaviour
- procrastinates until the 'time is right'

3 Impulsive behaviour (15 minutes)

In pairs, learners design a supermarket floor plan that they think would encourage impulse buying.

You could also take a vote on the best supermarket layout and discuss why. Round up by discussing the role of cafés in supermarkets, e.g. they encourage lingering, people may reconsider their buying decisions.

Suggested answer

It is well known that supermarkets put basic products like bread, dairy and meat at the back of the shop to encourage people to walk along the aisles and buy impulsively. Last-minute shopping decisions like batteries and products designed to catch the eyes of children are often placed near checkouts. Products on promotion and loss-leaders are often displayed prominently at the beginning and end of an aisle.

4 Executive summary (20 minutes)

Group learners to write an executive summary.

Suggested answer

Although there is not a set formula for a business plan, this one would have a definite audience, which is a bank. The executive summary should therefore be written with its readership in mind and include:

- a description of the business
- how they will manage and market the business
- financial projections
- some supporting data on its viability
- possibly some background information.

You could extend the activity by regrouping the learners and role playing a meeting between the supermarket entrepreneurs and the bank using the written plans. Copy the following role card for the bank onto the board.

Bank

- Is a case made for the ability to pay back the loan?
- Do the entrepreneurs believe in themselves?
- Are they fearful or optimistic about the future?
- How would they deal with slow business conditions?
- Are they sure about the goals to be achieved?

Writing 2: Business plan and executive summary

Overview of the unit

A *business plan* is a formal statement of a business's goals, how the team behind it plans to achieve them and why they are achievable. There is no fixed formula for writing a business plan, as this is influenced by the goals and the audience. However, it should contain an executive summary, a description of the business, a plan about how the team will market and manage the business and its financial forecast. It could also include background information to the company and the people behind it.

An *executive summary* is the first part of a business plan, but should be written after the details of the plan. This is because it provides a concise view of the plan and tells the reader why you think your company will be successful. It must attract attention and be interesting as it is the first section the reader turns to, before deciding to throw away the whole plan or to continue reading. It should therefore address the key questions *Who is the reader?* and *What is the purpose of the business plan?*

Introduction

1 Learners work in pairs to discuss the questions before feedback.

> ***Suggested answer***
> A written plan can be easily passed to other people and discussed and commented on. It acts as a point of reference where ideas and information are condensed into a single document. It can be easily modified and updated. Possible negatives of planning include the length of time it takes to write the plan and the risk that it is not translated into action – it remains simply a nicely written plan on paper.

2 Elicit the meaning of *kiosk*, i.e. a small open structure for selling newspapers and confectionary. You could elicit if any of them know its origin (Czech). Then learners work in pairs to write their lists. They will check these in the next exercise.

Writing skill 1: Outline structure for a business plan

1 Ask learners to scan the *What's included* part of the table and underline words they don't understand, e.g. *forecast, itemise, counter*. Elicit these words and give possible synonyms. Instruct learners to match the sections to the content, before pairing them to check answers.

> ***Answers***
> 1 d 2 e 3 h 4 a 5 f 6 g 7 b 8 c

2 Briefly elicit learners' answers to the question.

3 Hold a class discussion or pair learners to discuss the question and elicit their ideas.

Language focus: Key features of an executive summary

1 Learners match the paragraphs to the sections of the business plan before checking in pairs. Feed back.

> ***Answers***
> 1 d 2 e 3 b 4 f 5 c 6 a

2 Ask learners to read the characteristics then check understanding by asking some concept questions, e.g. *How could you illustrate a growing market? Which type of sources could you quote? What is a company's most important financial information?* Learners work in pairs to find the text reference, then form new pairs to check answers. Tell them to ignore the highlighting for this exercise – they will use it in the Writing skill 2 exercise.

> ***Answers***
> 1 Paragraph 1 (*the growing Asian population in the Vancouver area*)
> 2 Paragraph 2 (from beginning of paragraph to *monthly basis*)
> 3 Paragraph 2 (from *According to the Association of Canadian* … *to two years*)
> 4 Paragraph 2 (last sentence)
> 5 Paragraph 3 (from beginning of paragraph to *excellent prices*)
> 6 Paragraph 4
> 7 Paragraph 4 (from from beginning of paragraph to *awareness campaign*)
> 8 Paragraph 5
> 9 Paragraph 6 (sentence 1)
> 10 Paragraph 6 (sentence 2)

Writing skill 2: Executive summary writing

In pairs, learners rewrite the sentences for the ice-cream business they discussed in the Introduction, referring to the highlighted areas of the text. Elicit their ideas or ask learners to come to the board and write an example of each. Discuss any differences.

Output: Writing an outline for a business plan

Group learners to add any additional information for the ice-cream business and ask them to write the introduction. Display these introductions for learners to compare. You could make learners play the role of the bank and take a vote on the one to get the loan and why.

5 Crisis management

Overview of the unit

5.1 Theory: Dealing with crisis events

> 'This crisis exposed very significant problems in the financial systems of the United States and some other major economies. Innovation got too far out in front of the knowledge of risk'.
>
> *Timothy Geithner*

Crisis management is a summary of activities which aim to respond to a major threat to the organisation, its stakeholders or the general public. Crisis events are classed in two categories: events over which there is no control (e.g. extreme weather events) and events which could have been avoided with foresight and pre-emptive action (e.g. industrial disputes, computer data losses and product recalls).

Crisis management involves dealing with these threats after they have occurred, in contrast to risk management, which tries to predict and eliminate possible problems for an organisation. It involves preparing contingency plans which identify courses of action, creating a detailed standby procedure, planning how to limit possible damage, choosing a team or individual to deal with it and deciding how an organisation will continue when the crisis is over.

Most crises can be tackled by the realisation that short-term losses may have to be taken in order to maintain a healthy business environment. Failure to do this would make the organisation look incompetent, disorganised and even chaotic.

5.2 Practice: Successfully dealing with a crisis

Profile: Ceramic Fuel Cells Ltd

Ceramic Fuel Cells Ltd (CFCL) was formed in 1992 by Australia's Commonwealth Science and Industry Research Organisation and a consortium of energy and industrial companies. Based in Melbourne, Australia, it has over 100 staff in offices in Bromborough, UK and Heinsburg, Germany. It uses patented technology and strives for partnerships to manufacture, produce and use its fuel cells in Asia, Australia and Europe.

CFCL develops solid oxide fuel cell technology to provide reliable and low-emission electricity from natural gas and renewable resources. It aims to be the supplier for solid oxide fuel cell products, which can be integrated into micro, on-site, combined heat and power generation appliances (m-CHP). Domestic solid oxide fuel cells are no bigger than a dishwasher and are seen as a possible alternative for domestic power.

CFCL predicts that electricity demand will increase dramatically in the near future and believes that entry to the fuel cell market is restricted due to the high cost of research and development. It therefore forecasts high potential profitability for the industry.

5.3 Skills: Dealing with conflict

Conflict occurs when people have a clash of interests, values and opinion. If it is not resolved it can often deteriorate into acrimony, discord and active avoidance. For many, conflict is an inevitable state of being, but it is not always negative. If it is resolved correctly, it can lead to personal and professional growth.

To deal effectively with conflict, the best response is to focus on the underlying issues rather than the people involved, to listen actively, to remain polite and to look for viable solutions. It is also wise to stay calm, show patience and refrain from disrespecting the other party in order to prevent or overcome potential issues before they become major hindrances.

5.1 Theory: Dealing with crisis events

Introduction

1 Focus learners' attention on the crisis events. Ask them to underline any words they don't understand, e.g. *breakthrough*, *misconduct*, *bankruptcy*. Elicit if any learner knows the meaning and check in dictionaries if necessary. You could point out the use of illustrations to memorise new vocabulary, e.g. an arrow drawn through break, a face with a tongue sticking out, or a bank with water coming out of it. Pair learners to put the events into the categories before feedback.

Answers

1 A	6 B
2 A	7 A
3 B	8 A
4 A (and possibly B)	9 B (and possibly A)
5 A (and possibly B)	10 A

2 Learners work in pairs to discuss the questions, before forming new pairs to report back on their discussion.

Suggested answer

Organisations can make various contingency plans and conduct 'What if ..?' scenario planning. However, it will not be possible in practice to prepare for all possible crisis events. Many crisis events are unknown until they hit you.

Reading 1: 'Black Swan' metaphor

1 Pair learners to select the answers. Encourage them to underline the words or phrases in the text that helped them choose, e.g. *before the discovery* and *fragility of our knowledge*.

Answer

B and C

2 Learners choose the correct answer before checking in pairs and feeding back.

Answers
1 impossible 2 huge 3 mistakenly

3 Group or pair learners to discuss the question. Then elicit their ideas.

Answer
He means that it is always easier to see what to do after the event has already happened.

Reading 2: Dealing with unknown crisis events

1 Ask learners to predict if the statements are true or false, before reading the text and feeding back.

Answers
1 True
2 False (they should not underestimate the fear factor associated with having a problem with no known solution)
3 False (they may require a response before the size/scope of the problem has been fully assessed)
4 False (falls in the stock price may cause problems in cash flow, credit, liquidity etc.)
5 True
6 False (it is not simply about helping the company regroup but more about facing the event and making the best of the situation)
7 False (the company leadership must take emotion out of the equation)
8 False (they should concentrate on both)

2 Tell learners to scan the text, find the words in bold, and write them down. They can then match them to the phrases, before checking their answers in pairs in feedback.

Answers

1 paramount	5 give breathing room
2 an absolute must	6 day-to-day business
3 tunnel vision	7 cascading effect
4 figuring out	8 plummet

3 Pair learners to discuss the question. Then elicit one or two of their ideas.

Language focus: Comparison of strategy and tactics

1 Learners match the adjectives to 'strategy' and 'tactics' before checking in pairs and feedback. Encourage use of monolingual dictionaries if necessary.

Answers
A strategy B tactics

2 Learners work in pairs to discuss the question. Elicit their ideas on the board.

Answers
The word *tactics* sometimes has negative associations. There is a sense that tactics can be opportunistic – taking unfair advantage of opportunities that present themselves in that moment. The word can also have positive associations too, as seen from the partnerships with *useful*, and *effective*. The word *strategy*, on the other hand, has more positive connotations, being associated with something that is solid and properly thought out with due care and attention. Strategy is generally seen as a plan that is in operation for a long duration of time, whereas tactics are planned for a relatively short period of time, e.g. a specific meeting or crisis event.

3 Learners match the types of tactics to the strategies before checking in pairs and feedback.

Answers
1 e 2 d 3 a 4 b 5 c

4 & 5 Re-pair learners to discuss the questions. You may wish to elicit a few ways of dealing with the tactics.

Answers
1 a good strategy
2 good tactics
Planning to be market leader of your industry sector from being the number 4 in the sector is a medium- to long-term plan and will be wide-ranging, involving all aspects of the company's business in this sector. These are characteristics of strategic planning. A plan to achieve a successful outcome in the next stage of negotiations is tactical as it refers to only one part of the negotiations. the organisation might well have a negotiating strategy, but how it is implemented in a particular stage of negotiations will be tactical.

6 Check that learners know the adjective forms of *strategy* (*strategic*) and *tactics* (*tactical*). Pair them to complete the task and check answers from the text. Discuss as a whole class whether they agree with the author's advice.

Answers
1 tactical
2 tactics
3 strategy
The author states that tactics should align with strategy, which conforms to best practice business thinking (tactics are derived from strategy). However, questions could be asked as to the validity (or even existence of) a strategy in an unknown crisis event. This would be especially the case at the beginning of the crisis, where managers are 'thinking on their feet'.

Output: Deciding tactics to deal with crisis events

Stage 1

Group learners to choose a crisis event and brainstorm strategy. In one-to-one classes, choose an event appropriate to the student's situation and brainstorm strategy as a pair.

Stage 2

Regroup learners to present their ideas. Encourage them to find similarities between strategies for the events and focus on how ethical and legal they are. You could broaden the discussion on ethical behaviour with multilingual groups as a follow-on activity.

5.2 Practice: Successfully dealing with a crisis

Profile: Ceramic Fuel Cells Ltd

Introduction

1 Ask learners to predict possible answers and then read the text. Elicit their answers.

Answers
1 The probable loss of a financial investment of €7 million – a loss caused by the global financial crisis.
2 Product and technology development – the money was needed to fund this.
3 It wasn't; at this point the technology was at the product development stage, i.e. it hadn't yet been commercialised, with products available for sale.

2 Group learners to rank the list of action points. You could regroup them to come to a final ranking and elicit what is the most and least important to prioritise.

Suggested answer
Order of priority: d, b, a, e, c
The company's first priority would be to reassure staff and existing investors that the fundamentals of the company were fine. They would then need to move quickly to search for alternative finance to cover the €7 million lost. When the situation had calmed down somewhat they could start to devise a plan to speed up the product technology. Finally, when there was a small amount of 'breathing space' they could take time out to look back at past mistakes and find out why the company suffered this loss.

Language focus: Contrast financial terms 'investment', 'capital' and 'equity'

1 Books closed. Write the three financial terms on the board and check whether learners know the difference between them. If they do not, refer them to the text above the table. Learners match the columns to create word partnerships and then to the definitions. Elicit the definitions for each.

Answers
1 b i 2 c iii 3 a ii

2 Learners complete the questions, and then compare answers in pairs, before asking them.

Answers
1 investment horizon
2 equity stake
3 raise capital

3 Learners put the correct words in the text.

Answers
1 investment
2 investments
3 equity
4 investment
5 capital

4 Pair learners to discuss the statements. Elicit their ideas or discuss in smaller groups what they show about the company.

Answers
1 The company spent €12.4 million on a new factory in Germany; this shows evidence of expansion and continued progress.
2 The company sold some of its investments. The company needs to fund its activities from its investments.
3 The company offers shares in itself to staff and Directors to align their interests with the interests of the company and incentivise performance and staff loyalty.
4 The company receives monthly reports on how much its investments are worth and whether they have increased or decreased in value. The company needs to carefully balance the money it needs to fund its everyday activities with available cash.
5 The company successfully raised £36 million finance in London when it listed on the London Stock Exchange. This money would be essential to fund the next phase of product development. The successful raising of capital indicates that investors had confidence in the company at that time.

Listening 1: In search of funding 1.30

1 Quickly brainstorm ways of raising capital. Direct learners to the question and play 1.30 . Pair learners to check answers.

Answer
He mentions 2, 3, 5 and 7.

Audio script
Interviewer: When the company suffered a serious crisis and lost seven million euros, how did you manage to survive?
Brendan Dow: Well, since the crisis we have survived successfully having raised a substantial amount of further capital, to progress our commercialisation. At the time of the crisis the company hadn't yet delivered its first product. Throughout the crisis it was really critical to continue progress towards developing and then releasing the product, as the investment horizon of investors that were coming in was much shorter than those that had previously invested.
Interviewer: Right.**Brendan Dow:** The Board was of the opinion that, having reached a critical stage of commercialisation, maybe the State, or even the Federal Government, might support the company during the crisis. And, predictably in hindsight, the government sat on its hands. So one of the lessons there is save yourself, because nobody else will. The next thing we did was approach our commercialisation partners, the big utility companies like Gaz de France, E.ON in the UK, Nuon in Holland …
Interviewer: Huge companies.
Brendan Dow: And we thought that, given their size, they would continue to support us, with a relatively small amount of capital required to see us through. At the same time we would give them a generous share of the future upside. I guess, when we look back, none of the utilities could move quickly enough. I mean, a crisis happens quickly, the utilities move slowly, and we already have a disconnect. So we looked at a careful selection of existing investors and we approached them in December for additional equity, but unfortunately we weren't able to raise money here either. We re-approached existing investors, but this time with a new cornerstone investor in place. Someone who had come out of the woodwork, and we convinced him that this might be a good investment for him. He'd looked at a number of other fuel cell investments globally. He had done his homework on it and was happy to invest.

Answer
They tried to raise money from existing investors together with a new investor.

3 Play 1.30 again and elicit the details of each source of finance on the board.

Suggested answer
The investors coming in were investing on a shorter horizon than was needed. The State and Federal Government were approached, but didn't support the company.
They also approached the big utility companies that they were working with, as it was only a small amount of money they needed – however, the companies were slow to respond and the crisis happened quickly.
They also looked at their current investors, but they couldn't help. In the end they approached an individual who was happy to invest.

4 Tell learners to scan the audio script for the idioms. Discuss possible meanings in pairs or as a class and elicit other examples of usage, e.g. *They didn't know what to do, so they just sat on their hands*; *We have enough food to see us through*; *They all come out of the woodwork when something free is on offer.*

Answers
1 They took no action when action was required.
2 enable us to overcome the present difficulties
3 appeared after being hidden for a long time
4 He had done thorough research.

Listening 2: Lessons learned 1.31

1 Elicit any predictions learners can think of.
2 Play 1.31 for learners to check how many of their predictions were correct.

Audio script
Interviewer: What lessons do you think the company has learned as a result of going through this crisis event?
Brendan Dow: That cash is key. So, whilst we thought we were investing our money and using an external adviser to do that, at the end of the day we would have been better off just leaving it in cash, or some sort of government bond. And not putting it in the hands of someone else who thought they could do a better job. I think one of the main lessons we learned was you shouldn't expect that a white knight just comes out of the blue. White knights are unlikely to emerge in a crisis. You know, people often think well, there's a crisis, so there must be something wrong. There wasn't anything fundamentally wrong with the technology, or the company, or our strategy, it was just something fundamentally wrong with what had happened to the cash that was going to fund our way forward.
Another lesson we learned was when you are looking for new capital in a crisis, you need to operate on many fronts. You can't rely on a single investor or shareholder, or target. You need to have many in play at a particular point in time.
We learned to communicate with employees, because what we didn't want was to lose key employees in the crisis, and make a bad situation worse. So we brought them into our trust. In a crisis I think you have just got to convince people that if they save the company, then we are all going to be better off – rather than just everybody saving themselves.

3 Discuss possible answers first, then learners listen again to check their answers.

Answers
1 key
2 someone else
3 unlikely to emerge
4 a single investor
5 trust

Listening 3: Leading out of a crisis 1.32

1 Ask learners to predict possible answers. Then play 1.32 for learners to check in pairs.

Answers
1 He felt as if he was under siege and as though he had lost control of the situation.
2 He put in more hours and he did a lot more overseas travel to Europe.
3 Use positive body language – keep smiling, stand up straight, keep your head up, keep your shoulders up.
4 Talk about the future, the breakthroughs in the technology; tell suppliers they are going to get paid.
5 investors and suppliers

Audio script
Interviewer: How did it feel personally to be running a company in the middle of a crisis?
Brendan Dow: Well, it felt like you were under siege. You put in a lot more hours, particularly after hours. I mean, travel for me became quite onerous – between October and February I was in Europe on six occasions. So I probably spent about three out of the four months overseas, so that was always difficult. So you feel as though you've lost control of the situation. But I think it's important – I mean, the things that I did was really focus on keeping your body language positive. Keep smiling. Stand up straight. All the basic things that you don't think of when you feel really down: the shoulders go down, and the head goes down, and all that sort of stuff. Well, really focus on keeping your head up, your shoulders up, keep smiling, talk about what is happening, the future, the breakthroughs in the technology. Those sorts of things.
Interviewer: So confidence as well as cash is key.
Brendan Dow: You need to demonstrate confidence. One of the reasons for doing the travel was also to face the investors, so they could make sure that they could see that you were still … you know, there was a process going on. Go and see suppliers and tell them they are going to get paid, because the last thing you want is them to stop supplying you, because they know you're in a bit of trouble.

2 Pair learners to discuss the question. You could elicit advice for dealing with stress.

Suggested answer
Stress reduction techniques might include slow breathing at the moment of critical stress, doing sport or being physically active.

Transferable skill: Confident and insecure body language

1 Books closed. Elicit what learners understand by 'body language'. Pair or group them to discuss and fill in the table. In one-to-one classes, you could extend and discuss how they think other cultures communicate.

Suggested answers

The following answers are typical for a western culture such as the UK or the United States, and may be different for learners' own culture.

Body language type	Communicates confidence	Communicates insecurity
eye contact	consistent eye contact (but avoiding staring)	darting eyes or looking down a lot
facial expression	natural smile	forced smile
gestures	keep hands still or make slow movements with hands	hand wringing, hands in constant motion
the way you stand or sit	stand straight with head up and shoulders slightly back; keep your hands out of your pockets	head down, shoulders down, crossed arms
the way you greet someone	firm but not 'iron grip' and don't hold on too long	limp

2 Group learners to discuss the questions. Then elicit their answers. You may wish to build up a list of advice for learning about body language or role-play an introductions meeting (e.g. a guest arriving at an office) where learners use different body language.

Suggested answers

1 Culture A may think culture B is weak or passive. Culture B may think culture A is aggressive.
2 Culture A may think culture B is dishonest or embarrassed. Culture B may think again that culture A is very aggressive, and perhaps angry.
3 Culture A may think culture B is very unfriendly and cold, whereas culture B might think that culture A is behaving strangely, or is far too friendly.

Output: Preparing for 'What if...' scenarios

Stage 1

Briefly discuss possible crisis management techniques the learners may know of: role play, writing contingency plans, team-building events, etc. Then group learners to discuss the table. You may wish to concept check understanding of *patents*, e.g. *How can companies protect newly developed technology?*

Stage 2

Put learners into larger groups to exchange their scenarios. Then, in their original groups, ask them to devise plans to deal with them, noting their ideas in the table.

Stage 3

Regroup learners into the larger units to present their solutions to the scenarios. You could either record or ask one student to monitor the use of body language and report back.

5.3 Skills: Dealing with conflict

Introduction

1 Group learners to brainstorm answers, elicit a few of their ideas, and discuss with them whether conflict is inevitable or not.

2 Elicit synonyms for *tips* (e.g. *hints*, *advice*) and ask learners to match them to the explanations before checking in pairs.

Answers

1 e 2 a 3 f 4 d 5 c 6 b

Language focus 1: Conflictual turn-taking 1.33

1 You could elicit possible examples for each type of response for what each speaker says before asking them to do the question, e.g. for situation 1:

a *The rent's reasonable.*

b *No it isn't.*

c *Really? Not as stupid as the tenants.*

Answers

1 throwing back the criticism
2 direct refusal
3 interrupting

2 Learners listen to check their answers. Elicit what the second speaker says.

Suggested answers

Making predictions here is possible because usually people respond in similar ways, and the language also gives us hints. David's comment in 1 is a criticism, therefore we can predict John will try to react directly to the criticism. Comment 2 involves a request, therefore accepting or refusing it is very likely. In 3, we can see that John has not finished his message, which suggests he has been interrupted.

Audio script

1
David: ... and the rent's stupid.
John: Not as stupid as I was trying to make it.
2
David: So what else can we get out of you other than this?
John: Absolutely nothing.
3
John: Well, if you have an extreme problem with it then I can, er ...
David: I have got an extreme problem with it, yeah.

3 You may wish to elicit an example for each technique then group learners to discuss them.

Answers

Answers 1, 2, 4, 5, 7, 8 and 10 are appropriate.
The following are not:
3 avoid eye contact (this is highly dependent on culture – in some cultures this can help reduce conflict, but in other cultures it may be interpreted quite negatively)
6 don't respond at all
9 keep your intonation flat (in English, this can be interpreted as aggressive, or bored)

4 Elicit any other examples. Then pair learners to practise the techniques. You could ask more capable classes to use different examples.

> ***Answers***
> Other ways of reducing conflict include apologising and being a supportive listener (through body language and the use of positive words like *sure* and *absolutely*).

Listening 1: Opening the meeting 1.34

1 Tell learners to predict possible answers. They then listen to check their answers.

> ***Answers***
> 1 False (they introduce themselves)
> 2 False (he says he's in the dark and John explains the situation)
> 3 False (it has reached the end of the five-year term)
> 4 True

> ***Audio script***
> **David:** Nice to meet you, John.
> **John:** And you, David.
> **David:** Dive in. Grab a chair.
> **John:** Thank you.
> **David:** Right now, John, I have to say I'm a little bit in the dark here.
> **John:** OK. I'll give you the story then, shall I?
> **David:** Please.
> **John:** From the beginning, you know both the restaurants you operate are owned by us and we supply drinks to these restaurants.
> **David:** Mm.
> **John:** So you rent two properties at the moment with our basic range of drinks package. Now, you have received very good discounts on this range since you started renting the restaurants from us.
> **David:** Mm.
> **John:** So that was all fine. That agreement was put in place for a period of about five years. When you started renting the properties, which was just over five years ago, we guaranteed the discounts on the drinks until the end of this calendar year. We said that we would honour that agreement, then after that we probably wouldn't. Right. So this is the 'probably wouldn't' bit.
> **David:** Right.
> **John:** So what we've done is put into operation a scheme to give you discounts on …
> **David:** But not ones that I'll notice.
> **John:** … most of your range. No, no, no. You'll notice it. I'll talk you through it. It's all fairly logical. It's not rocket science – because we're a supplier, we're not keen on you selling other people's products.

Listening 2: Disagreements 1.35

1 Discuss which words could fill the gaps, before playing 1.35 and checking answers.

> ***Answers***
> 1 no opportunity whatsoever to get any benefit
> 2 meaningless
> 3 business sense whatsoever

> ***Audio script***
> **David:** I've got to try and figure out what we can do about this, 'cause that contract is giving us no opportunity whatsoever to get any benefit from increased volume.
> **John:** No. It's supposed to be protecting you, though.
> **David:** The wholesale price is – well, it's not protecting us at all, because in real terms the percentage of the discount's gone down. And will continue to go down every year. So soon, the discounts will be meaningless.
> **John:** Yeah.
> **David:** And the rent's stupid.
> **John:** Not as stupid as I was trying to make it.
> **David:** It's ridiculous already. The amount you were trying to make it was absolutely beyond any business sense whatsoever. So what else can we get out of you other than this?
> **John:** Absolutely nothing.

2 Pair learners before discussing why learners believe the level of conflict has changed.

> ***Suggested answer***
> The level of conflict has increased a lot compared to the beginning of the meeting. For instance, they are disagreeing very forcefully with each other, and are using quite emotionally charged language: *stupid*, *ridiculous*, *absolutely beyond any business sense whatsoever*

Listening 3: Closing stages 1.36

1 Learners read the questions, predict possible answers and listen to check.

> ***Answers***
> 1 John's company will pay the legal fees, and David's company will pay the rent.
> 2 High – the men are very rude to each other.

> ***Audio script***
> **John:** Well, if you have an extreme problem with it then I can, er …
> **David:** I have got an extreme problem with it, yeah. Specially for hundred and fifty quid. It's absolute madness.
> **John:** You didn't let me finish the sentence. If you've got an extreme problem with the legal fees then we can pay them.
> **David:** Good. You can say that about the rent.
> **John:** No.
> **David:** Mm. OK. Well, thank you for your time, John.
> **John:** OK. So you're clear where we're sort of coming from.
> **David:** Yes. Clear.
> **John:** Yeah.
> **David:** John, I don't envy you. You must be welcomed up and down the country.
> **John:** Well, yeah. Most people are kinder than you are, but there you go.

2 Play 1.36 again before eliciting their answer to this question.

> ***Answer***
> They were not successful at all; the meeting really gets out of control.

Critical analysis

1 & 2 Pair or group learners to discuss the questions. Elicit the situations where conflict was appropriate and necessary. In one-to-one classes, you could discuss if they have been in such situations.

> ***Answers***
> 1 The dangers of conflict are that it can cloud people's judgement, and it can have long-term negative effects on the relationship between the speakers and/or their organisations. Many mergers and acquisitions fail because of irreconcilable conflict (see unit 11.1).
> 2 Making any kind of change will usually involve conflict at some level, and conflict is often seen as an essential part of making and implementing innovations.

Language focus 2: Cooperative and aggressive idioms and metaphors

1 Learners work in pairs to match idioms and metaphors to meaning.

> ***Answers***
> 1 h 2 c 3 b 4 d 5 e 6 g 7 a 8 f

2 In the same pairs, learners decide whether or not the metaphors are conflictual, before checking in pairs and feeding back.

> ***Answers***
> conflictual: 4, 5, 6, 7, 8
> not conflictual: 1, 2, 3

3 Pair learners to rewrite the sentences and check answers. You could discuss why they think the language is aggressive.

> ***Suggested answers***
> 1 Well, to be honest, there were discussions about raising it further.
> 2 We think this proposal needs reconsidering.
> 3 It's difficult to see how this can be implemented in practice.
> 4 (As this is a sarcastic comment, it is probably best to say nothing.)

Output: Dealing with conflictual situations

In pairs, learners read the instructions carefully before the first role play. You may wish to check their understanding. After the role play you could re-pair them to discuss the follow-on questions. Repeat with new partners for the second scenario.

Progress test 1 (See page 120)

Answers

Grammar 1
1 of 2 on 3 on/at 4 in 5 of 6 of 7 to 8 on 9 of 10 in/to

Grammar 2
1 Few 2 a limited quantity of 3 billions of
4 a fair amount of 5 A great number of

Vocabulary 1
1 d 2 e 3 a 4 b 5 c

Vocabulary 2

Verb	Adjective	Noun
adapt	adaptable	adaptation/ adaptability
differ/differentiate	different	differentiation
minimise	minimal	minimum
globalise	global	globalisation
standardise	standard/ standardised	standard/ standardisation

Vocabulary 3
1 common 2 broad 3 strong-arm 4 coherent 5 underhand
6 long-term 7 integrated 8 illegal 9 delaying 10 Effective

Writing
Allow 2 marks each for task achievement, organisation, grammar, vocabulary and coherence.

Worksheet 5 (See page 131)

Improve your knowledge of fundraising

Level **C1 +**

Time **55–60 minutes**

1 Lead-in (10 minutes)

Pair learners to discuss the questions.

Suggested answers

1 *Shares* are issued or bought and sold. *Stakes* can be raised at a gambling table or metaphorically when increasing your risk level.
2 *Funds* are cash set aside and can be drawn upon quickly. *Capital* is cash and other forms of wealth used for business and investment purposes.
3 a person or event aimed at raising money for a particular purpose
4 *Funds*. *Shares* are issued to raise capital for private firms, the others are issued by governments to fund expenditure. UK gilt-edged securities or *gilts* are known as *Treasury bills* in the USA.
5 An *NPO* ploughs any surpluses from its activities back into the organisation and does not distribute them as profit or dividends. An *NGO* is an organisation that is not part of a local, regional or national government. Although it may be funded totally or partially by governments, an NGO excludes government representatives from membership in the organisation. A *charity* is an organisation created to promote the public good and can be either private or public.

2 Verbs, prepositions and *money* (15 minutes)

1 Ask learners to match the verbs, *money* and prepositions to make a phrase. They could check in pairs or you could elicit their ideas.

Answers

borrow	money	from	an unscrupulous loan shark
save		for	a rainy day
invest		in	a second home to let to tenants
raise		for	a charitable good cause
spend		on	a new outfit for an office party
waste		on	underperforming shares
put		in	the kitty

2 Pair learners to discuss other possible collocations and their dependent prepositions and examples. Elicit any ideas, e.g. *win/lose money on a bet, throw money at a problem.*

3 Private and public sector funding (15 minutes)

1 Pair or group learners to discuss similarities and differences in how the private (PV) and public (PU) sectors can fund themselves. You could extend the activity to include the voluntary sector.

Suggested answers

Bankruptcy: used by PV to raise funds to pay off creditors when a business collapses.
Donations: neither sector relies on these for funds. Used more to fund the voluntary sector.
Fundraising events: neither sector raises funds this way, although the voluntary sector does.
Government grants: both sectors – PV has tax breaks, PU is given funds to cover operating costs.
Internal market: used by PU bodies with different components to reduce costs and generate funds.
Outsourcing: both sectors can save costs in cleaning, security, etc. to generate funds.
Profit dividends: are recycled in PU and distributed to shareholders in PV.
Reclaiming taxation: both sectors can reclaim VAT paid on purchases under certain circumstances.
Renting buildings: both sectors can generate funds renting unused space.
Restructuring loans: both sectors use this instrument to reschedule interest payment on debt.
Selling assets: both sectors can generate funds selling buildings, vehicles, etc.
Selling shares: only available to PV to raise capital.

2 Re-pair learners or discuss this question as a whole class. Alternatively, extend the exercise and hold a debate. Some people argue that a large public sector 'crowds out' private investment. Others argue the public sector, including administration, education, health, police, military and welfare is the only viable employer in some regions of both developed and developing countries.

4 Fundraising role play (20 minutes)

1 Pair learners to discuss the ideas, justify their reasons and come to an agreement on six fundraising ideas. Encourage them to think of other reasons why some activities and events are better than others.

2 Re-pair learners to report back on their original discussion.

6 Leadership

Overview of the unit

6.1 Theory: Leadership styles and qualities

> 'A good objective of leadership is to help those who are doing poorly to do well and to help those who are doing well to do even better.'
>
> *Jim Rohn*

The leadership skills that a manager uses can often depend on the type of team that he or she is in charge of. A good leader will be able to judge the ability of their team and alter their style accordingly. In this way, leadership becomes more of a strategic choice than a function of personality. There are six styles of leadership: coercive, authoritative, affiliative, democratic, pacesetting and coaching. The style used depends on the level of support and guidance needed as well as the situation that is being faced. For example, a coercive ('do what I say') style may work in a crisis situation or with problem employees, but in other circumstances it can inhibit flexibility and motivation. Conversely a democratic style may lead to flexibility and fresh ideas in some circumstances, but in others will leave employees feeling confused and leaderless.

Research has shown that the most successful leaders develop a range of Emotional Intelligence competencies with self-awareness, self-regulation, motivation, empathy and social skill being key in allowing them to have the flexibility to switch between leadership styles as the situation dictates.

6.2 Practice: Nikki King – a business leader

Profile: Nikki King

Nikki King is the managing director of Isuzu Truck (UK), which was launched in 1996 and has a nationwide dealer network of over sixty locations. King worked for several years at an Iveco Ford dealership, starting as an administrative manager and becoming a fleet director. She then moved to Lex Plc, a vehicle leasing company.

After a business trip to Japan, Lex offered her the chance to launch Isuzu's first UK distributor. In 2004, she led a management buyout for the Isuzu import business and became its managing director.

King is particularly interested in the situation of working mothers. She encourages working from home and job-share schemes. She also incorporates many of the skills associated with raising a family such as time management, persuasion and politicking into her leadership and management style.

She has gained and been nominated for many awards and is involved in the work of various charities.

6.3 Skills: Motivating staff

The link between job satisfaction and creativity is clear and is seen to depend on tangible financial rewards and the organisational culture.

As well as payment, common motivational factors include job security, feeling of personal accomplishment, recognition, a clear understanding of what is expected, consistent and genuine management behaviour, and participation in decision-making. These factors fall into the transactional and transformational leadership model developed by James MacGregor Burns in 1978.

Transactional leaders create strong expectations and give clear indications of rewards and punishment. Transactional leadership is found in all organisations in terms of the salary earned and dismissal clauses in a contract. Reward or punishment is seen as the overriding factor in motivation. This style works better in the more individualistic cultures rather than the more collective ones, where payment/punishment for the group's achievement/errors would be more usual.

Transformational leaders inspire admiration, trust, loyalty and respect. They are able to mentor, to communicate vision easily, and to motivate followers to perform tasks beyond what is necessary to encourage professional development.

The model is important, as although pay is obviously an influential factor, the highest level of engagement and performance is also highly desirable.

6.1 Theory: Management Leadership styles and qualities

Introduction

1 Brainstorm some well-known leaders on the board. Pair learners and ask them to choose a leader that they admire. They should explain the reasons why they admire this leader.

2 Ask learners to look at the list of qualities and apply them to the leader that they previously described. They should also think of examples that demonstrate that the leader has these skills.

3 With a new partner, learners look at the pictures at the top of the page. They discuss which of the leadership skills each person needs. With weaker groups you could choose one of the photos and discuss it as a class activity as an example.

> ***Suggested answers***
>
> **Teacher:** needs intelligence to deal with her subject matter, good communication skills and a willingness to share her experiences in order to inspire her students. She needs respect for others and an ability to inspire her students to respect others. She sometimes needs to stay calm in difficult circumstances. With the increase in new technology in the classroom she needs to adapt to changes and learn new skills.
>
> **Football captain:** needs to have good communication skills with his team mates and an ability to inspire them.

He also needs to be single-minded and decisive. In some circumstances an ability to stay calm will be an asset. Self-awareness of his own strengths and weaknesses and those of his team mates is also a useful skill for him to have.
Politician: probably needs to use all of the different skills at different times during her career.
Manager: probably needs to use all of the different skills at different times during her career.

Language focus 1: Describing leadership styles

1 Learners match the leadership styles to their characteristics, compare answers in pairs, and then check their response.

Answers
1 d 2 f 3 b 4 c 5 a 6 e

2 Learners work in pairs to complete the sentences using the words in the box, before checking as a class.

Answers

1 resistant	5 competencies
2 adrift	6 inhibit
3 exemplify	7 hallmark
4 mastered	8 dampens

Reading 1: Leadership styles in practice

1 Focus learners' attention on the article *Leadership that Gets Results*. Give them a time limit of three minutes to complete the text with the six different styles from Language focus 1. Check the answers as a class.

Answers

1 coercive	4 democratic
2 authoritative	5 pacesetting
3 affiliative	6 coaching

2 Give learners five minutes to read the article again. They should decide whether the statements agree or disagree with the writer's point of view or if the writer's view is not given. After reading again, learners check in pairs and discuss the reasons for their answers.

Answers
1 D 2 D 3 A 4 A 5 NG 6 NG 7 NG 8 D 9 A

3 Put the learners in small groups to discuss the two questions.

Suggested answer
It is important because different leadership styles are needed for different circumstances and therefore it is important for managers to be able to adapt to the needs of their staff and the circumstances.

Reading 2: Leadership qualities and Emotional Intelligence

1 Check that learners understand what Emotional Intelligence is (the ability to understand the way other people feel and react and to use this skill to make good judgements and to avoid or solve problems). In pairs, they read the introductory paragraph to the article and complete the gaps.

Answers
1 consists 2 composed 3 corresponding

2 Learners work alone to analyse their own Emotional Intelligence. They should write the score that they would give themselves at the bottom of each column.

3 Learners compare their answers in small groups and discuss their personal qualities and capabilities based on the discussion questions.

4 Learners work alone to match the competencies listed to the correct column in the article, then check their answers in pairs.

Answers
1 SS 2 SM 3 SS 4 SM 5 SS 6 SS

5 In pairs, learners rank the six competencies in exercise 4 in order of importance. Put them in groups of 4 to discuss with another pair their answers and reasons.

Language focus 2: Word partnerships with 'self'

Ask learners to complete the sentences with different word partnerships with *self*. Check the answers as a whole class.

Answers
1 C 2 B 3 A 4 C 5 C 6 A

Output: Finding the right leader

Regroup learners to choose a type of company that they are all keen on working for. You could limit them to a choice of the type of organisations listed or designate a type of organisation to each group.

Stage 1

Learners should work as a group to analyse their strengths and weaknesses using the results from Reading 2 to form a basis for discussion.

Stage 2

Learners work together to find what type of leader they need, using the information from Reading 1 and Reading 2 to help them decide.

Stage 3

Learners create a profile of the type of leader they would like to work with. They could present this information to other groups and see if any other class members fit their profile.

6.2 Practice: Nikki King – a business leader

Profile: Nikki King

Introduction

1 Ask learners to read the profile box to find the answer to the question.

Answer
Nikki King was the first female managing director of a truck company in the UK and was the first female president of both the Society of Operations Engineers and the Institute of Road Transport Engineers.

2 & 3 In pairs, learners discuss the questions.

Suggested answers
1 Fewer women than men study engineering at university. There is also a general perception that the engineering and truck sector is a 'man's world' and as a result there is certain amount of sex discrimination at work which is often invisible, but is still real.
2 Determination, talent, strong communication skills, ambitious, a good motivator of people, a good networker (with reference to her posts in Industry Associations).

3 Learners work individually to complete the gaps and then compare answers in pairs before whole class feedback.

Answers

1 Leadership	4 managers
2 Management	5 manage
3 leaders	6 lead

Listening 1: The qualities of leaders and managers 1.37

1 Discuss the questions as a whole class.

2 Play 1.37 and elicit the answers.

Answers
1 Nikki King believes that a good leader has passion, vision and a long-term plan; is consistent and inspirational, and acknowledges that it is the people around him/her who enable him/her to be a good leader.
2 Nikki argues that leaders are born.
3 The example given by Nikki King is that good leaders are inspirational and lead their followers. Good managers make plans but then delegate someone else to do the job.

Audio script
Interviewer: What do you think are the attributes of a good leader, and do you think leaders are born or made?
Nikki King: I think passion and vision make a good leader. I think good leaders have to have a vision. They have to know where they are going in two years, five years, ten years. And then they can't deviate from that, so they have to be passionate about that vision.
Interviewer: OK.
Nikki King: And I think the one thing that denotes a good leader is somebody who is pretty consistent. I don't think, generally, people like leaders that run off in thousands of different directions.
Interviewer: Yeah, right.
Nikki King: So I think that's two attributes of a good leader. I think, to a degree, they are born. I don't think you can make a good leader.
Interviewer: Right.
Nikki King: Good leaders are inspirational in the way they behave. You know, you can have two sorts of general, can't you? The one that sits and plans an attack, and just hopes somebody else does it, which is generally probably a good manager.
Interviewer: OK.
Nikki King: But a good leader says, 'Come on, I'm jumping over this. I don't know what is on the other side of this, we might all die, but come with me anyway for the fun of it', and people go.

Listening 2: Leadership in different sectors 1.38

1 & 2 Focus attention on the headings in the table and discuss possible differences in the private and public sector. Pair learners in larger classes and elicit their ideas.Then play 1.38 once or twice for learners to complete the table.

Suggested answers
Leader communication: You can tell people what to do in the private sector. In social enterprises you need to be more persuasive.
Staff motivations: People's motivations are more varied in social enterprises.
Level of 'red tape' (bureaucracy): There is a lot more bureaucracy outside of private enterprise.
Commercial mindset: Social enterprises tend to be non-commercial.
Rules: There are rules and regulations in the local government sector.

Audio script
Interviewer: How does leading and managing in the private sector and in, say, social enterprises – or NPOs, charities – compare?
Nikki King: Oh, it's completely different. In the voluntary sector, you're dealing with volunteers and not people who work for you. So you have to be much more persuasive and far less ... not necessarily dictatorial, but you can't actually tell people what to do, and you have to be very, very careful on that one.
Interviewer: Yes.
Nikki King: You also have to really analyse why people are doing it, because people tend to work for the voluntary sector for many different reasons. It might be because they are just generally all-round good eggs who really want to help, or because they want their OBEs, or because they want some sort of kudos, or it looks good on their CV. And so you have to analyse it before you actually motivate them, which is very different to having somebody working for you.
Interviewer: Yeah.
Nikki King: In the local government sector, there is so much red tape that you don't have as a leader of your own business. So, you know, tremendous amount of committees for the sake of it, rules and regulations around health and safety and HR, and all these other things that we don't generally have so much of in the private sector.
Interviewer: Are there any other differences?
Nikki King: The major difference is that, unlike the private sector, the public sector and charities are not commercial at all.
Interviewer: Yes.
Nikki King: Which really works against them. So to actually bring somebody in with a commercial mind would normally have a very beneficial effect on both.

Listening 3: Advice for business leaders 1.39

1 & 2 Learners note their ideas, before listening to the speaker. Elicit the answers and if any learner predicted them correctly.

Answers
1 Be honest, be yourself.
2 Practise what you preach.
3 Don't deviate from your vision.

Audio script
Interviewer: What advice do you have for people wanting to be good leaders?
Nikki King: First of all be honest, be yourself. You can't keep up a pretence of being somebody else for your whole life. If you are a woman, don't try and manage like a man or be a male leader, because you are a woman, and behave like one because it's very unattractive otherwise.
Interviewer: Yeah.
Nikki King: Practise what you preach. Don't say one thing and do something else.
Interviewer: OK.
Nikki King: And really, really ... that's back to the vision and passion. Set your vision, do it with passion, and don't be deviated, and just keep going. And that's all I can say about it really.

Language focus 1: The language of leadership

1 Learners work individually, then check in pairs. You could elicit which form of the word is used.

Answers
passion: be passionate about / have a passion for / passions run high
vision: have a vision / have visions / be a visionary
consistent: be consistent / act consistently / lack consistency
inspire: seek divine inspiration / be inspirational / inspire your followers by example
dictator: avoid a dictatorial approach / be a dictatorial ruler / be a real dictator
persuade: be persuasive / have persuasive arguments / lack powers of persuasion
motivate: have the ability to motivate others / be highly motivated / be motivated by greed

2 Learners work in pairs to discuss the question.

Answers
The inappropriate ones are:
passions run high (= get upset)
have visions (usually associated with unreal mental states)
lack consistency
seek divine inspiration
be a dictatorial ruler / be a real dictator (the term *dictator* is negative; *strong leader* is a more positive expression)
lack powers of persuasion
be motivated by greed

3 Learners discuss those they consider important for leaders. Elicit any other qualities needed.

Suggested answer
All of these positive attributes are very important for leaders. Charisma is often cited as very important, as are self-belief and belief in the enterprise. A high degree of energy is also common among leaders.

Language focus 2: Understanding proverbs

1 Books closed. Write *proverb* on the board and elicit its meaning (traditional saying expressing generally accepted opinion, whose meaning is understood without further explanation). Discuss the meaning of the example proverb.

Answer
It means don't be a hypocrite – if you say staff should do something, you should also do it yourself.

2 & 3 In pairs, learners discuss the meanings of the proverbs, their L1 equivalents if there is one, quantity and frequency of use. In monolingual classes, you could ask them to translate the proverbs and discuss their meaning.

Answers
1 It is better to be late than to not come at all. It suggests that late results are better than no results.
2 Employees may blame their tools rather than themselves when something goes wrong. It is important to accept responsibility, even for mistakes.
3 You should value what you have, rather than value what you might get if conditions favour you. This relates to the importance of concrete results.
4 Developing autonomous or empowered employees is of great value. This relates to the importance of training.
5 Too many leaders or managers will lead to problems.

Critical analysis

Brainstorm possible issues that women could face at work, e.g. taking time off to care for a child. Learners read the text to find the answer to the first question. Pair learners to discuss the following questions. Elicit a few of their ideas for question 3.

Answer
The key issue is that women tend to face far more external (i.e. non-job related) pressures and demands than men – for example, dealing with family problems.

Output: Advising an organisation on leadership

Stage 1
Group learners to decide which points need addressing.

Stage 2
In their groups, learners brainstorm answers to the questions.

Stage 3
Groups develop a presentation. Regroup them to outline the NPO's new direction to each other. In one-to-one classes, ask the learner to give the presentation as if they were the president.

6.3 Skills: Motivating staff

Introduction

1 Discuss the pictures as a whole class.

Suggested answer
The pictures show two football managers. One is confrontational and the other is comforting a player.

2 & 3 Brainstorm a list of motivational factors on the board, then pair learners to discuss what motivates them. Then discuss how they think the managers in the pictures would behave.

Listening 1: Describing transactional and transformational motivation 1.40

1 Focus learners on the text and elicit the difference between the two types of motivation. Ask them to predict the classification of the factors. Then play 1.40 and feed back.

> ***Answers***
> Transactional: do what the boss says; experience tells us what to expect; telling; doing; pointing
> Transformational: need to work in new ways; consulting; togetherness

> ***Audio script***
> **David Prasher:** The reason this motivation thing is so interesting at the moment is I think what many businesses are going through, especially media businesses like ours, is transformation. And in the old business model, which everybody understood, leadership and management were fairly transactional. Which is 'I am the boss. You work for me. I have done your job before. There's only a limited set of outcomes, and, you know, experience tells us what they are. Therefore, if you do this you will succeed.'
> **Interviewer:** Yeah.
> **David Prasher:** And I think that leadership and management now have to change from transactional to transformational, which is 'We have a vision. The world is changing. We're asking you to work in new ways. We think we know the outcome, but we're not all one hundred percent sure. And we don't all know what it takes to get there.'
> **Interviewer:** Right.
> **David Prasher:** Technology is driving rapid change, and therefore that leadership and motivation can't be transactional. And so the language then needs to move from transactional language – which is telling, doing, pointing – to transformational, which is about consulting, joining, togetherness.

2 Ask learners to write down *transactional* and *transformational* and to take bullet point notes under the headings. Learners listen again and write down their ideas.

> ***Suggested answers***
> Transactional managers have a very clear idea of what the job involves, because the job doesn't really change, and tell the staff exactly how they should do it. Transformational managers, in contrast, recognise that their work environment is dynamic and changing, and therefore approach their staff more as fellow team members. A transformational manager will encourage the team to understand and solve the problems they face together.

3 Play 1.40 again if necessary and elicit the answer.

> ***Answers***
> The change has come about due to rapid changes driven by technology.

4 Briefly discuss which picture portrays a more transactional approach and why.

> ***Answers***
> Photo A shows a more transactional manager who is directing the player, as opposed to working together with him.

Listening 2: Motivating different types of people 1.41

1 Before listening, discuss as a class the four personality types and what features of each might display.

2 Ask learners to predict which type goes in each quadrant. Then play 1.41 and feed back in whole class.

> ***Answers***
> a coaster c problem child
> b star d striver

> ***Audio script***
> **David Prasher:** We try to define our staff in one of four different ways – coasters, or problem children, or strivers, or stars – based on a group that has motivation going across the X-axis.
> **Interviewer:** Say those four again? Coasters?
> **David Prasher:** Coasters, problem child, star, or striver. So, if you want me to define those, that would create a quadrant, because you would have 'ability' going up the Y-axis, with high ability at the top, low ability at the bottom.
> **Interviewer:** The 'motivation' going across the X-axis. Right?
> **David Prasher:** Yes, low on the left, high on the right. And, therefore, if you are top left you're a coaster. If you are bottom left you're a problem child, because you have got low motivation and/or low ability. If you are top right you are a star: high ability, high motivation. And if you are bottom right you are a striver.
> **Interviewer:** OK.
> **David Prasher:** So, the way that you motivate those people, and coach those people – and I think a lot of motivation comes from coaching nowadays – is different. So, for a star, the job is to keep them motivated. You probably have a higher frequency of contact. Give them real praise. Give them projects, and just harness their talents really. Whereas if you've got a problem child, there's far more of a building job required with a problem child, to move them up the scale. You might do more telling with those people.
> **Interviewer:** Right.
> **David Prasher:** You give them a detailed sort of plan of action. Concentrate on their skills. So, you know, they'll feel motivated if they think that you are improving their skill set.

3 & 4 Pair learners to discuss the questions. You could re-pair them to discuss again and decide on their own personality type.

> ***Answers***
> Stars need lots of contact and a manager who praises them. They should be given projects that harness their ability. Problem children mostly need telling what to do. A manager should make a plan of action and help them use and improve their skills.

Listening 3: Team-building meeting in a hotel

1.42

Books closed. Play 1.42 and discuss whether or not it was motivational. Allow them to listen again as they read the audio script on page 61. Then ask learners to read the quote from David Prasher. Elicit whether Brad's use of words and phrases such as *I am singing from the rooftops* and *the talent is here so we can win* makes them want to be part of his team, and why/why not.

> ***Suggested answer***
> It seems unlikely that this manager will motivate this team, due to both his style of speaking and the content of his talk. This group of employees probably will not relate to the football analogy, and his use of very idiomatic expressions like *singing from the rooftops* and speed of speaking may confuse English speakers of this level.

Language focus: Using transactional and transformational language

1 Pair learners to decide if the comments are transactional or not, before re-pairing them to check answers. You might wish to check if they understand '*proactive*' and '*worthwhile + ing*'.

> ***Answers***
> Transactional: 2, 3, 4, 7, 10
> Transformational: 1, 5, 6, 8, 9

2 Group learners to discuss how to approach the scenarios and what they would say. In smaller classes you could focus on one scenario only and build up a list of what to say.

> ***Answers***
> a A more transactional approach may be good, and the manager may say something direct like *You need to meet these deadlines, otherwise (the team will suffer / your position may need to be reviewed …).*
> b A more transformational approach here may be good. For instance, the manager can ask what projects the star wants to work on, and what he/she can offer.
> c A transactional approach, perhaps with a slight warning. The manager could remind the employee of his/her obligations.
> d Perhaps a transformational approach, with the manager exploring how the employee would like to be rewarded (e.g. with more responsibility).

Intercultural analysis

1 Pair learners to discuss the question before eliciting their ideas, e.g. transactional styles are found in industries where quick decisions have to be made (airline pilots, fire fighters, etc.); a possible disadvantage of transactional style is procrastination.

> ***Suggested answer***
> 1 A strongly transactional approach might be best in a workplace where doing the task in exactly the right way is essential, for example, in some factories where safety is an issue.

2 Form new pairs for learners to discuss the second question.

> ***Suggested answer***
> Some people might find the lack of clear direction offered by a transformational manager frustrating, and it may appear that the manager does not know what he/she is doing.

3 Re-pair learners to discuss the question. Encourage them to come up with a few adjectives or phrases to describe the two situations, i.e. bossy, authoritarian, clueless, over-elaborate, etc. and elicit them as feedback.

> ***Suggested answer***
> In both situations, there is likely to be a lot of friction and misunderstanding. The transactional manager might appear dictatorial to the transformationally minded staff. A transformational manager may seem to lack direction and clarity to transactionally minded staff.

Output: Motivating a staff member

Pair learners. Refer A (Manager) to page 139 and B (Employee) to page 143 and ask them to prepare for a meeting role play. If you have an odd number of learners, you could arrange a 'panel' interview of the employee of two managers. If you do, elicit how the employee felt in this situation.

Stage 1

Student A prepares to discuss the problems with the employee. Encourage them to think of what to say to motivate using their own experience. Encourage Student B to think of what would motivate them to change behaviour.

Stage 2

Learners hold a second meeting in their pairs, with one group of three if necessary. You could discuss how they would feel in this situation before asking them to role play.

> You may want to watch Sequence 3 on the DVD to find out more about Management and leadership in class or ask learners to watch it for homework. There is an accompanying worksheet on page 151.

Worksheet 6 (See page 132)

Improve your knowledge of leading and managing

Level **C1 +**

Time **55 60 minutes**

1 Lead-in (10 minutes)

Pair learners to discuss the questions. You could re-pair them to report back. Elicit their answer for question 4.

Suggested answers

1 A coach usually a sports instructor or a tutor in a specialised subject (e.g. a lifestyle coach).
A manager organises the training of a sports team or to be in charge or direct a business.
2 Yes. Coaches have to earn 'badges'. Managers can study 'management courses'.
3 establishing direction, aligning people, motivating and inspiring
4 The idiom originates from how to get a recalcitrant donkey to work. The carrot is the reward, the stick is the punishment.
5 Business Studies courses are perceived to help graduates get the job they want.

2 Describing a manager's and a leader's points of view (15 minutes)

1 Pair learners to discuss the words and phrases. It may help to describe the leader's style as transformational and the manager's style as transactional before learners do this exercise. You could re-pair them to check answers or elicit their ideas on the board.

Answers

Points of view	Leader (L)	Manager (M)
Relationship with co-workers	followers	subordinates
Organisational culture	shapes	represents
Risk	takes	minimises
Rules and regulations	breaks	makes
Outlook for the future	long-term	short-term
Persuasive technique	sells	tells
Source of power	charisma	authority
Strives for	vision	achievement of objectives
Dynamism	proactive	reactive
Zeal	passion	control

2 Discuss this question as a class. Arguably, all of the 'L' words could be used to describe a modern manager depending on the immediate business situation.

3 Satisfaction & dissatisfaction with management (15 minutes)

1 Learners decide if each employee is satisfied or dissatisfied and why. Pair them to compare answers. Elicit a few ideas as to why for feedback.

Suggested answers

1 dissatisfied – likes to do the minimum
2 dissatisfied – may not like being managed by a younger person
3 satisfied
4 dissatisfied – hasn't bought into changes
5 satisfied

2 Group learners to discuss how they would approach each dissatisfied employee. Elicit their ideas.

Suggested answers

1 Renegotiate contract or sell changes to work schedule.
2 Take a more participatory approach.
4 Could follow a delegating or a selling approach.

4 Ideal Business Studies course (20 minutes)

1 Group learners to discuss what would make up an ideal curriculum for a Business Studies course.

2 Ask the groups to present or write up an overview of the content of their ideal Business Studies course. You could discuss which would be the most popular.

Writing 3: Writing effective emails

Overview of the unit

There are many etiquette guides and rules for writing emails, but they are often inconsistent because of differing business and corporate culture. However, professionalism, efficiency and protection from liability are always constant.

It is recommended that all emails have subject lines, as 'no subject' emails will often be treated as spam and are immediately deleted. There should be one point per email, so they can be organised into those that need a quick reply and those that need more thought. If there are a number of points relating to the same project, the same email can be used, but paragraphs help to increase the likelihood that the points will be addressed.

Other recommendations include the KISS or Keep it Short and Simple principle, using gender-neutral language, refraining from overusing words like *important* and *urgent*, a very good level of spelling, grammar and punctuation and not hitting the 'reply to all' button to every email.

Introduction

1 Pair learners to discuss the questions. Ask learners if they have any personal experience of being misunderstood in an email.

> ***Suggested answers***
> 1 Meeting face-to-face includes body language, facial expression, tone of voice and hesitation, which all add meaning and allow participants in the conversation to adjust their replies accordingly.
> 2 Email misses all the features of face-to-face communication, so misunderstandings increase. Long explanations are particularly difficult to communicate via email. Compared to face-to-face communication, it is a less interactive medium.

2 Elicit any difficulties, or group learners to produce a poster on difficulties writing emails. Their difficulties could then be addressed more easily.

Language focus: Features of effective emails

1 Learners assess the guidelines individually. You may want to concept-check *in a dry way*: *What kind of writing would you consider dull? tedious? uninteresting?*

> ***Suggested answer***
> The guidelines presented here are general ones relevant for most situations. Some of these rules might not apply however depending on the 'house style' and culture of organisations. It might be perfectly acceptable, for example, for internal emails between colleagues within the same organisation to be dry, highly transactional messages that simply convey the necessary information.

2 Pair learners to discuss any similarities and differences in their assessments.

3 Learners match the phrases before feedback.

> ***Answers***
> 1 f 2 h 3 b 4 c 5 a 6 g 7 d 8 e

4 Pair learners to think of other phrases. Elicit on the board for others to take notes.

> ***Suggested answers***
> 1 In reference to [your letter dated 2nd July ...]
> 2 I look forward to hearing from you soon.
> 3 I'd be happy to help out with ...
> 4 Do you think we could ...?
> 5 Please refer to the documents attached.
> 6 With regards to [your last email / your idea ...]
> 7 Following on from [the conference call last night, I'd like to emphasise ...]
> 8 Please let me know if this is convenient.

Writing skill 1: Writing short messages in fast email exchanges

1 Elicit what an *email thread* is, i.e. a group of emails with the same subject. Then tell learners to order the emails before checking their answers.

> ***Answer***
> The correct order is E, A, C, B, D

2 & 3 In smaller classes discuss the answers and reasons why. In large classes, pair learners to discuss.

> ***Answers***
> Style b
> The guidelines are generally followed although there are some punctuation mistakes: the double full stop in the first sentence of email A and the missing apostrophe in *lets* in email B. The language recognises and builds relationships between the correspondents – this is not simply a dry communication of information.

4 Learners scan email A to find the examples. Elicit their ideas as feedback on the board.

> ***Answers***
> a Hi Marlene, All best
> b good job, bit (email A)
> c – good job – the last bit works very well too – concise
> d – concise
> e gets across message, All best
> f I've, I'll

5 Learners re-write the examples. They could come and correct them on the board.

> a Dear Marlene; with best wishes
> b Well done *or* You've done a good job; bit = part
> c Well done. The last part works very well too, as it is concise
> d it is concise
> e gets across the message; with best wishes
> f I have, I will

6 Ask learners to re-write emails A, B and C more formally. You could put them into three groups to re-write one email each and then re-group to tell others how to write their email more formally.

> ***Suggested answers***
> A
> Dear Marlene
> Well done. The last part works very well too as it is concise and gets across the message that the clients are getting a lot here.
> I have put a few comments down with a couple of alternative wordings in a few places (please see the attached document).
> I will leave it to Sylvie to decide which ones she likes.
> With best wishes
> Max
>
> B
> Dear Sylvie
> I think this looks very good so suggest that we go ahead with it. This is another part of the job that has been done well.
> Best wishes
> Max
>
> C
> Dear Max and Marlene
> Please find my comments attached. The introduction in particular is very nice.
> All the best
> Sylvie

Writing skill 2: Writing a longer email

1 Learners scan the email. Elicit the purpose for each paragraph.

> ***Answers***
> Paragraph 1: State purpose of writing
> Paragraph 2: Explain issue in detail
> Paragraph 3: Request action

2 Ask learners to underline examples of informality. Elicit and discuss their ideas.

> ***Answers***
> Months of the year which have more than one syllable have been shortened: *Nov/Oct/Sept*. The words *at the* have been omitted before the words *end of Sept*. No other 'informal professional' email features are used, indicating that a more formal and polite style is being used here.

3 Learners scan the email and match the formal phrases to the informal ones, before checking their answers in pairs. You may like to discuss other formal words and phrases, e.g. *characteristically*, *subsequent*, *extremely eager*, *dramatically affect*, *speeded up*.

> ***Answers***
> 1 typically
> 2 the following
> 3 are very keen
> 4 considerably influence

4 Briefly discuss what learners understand by writing 'directly', i.e. use of *will*/simple present tense instead of *would*/*could*/simple past tense. Pair learners to discuss and re-write the underlined parts of the email more directly. You could group them to compare their answers.

> ***Answers***
> I want to follow up on ...
> let you know there is a problem with the planned launch dates
> we will lose a whole year of sales.
> we need to give these customers what they want – it will have a big impact on sales.
> Please look at the dates again and see how you can tighten the schedule.

Output: Write a fast email exchange to make an agreed decision

Stage 1

Put learners in threes, ask learners to choose a role and prepare to write an email exchange. You could do this passing paper between them, but a computer room or SMS messaging would be more authentic. If your class does not split into three, ask the extra learners to play assistants to the main characters.

Stage 2

Learners write, type or text the email exchange.

Stage 3

Learners review the language and style used. You could display them on a screen for the class to discuss if you use a computer room.

7 International communication

Overview of the unit

7.1 Theory: Culture in international business

> 'Yes, we are all different. Different customs, different foods, different mannerisms, different languages, but not so different that we cannot get along with one another. If we will disagree without being disagreeable.'
>
> *J. Martin Kohe*

Defining culture is notoriously difficult, but everybody has culture if it is defined as an idea, behaviour or something that is shared by human national, family, leisure, company or social groups and is passed on to the young and new members or recruits to that grouping.

Cultural differences go far beyond meeting, greeting and gift-giving in international business. Cultural issues that relate to punctuality, space orientation, power relationships, dealing with conflict, body language, and whether a culture is seen as individualistic or collectivist or not, all can have a positive or negative impact on the success of an international business.

Culture is also not static, but can change over time and is subject to internal and external influences such as economic change, borrowing and adapting from other cultures. This cultural transfer is implicit in international business. Entering new markets or introducing new work behaviours needs to be thought out carefully as this transfer process is selective, e.g. in many cultures a transformational style of management may be seen as weak, as managers are expected to direct operations and in some societies, the use of direct speech in communication is not rude or arrogant, but an acceptable cultural norm. However, many cultures now share the notion that the customer is always right and having a meal with a business partner helps build a relationship.

Raising awareness of cultural issues directly impacts the success and profitability of a business. Therefore, building cultural competence in a workforce is imperative when doing business on a global basis.

7.2 Practice: Internationalising a company

Profile: Rakuten

Rakuten Inc, founded by Hiroshi Mikitani in 1997, its subsidiaries and affiliates, are collectively known as the Rakuten group of Internet service companies. They range from an Internet shopping mall (Rakuten Ichiba), to an Internet banking service (Rakuten Bank), to an online travel reservation service (Rakuten Travel) to a baseball team (Tohuku Rakuten Golden Eagles). Rakuten has evolved an e-commerce business model centred in Japan and has now begun to expand internationally through acquisition of companies in Asia and in Europe. To facilitate this expansion and because of the increase in the number of non-Japanese speaking employees, the company announced its intention to make English its official language, even in meetings where all participants are Japanese.

Megumu Tanefusa, Rakuten's Public Relations Chief, was quoted in *The Japan Times* as saying 'in order to globalise the company, everybody from top management to regular employees should be able to speak English'. To this aim, the company provides in-house English language training for its employees and rewards proficiency, measured by an internationally recognised examination, with promotion.

7.3 Skills: Conducting successful intercultural communication

The key to successful intercultural communication is anticipating the right balance between shared and different cultural behaviour and the avoidance of ethnocentrism. An overemphasis on things shared such as coffee-drinking could lead to looking for similarities that are not there, while an overemphasis on differences may hinder cultural understanding and give rise to the belief that 'our' way of doing things is the 'only' or 'best' way.

Effective global communication means adapting to other cultural rules and an ability to see everyday things from another perspective. Language is important, but its nuances can be misinterpreted when business partners do not share the same level of control. There are also dialectical differences within languages where attitudes to accents reinforce both international and regional prejudices in terms of business ability and overall intelligence.

An understanding of the nature of successful international communication has to include the familiarisation of the business person to the cultural norms of the target market in terms of body language, clothing, eye contact, punctuality, space orientation, touching, power relationships and an awareness of cultural prejudices embedded in language.

7.1 Theory: Culture in international business

Introduction

1 Books closed. Write *culture* on the board. Elicit possible definitions from learners, who then work in pairs to discuss the question.

> ***Suggested answer***
> Most obviously relevant to business communication are those which might affect our behaviour with business colleagues in the workplace: dress at work, customs of professional groups, punctuality, directness of communication, decision-making, national customs, attitudes to power and customs of organisations. However, traditional aspects of culture such as art and music can be relevant in providing events where business people can socialise and build relationships.

2 & 3 Learners with experience of working in different cultures could compare their experiences in pairs before feeding back to the whole class. Learners without work experience could discuss experiences of meeting people from different cultures and imagine how this might affect working relationships.

> ***Suggested answer***
> Different cultures may have different ways of doing or expressing the same thing, such as showing approval, or may do the same action but with different meanings, such as a gesture. This means the possibility for misunderstanding is higher than in homogenous groups. Increasing our understanding of these areas means we are less likely to misunderstand or attribute incorrect interpretations to each other.

Language focus: Key intercultural words and concepts

1 Discuss what knowledge learners would expect to gain from a consultant on cross-cultural communication. Ask them to match the terms, check their ideas in pairs, and then check answers.

> ***Answers***
> 1 e 2 b 3 h 4 j 5 g 6 i 7 k 8 f 9 c 10 a 11 d

2 Learners work in pairs to put the steps in order.

> ***Answer***
> The order is: Recognition, Respect, Reconciliation, Realisation.

3 Still in the same pairs, learners match the statements to the steps. Re-pair them to check answers before whole class feedback.

> ***Answers***
> 2 Reconciliation – The person has started to understand that there are differences, but has not yet realised what the cause of the problem is or how to solve it.
> 3 Realisation – the person realises that there is a need to understand the different cultures before differences and conflicts can be resolved.
> 4 Respect – the person realises that as well as being aware of differences it is important that all parties have a chance to express their opinions and be listened to.

Listening 1: International organisations and their cultures (1.43)

1 Learners predict the differences in the types of organisation. Elicit their ideas.

2 Ask learners to try and match the points to the organisation type. Play 1.43 for learners to check answers in pairs, then elicit their answers.

> ***Answers***

1 a	5 a
2 c	6 c
3 c	7 b
4 b	8 c

> ***Audio script***
> **Interviewer:** You talk about three types of companies – what are they?
> **Fons Trompenaars:** Let me start with 'globalisation' – when everything is universal and you think only about 'one size fits all'. It's indeed very cynical when American firms come to Europe and Asia and say 'Oh gee, that's the way we do things around here.' And you don't have any freedom to do things differently.
> **Interviewer:** OK.
> **Fons Trompenaars:** The opposite is what we call the 'multi-local organisation' – an organisation that has, for example, a shared brand. But the local offices have complete autonomy. They have different approaches in different nations. A good example is Walt Disney's amusement parks. In the parks you see the major themes are the same, in Japan, in Paris, in Florida, but there are slight differentiations to make it more attractive to the local audience.
> **Interviewer:** Yes.
> **Fons Trompenaars:** Now, how do you recognise a trans-national firm and what are good examples? A trans-national firm is a firm that is always keen on learning locally, then taking the best practices which they globalise. So a trans-national team – even McDonald's nowadays – says 'Gee, what is the fastest-growing market? Oh, it seems to be Paris. How come? Oh, it is because of the architecture of the restaurant.' So what we have seen suddenly is that McDonald's took the French architect to Manhattan to refurnish their restaurants. So, you take local best practices which you then globalise. The second characteristic is the top management is very often very multi-cultural. At one stage Applied Materials, a company based in California, had seven people in the management team with nine different nationalities, because two had a double passport. Now that kind of management team is very often a sign of a trans-national type of organisation. And interestingly enough they don't very often have one centre. They have multi centres, which is the third characteristic.
> **Interviewer:** Right. Yes.
> **Fons Trompenaars:** So there's not this dominant 'Here is Chicago or London calling'. The final characteristic is it's very often a value-driven organisation. But the values are very often sophisticated. Let's take PepsiCo International. They have values like 'We strive for teams that consist of creative individuals.' Reconciling individuals and the group. Values like 'We give direct feedback with diplomacy.' So that's the trans-national firm that copes with cultural differences in a much more sophisticated way.

3 Discuss the question before playing 1.43 again and checking answers if necessary.

Answers
Trans-national organisations, because their practices will allow them to cope with cultural differences around the world in a more sophisticated way and therefore be more successful.

4 Discuss the question as a class, or pair learners and elicit a few of their ideas as feedback.

Suggested answer
They need to be able to work effectively in a diverse environment with people from different cultures and with different ways of doing things, and to enjoy that challenge. They would need to have a wide range of negotiating and problem-solving skills, and be dynamic in the way they deal with people and issues. Knowledge of different languages would be of benefit.

Listening 2: Merging companies with different cultures 1.44

1 Elicit the difference between *merger* and *acquisition*, i.e. a combination of two or more commercial organisations / the buying of an organisation. Discuss whether or not cross-border mergers and acquisitions can create cultural conflict. You could elicit their ideas about conflicts caused by differences in management style, punctuality, behaviour in meetings, dress code, etc. Play 1.44 and elicit what Dr Trompenaars says.

Answers
He argues that culture can sometimes play a very big role in failed M&As, but he also points out that it is sometimes used as an excuse (for example, the mistakes a bad CEO makes).

Audio script
Interviewer: Research shows that acquisitions or mergers often fail. Can this be explained from a cultural perspective?
Fons Trompenaars: For sure. A lot of research also shows that between fifty and … eighty percent of the failed mergers are caused by misunderstandings on the human side. Now, I very often, also with our little consulting firm, help companies to integrate and in fact it is fifty percent of our business, so we do a lot of merger and acquisition work. And I am saying this because what we find is we clean up the mess of the technical type of consultants, because they just look at the better IT system. How many people can we kick out? The organisational structure, all the hard stuff. On the cultural side, I would say be careful because culture is nearly always taken as an excuse for mergers which technically fail. In other words the CEO is awful and they say 'Yeah. I don't know what it is so let's call it culture.'
Interviewer: Right.
Fons Trompenaars: However, the beauty of taking culture seriously in a merger acquisition is helping people talk to each other. We say even if you don't reconcile all the cultural dilemmas, at least you have a better dialogue between the cultures, which will help the business in the long run. So it can help, but let's not over-exaggerate.

2 Ask learners to predict the statements then listen to check their answers.

Answers
1 False (between 50% and 80%)
2 True
3 True
4 False (…even if you don't reconcile all the cultural dilemmas, at least you have a better dialogue…)

3 Pair or group learners to discuss the question. Elicit whether they agree.

Answer
He is arguing that while culture is important, there may be other factors at play as well.

Transferable skill: Avoiding stereotyping others

1 Books closed. Write *ethnocentrism* on the board. Elicit its meaning, i.e. a belief that the home culture is better than all others. Discuss as a whole class what they think Dr Fons Trompenaars means by the quote, then pair learners to find the stereotypes. You could brainstorm learners' stereotypes of their own cultures as a way to extend the activity.

Answers
1, 2, 5

2 Group learners into threes or fours to discuss the question. Ask them to decide on the most important for improving intercultural competence and elicit their ideas.

3 & 4 Pair learners to discuss both questions before re-pairing them to report back.

Suggested answers
Stereotypes affect the way we see other people, in that we may not see the reality of the other person, and in fact subconsciously look for behaviour that supports our stereotypes. As many stereotypes are negative, this means we are viewing the 'other' negatively, often unfairly. Given that trust and relationships are so important in business, having such an attitude means that we are less likely to trust the 'other' and develop a good relationship. Furthermore, the 'other' person may pick up on our judgements, which may further damage the relationship.
Understanding the culture of the country you are doing business with or in will allow for you to develop better relationships and will be appreciated by your partners.

Output: Advise companies on reconciling cultural differences

Put learners into small groups. Instruct them to prepare a presentation for each of the companies outlining the culture of both companies, predicting possible areas of cultural conflict and possible solutions to two of these areas. They could then present their ideas in new groups or to the class.

Alternatively, you could ask them to prepare one presentation for both companies and present to the class. Or you could divide the class into four groups and ask two groups to prepare for H.L Corp and two for Kripp. They could then form two groups to present their ideas to each other.

7.2 Practice: Internationalising a company

Profile: Rakuten

Introduction

1 Pair learners to discuss the points. Encourage them to think of opposing views if they agree. You could use one of the more controversial points as a basis for a debate.

2 Discuss the question as a whole class briefly, or re-pair learners in larger classes and elicit a few of their ideas.

Reading 1: Initiating policy

1 Learners predict possible answers, and then find the answers in the text. Ask learners to underline any words or phrases they do not understand in the text, e.g. *keep track of*, *merit*, *charismatic*, *enormous*. Elicit and discuss possible synonyms in context: *record*, *value*, *ability to inspire*, *very large*.

> ***Answers***
> 1 Very strict; employees will be fired if they do not have the required English level.
> 2 None
> 3 The level of staff commitment will dictate the success of this policy.
> 4 1 in 15 (200 of the 3,000)

2 Pair learners to discuss the question. If they think the company does not offer sufficient support, discuss what the company could do, e.g. provide grants to study English abroad, specify a level of English needed for higher positions, or pay for classes at an English language school.

Reading 2: Other companies and reactions

1 Ask learners if they know anything about Uniqlo, Nissan and Nomura and why they have English language programmes, e.g. Uniqlo has a strong American presence in the fashion market, Nissan is allied to Renault of France and has a strong American presence in the automobile market, Nomura has a strong American presence in the financial market. Ask them to predict possible answers, and then read the text to check them.

> ***Answers***
> Uniqlo: English will be the official language, but when the participants are all Japanese, using only Japanese is acceptable.
> Nissan: It has no official policy, but when non-Japanese are present, English should be used (Nissan's CEO does not speak fluent Japanese and the company owns European business).
> Nomura: No rules, but English is needed for dealing with non-Japanese.

2 Ask learners to scan the text to find Giri Suziki's view and elicit the difference in opinion.

> ***Answer***
> Giri Suzuki thinks that the Rakuten policy will fail, but Hiroshi Mikitani seems to see it as essential for the company's success.

3 & 4 Pair learners to discuss both questions. Re-pair them to report back on their initial discussion. Elicit a few of their ideas as feedback. You could extend the activity by discussing what has motivated your learners to study English to this level.

Critical analysis

Learners discuss the questions in pairs or groups depending on the size of the class. Alternatively, organise groups to discuss one of the statements, before presenting their view to the others and then holding a question-and-answer session on what they present.

Language focus: Linking ideas and information together

1 Learners scan both texts to find the linking words. Elicit them on the board. Learners match the words to what they are used for and then check in pairs and get feedback.

> ***Answers***
> **Adding extra information or explanations:**
> whether
> of whom
> by
> saying it
> adding that
> as
> and thus
> **Adding contrasting information:**
> while
> but none has gone as far as to
> though ... and
> but

2 Elicit which words are more common in spoken English. You may wish to discuss whether *of whom* is a dying part of spoken English and whether the sentence: *The Rakuten group has 400 non-Japanese employees out of 6,000 globally* would be more natural currently.

> ***Answers***
> Apart from *but* and perhaps *as*, all of the examples are quite formal, and may therefore be unsuitable in less formal spoken situations. The phrases *of whom*, *adding that* and *and thus* are very unusual in informal spoken language.

3 Pair learners to make sentences. You could group or re-pair them to check answers.

> ***Suggested answers***
> 2 Whether we are present or not, new markets will want these products.
> 3 We have 2,000 employees, 700 of whom speak good English.
> 4 Many companies move their manufacturing plants abroad, but none has gone as far as to move its head offices (until now).
> 5 Staff will receive support, and thus they will be expected to reach a satisfactory English standard.

Output: Developing an English policy for an international company

Stage 1

Put learners into two groups of roughly equal size. Refer Group A (managers) to page 140 and Group B (staff) to page 143 and ask them to read their roles. Ask them to underline the information in the text with reference to the issues and check understanding, while you monitor. You could either form smaller groups for the meeting or keep the original groups for the meeting role play.

Stage 2

Tell the groups to write a summary of the results of the meeting. You could pair them to check their written work while you monitor.

7.3 Skills: Conducting successful intercultural communication

Introduction

1 Brainstorm topics that could be *small talk*, e.g. the weather, hobbies, food preferences, sports. Ask learners to stand up and talk to each other at varying distances using these topics. Do this a few times with different partners. Elicit how comfortable they feel at different distances and possible problems if people from cultures with different space orientation meet.

2 Learners work in pairs to discuss the questions.

3 Re-pair learners to sort the questions into categories and discuss the following questions. Elicit a few ideas from different nationalities if possible.

> ***Suggested answer***
> touching: 1, 2
> distance between speakers: 3, 4
> humour: 5
> time: 6, 7
> dress: 8
> It is often argued all these are affected strongly by culture, far more than people often realise. For instance, people in Japan tend to stand much further apart than people in Saudi Arabia in similar contexts, such as colleagues talking in the workplace.

Language focus: Collaborative turn-taking 1.45

1 Elicit what learners understand by *turn-taking*. You could discuss if this is common in their culture as some cultures prefer to let 'senior' speakers finish first, before adding comments. Learners match the strategies with the phrases; check their answers in pairs before feedback.

> ***Answers***
> 1 a 2 d 3 f 4 c 5 b 6 e

2 Learners listen to the extracts and match to the strategies.

> ***Answers***
> Extract 1: Handing over to another speaker
> Extract 2: Reformulating another person's meaning
> Extract 3: Repairing misunderstanding about your intended meaning
> Extract 4: Summarising the discussion so far
> Extract 5: Checking shared viewpoint
> Extract 6: Actively supporting the speaker

> ***Audio script***
> **Extract 1**
> **Speaker:** Helen, run us through this if you would.
>
> **Extract 2**
> **Speaker:** Deborah said not being vigilant on the standards, which in other words means not always following the sequence which is described.
>
> **Extract 3**
> **Speaker 1:** So, if you have considered another Yokohama bridge you might consider this, er ...
> **Speaker 2:** Oklahoma?
> **Speaker 1:** No, Yokohama.
> **Speaker 2:** Yokohama Bay Bridge. Okay.
>
> **Extract 4**
> **Speaker:** Thanks, Dan. Our goal today was to explain the growth opportunities available to Kodak and to make a strong case for the higher valuation we think Kodak deserves. To sum up: Kodak plans to achieve an annual top-line growth rate of eight to twelve percent by the end of our annual planning period.
>
> **Extract 5**
> **Speaker 1:** If we go and do this it, it, it doesn't work. Is that correct?
> **Speaker 2:** That's correct.
>
> **Extract 6**
> **Speaker 1:** It's actually, erm, an Internet TV site as well.
> **Speaker 2:** Oh, is it?
> **Speaker 1:** Yeah.
> **Speaker 2:** Oh, right.
> **Speaker 1:** Mm.
> **Speaker 2:** Okay. I see. So what's the business it's been doing?

3 Pair learners to discuss the problems and decide on a strategy. They could check their ideas in small groups or you could elicit their answers.

> ***Answers***
> a 5 b 1 c 3 d 6 e 4 f 2

4 Hold a class discussion on the importance of strategies. Emphasise the international context.

> ***Suggested answers***
> These strategies are commonly used in many types of meetings because they help guarantee successful understanding and the smooth flow of communication. Because of the greater challenges involved in international communication (such as the range of different accents), these strategies are arguably even more important.

Critical analysis

Ask learners to discuss how *silence* is interpreted in multilingual groups if possible. In a monolingual class you could brainstorm their ideas for other cultures as a whole class. Pair learners to discuss both the questions. Elicit their solutions to the problem. You could repeat the small talk exercise, encouraging learners to interrupt each other to varying degrees.

> ***Suggested answer***
> 2 The relationship may suffer, as both speakers may develop a negative impression of each other: the former person is likely to think the latter has nothing to say or is in a bad mood, whereas the latter may think the other person is rude. One possible solution is to notice how you tend to communicate, and to adapt your style when you are talking to others who communicate differently.

Listening: Expert advice

1.46

1 & 2 Tell learners they are going to listen to advice from three people. Ask them to predict what they will say. They then listen and take notes. Elicit the key point for each speaker as feedback. You could ask them if they agree with the speakers.

> ***Answers***
> Speaker 1: Smile sometimes (especially if you are from a culture where people may not smile so much in communication).
> Speaker 2: Learn the history of the other culture.
> Speaker 3: Use small talk to evaluate the other person's English level.

> ***Audio script***
> **Speaker 1:** Hiro Tanaka
> **Hiro Tanaka:** Very often I find Japanese people's interaction to be very monotonous, including their facial expression. So sometimes I encourage them to smile, and it works very well. A person may know their job very well, and be intelligent, but when that person smiles, the personality comes out. I think smiling helps a lot.
>
> **Speaker 2:** Nikki King
> **Nikki King:** Well, the first tip is always to study the history of a country before you start, because I don't believe you can understand the country's culture until you understand its history. You understand its DNA, what made it what it is. I think that's really, really important. I think you must try and learn the language, even to a small degree. And I think the other thing is to watch very carefully, and listen to the way people are dealing with you, because it's quite a good pointer on the way you should be dealing with them.
>
> **Speaker 3:** Charlie Peppiatt
> **Interviewer:** Is it true when people meet somebody for the first time they'll use the kind of pre-meeting chat time, the small talk preceding the meeting, quite strategically in order to gauge the other person's English. Is that right?
> **Charlie Peppiatt:** Yes, I think rather than people finding out about people's background and interests, which might be the typical context for a meeting amongst native speakers, you find that people spend the first few minutes just feeling out the ability with which they can communicate with each other in English.

Intercultural analysis

Group learners to select appropriate advice. You could regroup them to report back or elicit their ideas from a group secretary. Pair them to role play the situations.

> ***Answers***
> 1 Speaker 3 (use small talk at the beginning of the meeting)
> 2 Speaker 2 (learn about the culture and a bit of the language first)
> 3 Speaker 1 (maybe try to do the same yourself) and Speaker 3 (check with your host as small talk).

Output: Intercultural consultancy work

Stage 1

In groups, learners discuss possible solutions. Brainstorm some American idiomatic expressions, e.g. *a ball-park figure*, *a no-brainer*, *nip and tuck*, and ask why using idiomatic language and cultural references can cause bad feelings.

Stage 2

In larger classes, you could regroup learners to report back, or you could ask a group to summarise their discussion for an individual point and discuss whether the others agree.

Worksheet 7 (See page 133)

Improve your knowledge of intercultural competence

Level **C1 +**

Time **55–60 minutes**

1 Lead-in (10 minutes)

Pair learners to discuss the questions and elicit a few of their ideas.

Suggested answers

1 Depends on learners' experience.
2 Definitely. Note the concept of 'seniority' in Asian cultures and respect for elders as well as the concept of 'a glass ceiling' in Western cultures, i.e. the point above which women cannot go to improve their position at work.
3 Perhaps, especially when there has not been any contact with that nationality, though as with all stereotypes should be treated with great care.
4 Arguably the importance of family, although attitudes towards different elements within family life will vary, e.g. child rearing, care of the elderly.
5 Definitely. Note the use of 'polite' rather than 'direct' language in British English

2 Cultural expectations in meetings (10 minutes)

1 Learners work individually to match the expectations to the nationality, then compare their answers in pairs.

Answers

Nationality	Quotes about meeting behaviour
Argentinian	'Punctuality is better than in other places in Latin America.'
Nigerian	'Things are slower here. It is vital to get to know your hosts.'
Japanese	'There's polite conversation about mutual contacts and good small talk.'
Polish	'Meetings are directed with attendees speaking one at a time.'

2 Keep learners in their pairs and ask them to discuss the question.

Suggested answer

Some kind of neutral small talk is applicable to all nationalities, but you would expect its length to be shorter in Northern Europe and North America, as they prefer to get down to business sooner.

3 Attitudes to management styles (10 minutes)

Pair learners and encourage them to use their experience and knowledge to discover the answers.

Answers

Nationality	Quotes about preferred management style
Indian	'My manager is the boss: he gives explicit directions which must be followed fully, even if everybody disagrees.'
Taiwanese	'Seniority and the managerial position command respect. My manager gives instructions to us and we obey.'
Swedish	'My managers are transformational. They act as facilitators and include everybody in the decision-making processes.'
British	'Our manager values interpersonal skills and a "hands-on" approach. She prefers to request assistance to being direct.'

4 Improving cultural competence (10 minutes)

Put learners into small groups to discuss what they would like to learn about the nationalities. Encourage them to discuss questions they would like answered. Alternatively, assign a nationality to a group of learners, and re-group them with members of other groups to report back.

Suggested answers

What's the appropriate dress code? What topics of small talk could cause offence? Is it a good idea to make jokes in meetings or presentations? Which colours carry meaning? How do I greet women? How close is too close? What does 'punctual' actually mean? Which gestures are offensive?

5 Cultural competence programme (20 minutes)

1 Group learners into threes or fours. Decide on a secretary and ask them to come to an agreement on the programme, using the subjects submitted by the consultant. Encourage them to discuss what they think the content could be and why it would be useful.

2 Ask the secretary to outline their group's programme and why it's important. You could decide as a whole class on which subjects to ask the consultant to present.

8 International outsourcing

Overview of the unit

8.1 Theory: Avoiding outsourcing pitfalls

> 'Outsourcing and globalisation of manufacturing allows companies to reduce costs, benefits consumers with lower cost goods and services, causes economic expansion that reduces unemployment, and increases productivity and job creation.'
>
> *Larry Elder*

Outsourcing is when an organisation concludes that some of its activities can be separated and given to other local or international organisations to manage. It involves the contracting out of activities such as catering, payroll, information technology and maintenance. The careful choice of the right activities to outsource is beneficial for a successful and sustained management of change in the business and technology sector. However, successful outsourcing involves a strict analysis of the work to be done and writing explicit instructions. Indeed, it is vital that a company examines all the variables of outsourcing before deciding to use it as an engine of growth.

The pitfalls associated with outsourcing stem from choosing the wrong outsourcing provider, losing control of the activities outsourced and a poorly researched and written contract. For example, the provider may have an inability to cope with the volume of activities, employ staff that lack the required skills, different working practices to the organisation, or be unsure of what constitutes a satisfactory job contractually. The organisation's exit strategy may be inadequate when the provider does not meet expectations.

A company can outsource core activities like Human Resource projects and technical planning and technical infrastructure, but these may be better managed by an in-house team with an investment in the future of the organisation, rather than risking a loss of control. Outsourced workers do not work for your organisation; they work for another one with a separate career structure and company culture. They may even also work for a competitor in the same field, which could adversely affect your organisation's business.

8.2 Practice: Offshore outsourcing provider's perspective

Profile: Business Processing Association Philippines (BPAP)

BPAP is the overseeing organisation for Information Technology – Business Process Outsourcing (IT – BPO) and Global In-house Centres (GIC) in the Philippines. It was founded in 2004 and includes the Philippines government and chambers of commerce and trade as its stakeholders. It has expanded within the outsourcing industry, reaching 525,000 employees in 2007, to having a projected increase to 1.3 million employees within the next two decades.

It provides information technology services such as application development and maintenance, network management, software development and hardware maintenance. Its business process outsourcing includes voice services such as customer care, technical support and sales, as well as non-voice services such as finance and accounting and writing official copies of medical and legal proceedings.

As it is involved in cut-throat competition with India in this sector, BPAP makes much use of the Philippines' long association and cultural affinity with the USA and offers a conducive regulatory environment as well as tax breaks to companies looking to outsource activities.

8.3 Skills: Dealing with Q&A

Q&A (questions and answers) is the interactive part of any meeting or presentation and are very important. It should be seen as an opportunity to support your arguments and reinforce your message rather than a hindrance. In presentations, some presenters prefer to take questions during or after the presentation, while some secretly wish that they did not have to face Q&A sessions at all.

When dealing with Q&A sessions, you do not have to answer all questions, as some may be off topic, some may have been already answered in the presentation, others may be difficult because you do not have the information at hand to answer them, and some may be extremely hostile and the questioner may be looking to promote themselves.

Preparing for Q&A sessions requires trying to anticipate questions before the event and thinking of a few phrases to use to comment on the question first, e.g. saying 'that's a good question' and 'I see what you mean' to give you time to think about the answer.

There may even be a lack of questions, in which case you could stimulate discussion by asking for opinions.

8.1 Theory: Avoiding outsourcing pitfalls

Introduction

1 Books closed. Elicit a definition of *to outsource*. Find out if learners have had any experience of outsourcing. Pair them to discuss the first question or, in smaller classes discuss as a whole class.

> ***Suggested answer***
> They fear job cuts and deterioration in pay and working conditions for employees.

2 Learners discuss the second question.

> ***Suggested answer***
> They would be looking for cost benefits and might not have the skills in-house to run these services at the required quality standard.

3 Check that learners understand *offshore* (based in another country with more beneficial tax laws) before discussing the question.

> ***Suggested answer***
> Companies tend to use local outsourcing providers when they need day-to-day control or contact with the providers, such as cleaning companies. Offshore outsourcing is more popular for activites such as data entry, or where face-to-face contact is not needed.

Language focus: The language of outsourcing

1 Ask learners to match the words and phrases to definitions, then compare in pairs and check answers.

> ***Answers***
> 1 e 2 h 3 f 4 b 5 g 6 c 7 a 8 i 9 j 10 d

2 Group learners in threes or fours to brainstorm reasons. You could give each group a type of brainstorming structure, e.g. lateral association or provocation. (see pages 137 and 142 of the Student's Book) and ask them to present their ideas.

> ***Answers***
> 1 to cut costs, improve performance, or refocus on the core business
> 2 because the company requires fewer personnel in-house
> 3 They are too close to the core business.
> 4 They may have failed to plan an exit strategy.
> 5 They may have overlooked hidden costs.

Reading: Issues facing outsourcing companies

1 Discuss the use of *sin* in this context, i.e. an offence, a fault, etc. Ask learners to scan the executive overview to find the 'seven deadly sins' underlying failed outsourcing. Learners answer the questions individually, then check their answers in whole-class feedback. In smaller groups, you could discuss why each of the seven are 'sins', then ask them to answer the questions.

> ***Answers***
> 1 The three reasons stated are: cut costs, improve performance, and refocus on the core business.
> 2 a survey of nearly a hundred outsourcing efforts in Europe and the United States
> 3 Firms are reluctant to publicise outsourcing failures.

2 Pair learners to match the titles to the correct paragraph. Re-pair them to check answers. Ask them to underline any vocabulary issues they have in each text, e.g. *turn out*, *stood at*, *rumour*, *reluctant*, *upfront*, *a third-party*, *dismantling*. Discuss whether they needed to understand these words to do the exercise, then elicit possible synonyms or give out dictionaries.

> ***Answers***
> 1 Writing a poor contract
> 2 Outsourcing activities that should not be outsourced
> 3 Overlooking personnel issues
> 4 Failing to plan an exit strategy
> 5 Overlooking hidden costs
> 6 Selecting the wrong outsourcing provider
> 7 Losing control of the outsourced activity

3 Learners individually answer the questions, compare answers in pairs and then give the answers in whole-class feedback.

> ***Answers***
> 1 The contract was not precise.
> 2 6–7%
> 3 Because retiring personnel were not being replaced, which helped to fuel rumours.
> 4 Because reintegrating the activities back into the company would take longer than switching to another outsourcing provider.
> 5 The upfront cost of finding the outsourcing provider; the legal costs to negotiate the initial contract and the annual management costs involved in ensuring the outsourcing provider fulfils its contractual obligations.
> 6 Management at the US HQ thought its subsidiary did not have the expertise to run a just-in-time logistics operation.
> 7 'A total and dangerous loss of control over IT, inability to cope with the changing environment and command over the future.'

4 Pair learners to discuss the question then elicit the two sins in circles on the board. Re-pair them to discuss reasons if they did not get the answer or elicit the reasons for the author's opinion.

> ***Suggested answer***
> The two most deadly sins identified by the author in his research are: 'Writing a poor contract' and 'Losing control over the outsourced activity'.

Transferable skill: Considering the other side of the argument

1 Learners rank the benefits and then compare in pairs and come to a collaborative agreement. They might, for example, prioritise points 3 and 4 which are more general, while points 1 and 2 refer to specific work situations.

2 Check understanding of 'non-academic services'. Elicit which ones learners would not consider outsourcing then pair them to discuss the alternative argument. Elicit a few of their ideas on benefits.

Suggested answers
All services could theoretically be outsourced. For example, the possible benefits of outsourcing canteen services include better quality, range of food options and eating experience for diners. One possible option would be to bring in branded food chains to run a franchise on the university campus.

3 Pair or group learners to discuss the question. Re-pair or ask a secretary to report back.

Suggested answers
Universities have not outsourced academic services as these are core services and the basis of the universities' competitive advantage. There would also no doubt be insurmountable legal blocks, as well as an orchestrated political, union and media campaign to stop any such move. Outsourcing possibilities include using of experts working in the field to teach courses – architects teaching architecture students, business people teaching business students, etc. This would ensure teaching is up to date and that skills are relevant to industry needs. Universities could outsource course design to expert management consultancy firms, who can afford to employ the brightest and best in the field to undertake this task.

Output: Discuss cases of extreme outsourcing

Stage 1

Put learners into small groups, and ask them to scan to find the difference between the two companies, i.e. one outsources all of its activities, the other none.

Stage 2

In their groups, learners decide the best activities to outsource either locally or internationally. Encourage them to note down their reasons in the table.

Stage 3

Regroup learners to report back on their decisions made in their original groups using the table.

8.2 Practice: Offshore outsourcing provider's perspective

Profile: Business Processing Association Philippines (BPAP)

Introduction

1 Pair learners to discuss the questions. Elicit a definition for *voice and non-voice* business process outsourcing (BPO). If you have a multinational group, elicit what they know of any government departments that promote this in their countries.

2 Pair learners to discuss possible advantages and disadvantages of offshore outsourcing. Instruct them to think in terms of the end user. Elicit a few of their ideas. You could expand the exercise and tell them to also consider the company and the country.

Answers
Advantages for the end-user customer
The company will save money locating these services in low-cost countries, which means there is less cost to pass on to the customer. Also, as offshore providers are in different time zones they can more easily and cheaply supply service outside working hours in the US and UK.

Disadvantages
Customers resident in the US or the UK might experience problems understanding call centre operators' English. The level of shared understanding between call centre operators and callers will be lower compared to local call centre operators – for example, their knowledge of UK towns and cities, which is important when giving information for train enquiries, etc.

Listening 1: Benefits of offshore outsourcing 2.02

1 Discuss reasons why a country would wish to promote itself as a BPO destination and then ask learners to predict possible reasons before listening to check.

Answers
2, 3, 5

2 Tell learners to listen for an example presented for illustration and as fact. Play 2.02 and elicit learners' answers.

Answers
The example (recruiting 2–3,000 accountants) is for illustration purposes.

Audio script
Interviewer: What benefits are companies looking for when they outsource offshore?
Gigi Virata: Basically they are looking for skills: human resources and a mix of other skills. Some of them are looking for a certain number of new recruits in order to scale up their business – sometimes in the thousands. Or they are looking for a certain depth of skills that are getting harder to come by in their home base.
Interviewer: Can you give us some examples of that?
Gigi Virata: Well, you might have back-office needs: maybe two to three thousand accountants just doing simple transactional work, like payroll processing or accounts receivable. That can be a challenge in, for example, a smaller city in the United States – and so they come to the Philippines or India where they can find these people easily and quickly. So part of the benefit is that they have the people and services available here. And there are, of course, cost savings doing it in low-cost countries like India and the Philippines.

Critical analysis

Focus learners' attention on the placards and briefly discuss why the people might be demonstrating, e.g. they have already lost their jobs or they fear losing their jobs. Pair or group learners to discuss the questions and then elicit a few of their ideas. You could round up the discussion by canvassing your class's opinion on the effectiveness of such workers' demonstrations.

Suggested answer
A number of groups would lose out, including individuals and firms in the outsourcing industry offshore. This would have a wider impact on their national economies. Companies in the industrialised world would also lose out as they would find it difficult to source skilled workers in sufficient quantities in their own countries. Consumers in the industrialised world would lose out as they would inevitably pay more for goods and services that are no longer supported by low-cost back-office operations.

Listening 2: Why companies choose the Philippines (2.03)

1 Learners predict possible answers to the questions, then listen and compare answers in pairs.

Answers
1 IT work
2 It does less IT outsourcing than India.
3 They are 'a little bit better than India'. The accent is easier to understand and they are culturally closer to the clients.
4 Hollywood and basketball
5 customer satisfaction

Audio script
Interviewer: Why should companies choose the Philippines in particular as an outsourcing destination?
Gigi Virata: We are the third-largest English-speaking country in the world. We have a hundred million people now, and we produce about four hundred thousand university graduates a year. And of those graduates about seventy percent speak English, and that's primarily why we have so many North American and UK companies working with us here. We have not had as much business from the non-English speaking countries. For companies from non-English speaking countries we do more work in IT, but we are not as big as India is in IT.
Interviewer: What about call centre operations?
Gigi Virata: Well, for voice services, companies tell us that we are a little bit better than India. Our accent seems easier to understand, for Americans or westerners, than most Indian accents. And then – well, you know, you could say India was an English colony, the Philippines really embraced western culture. We were an American colony for fifty years and we took everything, Hollywood, basketball and all that stuff. It seems that that is something the customers really appreciate. People feel more comfortable talking with our call centre agents. It's really all about customer satisfaction.

2 & 3 Elicit what learners think the figures refer to. They then listen again to check.

Answers
a the population of the Philippines
b the number of graduates every year
c the percentage of graduates who speak English

Intercultural analysis

Briefly discuss whether learners know anything about the Philippines, e.g. it is named after a Spanish king, was a former US colony, has US military bases, education is in English.

1 Pair them to discuss why cultural affinity is an important selling point for some sectors of BPO. Elicit a few of their ideas as feedback.

Suggested answers
Call centre agents with closer cultural affinity are better able to understand and interpret the subtleties of communication and build better personal rapport with the client.

2 Now do the same for the second question.

In the case of accounts, there is less direct interaction with clients. The communication required will be mainly written, where there is less room for misunderstanding compared to voice communications. Communication for both IT support and accounts will be based on technical competence and knowledge that is far less sensitive to cultural differences.

Listening 3: Challenges facing the industry (2.04)

1 Ask learners to predict the gaps, compare in pairs and then listen to check their ideas. Ask them if they would like to listen again, and then check the answers.

Answers
1 are applying
2 English and computing skills
3 hired (immediately)
4 intensive English training
5 training process
6 negative perceptions

Audio script
Interviewer: What do you see as the main challenges and problems facing the offshore outsourcing industry? Is it a bright future?
Gigi Virata: Our problem is a good one, but still it's a big challenge. We do have a lot of raw talent. There are people in the Philippines that would be very suited to work in our industry, but not everyone is applying to work with us. Also those who do want to work with us, not all of them have the skills. Either they haven't been practising their English – they've been learning it in school but they haven't been using it – or they're not up to speed with their computer skills.
Interviewer: I see.
Gigi Virata: So far what the companies are telling us is that, out of a hundred candidates who come to be interviewed, they are lucky to hire ten suitable ones. But we find that the next twenty to thirty applicants would only require maybe two weeks of intensive English practice to become hireable. So there are two things that as an association and as an industry we look at. First, how do we make the whole recruitment, hiring and training process more efficient? The other is, we want to change some negative perceptions of the industry that some people here have – that it's bad for your health, the work is too hard, and that kind of thing. So we need to have more awareness campaigns and to talk to parents, students and teachers to show the different kinds of careers that can be had in this industry. So that's another thing we have to tackle. That's a challenge.

2 Pair learners to practise presenting the information. You could record them, play back and discuss any differences.

Language focus: Taking different stances to intensify or tone down the message

1 Pair learners to choose two descriptors to describe all the sentences. Re-pair them to report back and elicit their answers.

Answers
objective/balanced, diplomatic/tactful. Note comments favourable to the outsourcing industry in the Philippines are presented objectively: *Companies tell us …*, so it would be incorrect to say the stance taken is highly subjective/one-sided.

2 Discuss which words prove the stance taken, then learners rewrite the sentences more directly.

Answers
1 Our accent seems easier to understand, for Americans …
2 … companies tell us that we are a little bit better than India.
3 That can be a challenge [in, for example, a smaller city] …

Suggested answers for intensified reformulations
Our accent is far easier to understand for Americans.
Companies tell us that we are significantly better than India.
It is extremely difficult to find in a smaller city.

3 Ask students to make the sentences less direct and elicit a few of their answers. Extend the activity and, in a monolingual class, discuss which style they prefer and if this is because of culture.

Suggested answers
1 I think you might need to look at this report again.
2 I'm not sure that's completely correct. We weren't really responsible for that.

4 Learners work in pairs to categorise the words and phrases.

Answers
A = sort of, kind of, basically, a (little) bit, like
B = very, completely, totally, so, absolutely, such

5 Ask learners to fill in the gaps, then check in pairs before feedback.

Answers
1 such
2 basically
3 kind of / sort of
4 absolutely / totally / completely
5 like / basically / sort of / kind of
(The underlined word/expression is the one that was actually used in the corpus.)

6 Pair learners to discuss the question and elicit their ideas.

1 softener
2 softener
3 intensifier
4 intensifier
5 intensifier

7 2.05 Learners listen and repeat. Briefly discuss the stress patterns as a whole class.

Answers
These four words are stressed (emphasised) when the speaker is using them as intensifiers.

Audio script
1 I'm just writing to ask if you could …
2 It's not a big seller really.
3 It's really easy to do.
4 You could actually smell all the smoke coming up …
5 It was quite an experience!

8 Learners decide when the words are used. Check answers. You could discuss if this is the same in learners' own language.

Answers
A describes the use of tone-down softening words.
B describes the use of intensifiers.

Output: Resolve misunderstanding between client and outsourcing provider

Stage 1

Group learners into threes if possible and assign each group role A or role B. Refer Group B to page 143. Ask them to read their roles and prepare for a meeting. You may wish to check understanding as they read.

Stage 2

Tell groups to assign a role to each person. If there is an extra student in any of the groups, ask them to play the role of a person who wishes to keep the atmosphere positive using a combination of the approaches. Put Group A with Group B to discuss a solution to each of the problems with a time limit of 20 minutes.

Stage 3

As a whole class, discuss which approach was more effective. If you have a multilingual class, you could discuss if they were comfortable with the approach they were assigned and why.

8.3 Skills: Dealing with Q&A

Introduction

1 Pair or group learners to discuss the advantages and disadvantages of both approaches. Elicit their ideas on the board as feedback.

Suggested answer
Taking questions during the presentation
The advantage of this approach is that it allows a closer connection with the audience and, when done well, often creates an informal, relaxed feel to the talk. The content and structure are quite loose, following the direction of questions. The disadvantage is that too many questions can distract the presenter and there is a risk of losing control of the presentation.
Taking questions in Q&A
The advantage for presenters is that they have more control and can determine a set time limit for questions. The possible disadvantage is a loss of spontaneous interaction with the audience, resulting in a more formal and structured talk. Note, however, that most presenters choose the Q&A approach as they want to limit spontaneous interaction from the audience.

2 Pair learners to discuss the question in the chart and follow the route. You might like to elicit a few ideas for questions faced by politicians, e.g. indirect questions, both of which are usually not answered directly.

3 Discuss the question as a class.

> ***Suggested answer***
> It is very important to try and anticipate what questions you may be asked, in order to minimise the risk of being 'taken by surprise', to appear professional and to give the audience confidence in what you have said.

Listening 1: Managing a Q&A session 2.06

1 Learners listen to choose the correct type of meeting. Elicit a few answers and why they think so.

> ***Answer***
> B

> ***Audio script***
> **Leo Dillon:** It's now time to begin our discussion period, our question and answer comment period, if you like, and before we open this part of the meeting for discussion, I want to review a few ground rules. We look forward to trying to answer to the best of our ability all your questions as fully as we can. We do, however, reserve the right to pass on any issues that might involve confidential information. And we really do not plan, because we can't effectively do it, to deal with personal issues related to the individual shareholder, although if you have personal issues, please write to us and we will try to deal with them. If you wish to ask a question or make a comment, go to the nearest microphone in the aisle and they will take your name and draw you to my attention. I have a little monitor here of which microphones are trying to get attention.

2 Learners listen again, and then check answers in pairs before feedback.

> ***Answers***
> 1 The two rules are:
> (i) They can't answer questions which involve confidential information.
> (ii) They can't deal with personal issues relating to particular shareholders.
> 2 They should go to the nearest microphone in the aisle and give their name.

3 Learners try to write in the endings, before they listen again. Elicit their answers.

> ***Suggested answers***
> 1 our discussion period / our question and answer period
> 2 a few ground rules
> 3 trying to answer (to the best of our ability) all your questions as fully as we can
> 4 pass on any issues that might involve confidential information
> 5 to deal with personal issues related to the individual shareholder
> 6 go to the nearest microphone in the aisle

4 Learners practise the Q&A set-up. You may like to ask them to stand up to do this.

Language focus 1: Inviting questions from the audience 2.07

1 Ask learners to predict the answers.

> ***Answers***
> 1 proceed
> 2 happy
> 3 hand
> 4 fire
> 5 start
> 6 open up

2 Play 2.07 and elicit answers.

> ***Audio script***
> 1 Are there any questions about how we're going to proceed?
> 2 I'd be happy to take questions at the end of the talk.
> 3 If you have any questions, please raise your hand.
> 4 So, any questions anybody? Please fire away.
> 5 Right, are there any questions before we start?
> 6 I'll move straight over to Graham and open it up for any questions from the floor.

3 & 4 Discuss as a whole class which sentences are formal and informal and the one unlikely to be in a Q&A session.

> ***Answers***
> Question 1 is more formal and Question 4 is more informal. Questions 1, 2 and 5 would generally be asked during the presentation, not at the end in a Q&A.

Listening 2: Dealing with different question types 2.08

1 Elicit what learners understand by the question types, i.e. non-question: questioner does not form a question; straightforward question: easy question to answer; difficult question: a question that cannot be answered immediately, etc. Learners listen and check answers in pairs before feedback.

> ***Answers***
> Non-question: 3
> Straightforward question: 1
> Difficult question: 4
> Hostile question: 5
> Multiple question: 2

> ***Audio script***
> 1
> **Shareholder 1:** Good morning. I have a simple question. I would like to know the future of the motor racing sponsorship.
> **Leo Dillon:** We think that motor racing – which is one of the, if not the, fastest-growing sports in the United States – is one of our best sponsorships, and we are happy to be associated with it. It's hard to measure what real money you get out of these things, but it's a very brand-loyal audience and we plan to continue with motor racing, and maybe move forward from the middle of the pack. Thank you.
> 2
> **Shareholder 2:** Good morning, Mr Dillon. Given the consolidation that is taking place in the commercial printing industry, what impact do you see on that vis-à-vis Zelig products in the years going forward? And on the cost side, speaking of folding cartons, has there been any thought given to outsourcing the manufacture of Zolig's little red boxes, and the collection and disposal of solid waste?

Leo Dillon: There are many questions there. On the outsourcing issue, we give consideration to outsourcing everything that we don't think is strategic. In some cases we find we can do it much better than anybody on the outside and we don't outsource those. So we look at that. I know we are looking at outsourcing some of the packaging efforts. Is Bill here? Do you want to comment?

3

Shareholder 3: Zelig changes their products and organisations to keep up with the times. It's time the old wage bands and the culture of the human resources and legal departments change also, to get in step with the Zelig values in our new value-based high-performance culture.

Leo Dillon: Your question was what?

Shareholder 3: Just a statement.

Leo Dillon: A statement. OK, thank you. We do make mistakes from time to time. I would be the first to admit that. When you have a hundred thousand people all over the world and you are changing a lot of the culture and the structure, we make some mistakes. But by and large, I am very, very proud of the people in our HR and legal functions, who have to manage through these very difficult times.

4

Shareholder 4: How do you plan to raise the morale of the few employees who are left to do the work of many, and who are fearing the loss of their jobs tomorrow?

Leo Dillon: That's a very serious issue, and one that we don't take lightly. First of all, when you have gone through as much restructuring as we have over many years, it has a damaging effect on morale. The good news is that, as people begin to see some progress, things change. You can do a lot of things to help, but there is nothing like business success today to build morale.

5

Shareholder 5: I would ask you what you're going to do about your management problem, because it's been written up in the national papers. I know of it personally. I have written you personally and offered to share comments with you, and you have not felt free to come back and find out about any of the incidents at all.

Leo Dillon: I haven't seen these recent articles you refer to in the national papers that talk about this management team. The articles I have seen and what I have gotten from my associates who are the analysts on Wall Street, is that they believe this may be the best team Zelig has ever had in its history. They are making the changes. Unfortunately, I know that some people, like yourself, have lost their jobs and we all feel bad about it. We don't like that. I don't know a person on this management team that likes to lay off good people. A lot of good people like you have lost their jobs. That is not a fun thing to do. Unfortunately, it is necessary to do to get our cost structure in line, in order to be competitive so that the remaining thirty-five to forty thousand people in Zelig have a viable future. Thank you.

2 Learners look at the table. Ask them to use their own words to describe the strategies and elicit an idea for each strategy. Play 2.08 again for learners to check answers in pairs and feedback.

Answers
1 a
2 a, b, c
3 a, c
4 a, c
5 a, b, d

3 Pair learners to discuss the question. Elicit which strategy might be ineffective and why, e.g. attack the questioner – not good for relationship building.

Language focus 2: Replying to questions

1 Learners match the strategies to the phrases, check answers in pairs then give the answers.

Answers
1 c 2 a 3 h 4 e 5 f 6 i 7 d 8 b 9 g

2 Pair learners to ask and answer 'difficult' questions. You may wish to elicit one or two examples, e.g. *How do you hope to gain promotion? Which lecturer would you fire?*

Output: Q&A session discussing staff redundancies

Learners scan the text and underline any words they do not understand. Elicit them and discuss synonyms, e.g. *inevitable* (certain, unavoidable). Divide learners into A and B groups. Refer Group A to page 139 and Group B to page 144 to read their roles. Monitor and discuss any misunderstandings, e.g. *ground rules* may include no self-promotion, introducing yourself (by name and position), and type of question style.

Ask them to rehearse their Q & A sessions before grouping them to hold the session for real.

You may want to watch Sequence 4 on the DVD to find out more about Globalisation in class or ask learners to watch it for homework. There is an accompanying worksheet on page 153.

Worksheet 8 (See page 134)

Improve your knowledge of regional development policies

Level **C1 +**

Time **55–60 minutes**

1 Lead-in (10 minutes)

Pair learners to discuss the questions.

Suggested answers

1 Defined as any government programme aimed at encouraging the industrial and economic development of regions suffering from unemployment or other economic problems.
2 Yes it can. The definition of regional development varies according to what is legally defined as a region, and how its boundaries are recognised both internally and externally.
3 It can provide funds to reduce differences between regions by supporting structural change and the redevelopment of former industrial regions. It can also fund vocational training and job-creation initiatives as well as transport infrastructure and environmental projects.
4 This will depend on where your learners are from.
5 ERDF aims to reduce regional differences in income, wealth and economic opportunities. OECD aims to promote policies to improve the economic and social life of people globally and provides a forum for governments to share experiences. ILO aims to promote employment opportunities and increase workforce protection.

You could brainstorm any more development organisations learners may know and discuss their roles.

2 Regional development policy of the European Union (10 minutes)

1 Check that learners understand this meaning of *pillar* (very important feature). Learners match the pillars with their purpose.

Answers

Pillar	Purpose
Convergence	reducing regional disparities
Regional Competitiveness and Employment	making regions more alluring to investors
Cross-region/country cooperation	improving territorial cohesion

2 & 3 Re-pair learners to discuss the two questions. Alternatively hold a class discussion on the questions. You could ask if your learners have had any experience of EU regional policy, e.g. the Erasmus education project.

Answers

1 The overall aim is to remove social and territorial disparities, restructure former industrial areas and diversify rural areas.
2 About one third of the EU's total budget is devoted to regional policy. However, this funding is not spread equally across the three pillars.

3 Regional development policy objectives and tools (10 minutes)

1 Check understanding of any new vocabulary, by asking them to underline new words and eliciting synonyms. Then pair learners to match the objectives to the tools. Use monolingual dictionaries if necessary.

Answers

Policy objective	Policy tools
Create sustainable jobs	free trade, tax policy, infrastructure investment
Stimulate economic growth	education, social stability, incentivised risk taking
Ensure environment and risk prevention	integrated conservation strategies in land use
Improve transport and telecommunications	added capacity, reduced bottlenecks, improved efficiency
Special assistance for remote areas	direct aid and investments in small/medium businesses
Promote innovation and knowledge	opportunities for R&D and entrepreneurship
Enhance cross-border cooperation	shared economic, social and environmental programmes
Advance interregional cooperation	networking and exchange of experience events

2 Re-pair learners to discuss the question, or in smaller classes hold a class discussion. Answers will depend on where the learners are living and what they see as important for their region.

4 Regional development policy role play (25 minutes)

Group learners into threes if possible. If not, you could pair them and either omit one of the roles or divide up role C between roles A and B. Give out copies of the role cards to each group. Check understanding of vocabulary, then tell them to think of a name for their country and region and then discuss how to improve the economic opportunities for their working population using *five* of the policies on the role cards.

Ask them to present their ideas to the rest of the class after about 15 minutes. The rest of the class can act as groups of possible investors, who must decide at the end of the presentation whether or not to invest. You could discuss why each policy was successful or unsuccessful as a follow-up activity.

Writing 4: Writing follow-up emails

Overview of the unit

Email is now the preferred medium for communication on transactional (work-related) topics and on relational (interpersonal) subjects. Follow-up emails should be concise as many people read them on smartphones. A transactional email is sent when you need to get something done, e.g. instructing. It is often governed by professional email etiquette and organisational templates. Interpersonal emails are something people do to socialise and build relationships and may be influenced by personal factors, e.g. how well you know each other. As a result of this increased use of emails for professional and personal reasons, communication is shortened and may seem curt or even rude. This can lead to miscommunication or even conflict as tone cannot be heard in written communication.

Introduction

1 Learners decide whether the phrases are transactional or interpersonal and then check in pairs. You may wish to discuss how well the people know each other in the two interpersonal ones.

> ***Answers***
> Transactional: 1, 4, 5 Interpersonal: 2, 3

2 Pair learners to decide on the nature of the views. You may like to elicit the similarities between the answers, e.g. transactional practices could be influenced by short-term considerations.

> ***Answers***
> Transactional: 2, 4 Interpersonal: 1, 3

Writing skill: Contrasting transactional and interpersonal emails

1 Learners choose the correct words, and then compare their answers in pairs. You might wish to discuss answers, e.g. name and address are two items, *had expressed* is in reported speech, and the reporting verb (stated) is in the past tense.

> ***Answers***
> 1 were referred
> 2 had expressed
> 3 requested
> 4 enclosing
> 5 itemizes
> 6 provide you
> 7 participating in

2 Discuss why the email did not receive a reply as a whole class. Ask learners for an example to support their opinion.

> ***Answers***
> The email has a very strong transactional focus, with almost no attention paid to developing the relationship.

3 Pair learners to discuss the question then elicit their ideas. You could ask them to discuss how personal they would make the email.

> ***Answers***
> All of the points suggested would make the email more interpersonal. How interpersonal you make communication depends on your own preference and how interpersonal you believe the culture of the addressee (the person you are writing to) to be. In general, it is always better to use the recipient's name at the start, if you know it.

4 Ask learners them to underline examples of the points in the email before checking in pairs. You could elicit examples of transactional writing, e.g. … *has informed me that you have expressed an interest in our products; I am also enclosing a price list.*

> ***Answers***
> The email uses all of the points in exercise 3 apart from point 4.

Intercultural analysis

1 & 2 Pair learners from different cultures if possible to discuss the questions. Discuss as a class whether stereotyping is useful.

> ***Suggested answer***
> While generalisations are useful in helping us understand tendencies across cultures, we cannot expect the next person we meet from the relevant culture to behave in exactly that way. There is often far more variation within cultures than between cultures.

Language focus: Reminding, explaining and requesting in follow-up emails

1 Learners order the stages and check in pairs.

> ***Answers***
> b, c, a

2 Learners match the language to the stages. Elicit answers.

> ***Answers***
> a 1, 7, 8, 9 b 4, 6 c 2, 3, 5

3 Discuss formality with the class and brainstorm other examples.

> ***Answers***
> Requests: we request your comments on … / Please let me know your … / If you could send us … that would be great
> Reminders: we remind you that … continues to be available / if you remember from our previous discussions …
> The answers are in order of formality (the most formal first).

Output: Writing to a potential client

Brainstorm what sample equipment a garden tool company could send, e.g. forks, spades. They then write their emails.

9 Affordable innovation

Overview of the unit

9.1 Theory: Affordable innovation through reverse innovation

> 'Innovation does not relate just to a new product that would come to a marketplace. Innovation can occur in processes and approaches to the marketplace.'
>
> *David Schmitten*

Innovation is an activity where people alter both themselves and their environment. In business, innovation is a series of changes that reflect market conditions, modify production facilities, increase the level of knowledge, improve technology, and displace organisational structure and culture.

'Affordable innovation' is the challenge to deliver high-quality products and processes at lower prices. 'Reverse innovation', a concept coined by GE Chairman and CEO Jeff Immelt and GE's Chief innovation consultant Vijay Govindarajan, refers to building technologies that respect local needs in developing regions, then distributing them globally. This contrasts with the usual innovation route of developing products for developed markets and adapting them for developing markets.

The most common concept of innovation is incremental, whereby existing knowledge is built upon. This enables the existing approaches to business to remain efficient and products to remain competitive. In contrast, radical innovation renders the present knowledge obsolete and results in the phasing out of old product lines and practices and the launching of new ones.

Top-down innovation is where charismatic leadership enables and promotes it, while bottom-up innovation comes from individual insights, which are transformed into ideas that might lead to an innovation that adds value to the organisation. Collaborative innovation is where companies share strategies and practices to identify and exploit new business opportunities.

History is littered with many innovations that have come about through sheer accident and luck. The best preparation for innovation could possibly be to prepare the ground for these unexpected opportunities to arise.

9.2 Practice: GE Healthcare – low-cost reverse innovation in practice

Profile: GE Healthcare

Headquartered in the UK, GE Healthcare is a division of the USA-based General Electric Company (GE) and currently employs over 45,000 people worldwide. It sells a wide variety of 'transformational' products that help to promote earlier diagnosis, detection and prevention of disease. These products include medical imaging, medical diagnostics, patient monitoring systems, medicine discovery and pharmaceutical manufacturing.

The company's biggest research and development centre is in Bangalore, India. However, it employs healthcare professionals worldwide to 're-image' new ways to predict, diagnose, inform about, treat and monitor disease. The company has a century-old tradition of innovative breakthroughs and of turning good ideas into technologies, and this is something it wishes to continue to foster in the future.

9.3 Skills: Dealing with criticism

Criticism may occur in conflict situations or can foster conflict. It can affect self-esteem and motivation and it can create self-doubt. It can be very negative and take the form of bullying, but it can also be very positive if it comes, in either a subtle or more direct way, from a work colleague with more years of experience than you.

Indirect criticism should not be confused with a type of criticism where anonymity is the chief weapon. It can be constructive through a subtle use of language to offer ways and suggestions for improvement, in contrast to direct criticism, which uses language in a more explicit way.

Automatically taking criticism personally is not the ideal response, as emotion clouds judgement and limits rational thinking. When receiving constructive criticism, emotion will hinder the learning that is the aim of the critic, and it is far better to detach this injured pride and perceived loss of face from the useful suggestions that may or may not lie behind the criticism. Coping with criticism professionally requires determining if the critic has all the information, explaining your actions or accepting the criticism as part of the learning process, and saying that it will motivate you to do better and change your approach.

It is important to see the benefits of criticism. The ability to deal with it and learn from it is an important aspect of successful personal and professional development.

9.1 Theory: Affordable innovation through reverse innovation

Introduction

1 Books closed. Write *R&D* on the board. Elicit what learners understand by the term and which industries invest in it the most. Ask learners to read the definition and rewrite it in their own words. Elicit a few examples and then discuss as a whole class which industries are portrayed in the photographs and which products or services they provide.

2 Pair learners to rank the factors and then group them to come to a collaborative ranking before giving the answers. Discuss as a whole class to discover whether the order changes after further discussion.

Answers
The top three drivers in order of importance are: 1 f, 2 a, 3 e

Language focus: Concepts of innovation

1 Learners fill in the gaps and then compare answers in pairs before feedback.

Answers
1 innovation
2 invention

2 Write *innovation* and *invention* on the board. Pair learners to discuss which words in the box go with which, using dictionaries if necessary. Elicit their answers and write them next to the correct word.

Answers
patented invention / ingenious invention / license (an) invention
foster innovation / marketing innovation / product innovation / encourage innovation

3 Elicit possible alternative synonyms or phrases for the adjectives in 1–6, e.g. *radical* (fundamental), *affordable* (cheap), *top-down* (from above), *bottom-up* (from below), *collaborative* (working together) and *incremental* (gradual). Pair learners to match the concepts with the definitions. Elicit one or two of their answers for each question and why they chose it.

Answers
1 f 2 a 3 b 4 d 5 c 6 e

4 Learners fill in the gaps individually and then compare answers in pairs. As feedback, you could discuss why they chose their answer.

Answers
1 radical innovation
2 affordable innovation
3 collaborative innovation
4 incremental innovations
5 top-down innovation, bottom-up innovation

5 Elicit a few companies that learners are familiar with in the sectors in the Introduction. Pair them to discuss the question and then re-pair them to report back. Alternatively, pair learners, assign a sector to them and ask them to discuss the question with reference to that sector. You could then re-pair them to report on their discussion.

Suggested answer
The type of innovation approach chosen will depend on the type of industry sector the organisation is a part of, the size of the company or innovation project, the corporate culture of the organisation and the demands of consumers. Companies with conservative cultures tend to avoid radical or bottom-up innovation, for example. Companies in fast-moving industries such as the IT sector are more likely to favour radical innovation. Where consumers are price sensitive, companies need to respond by presenting low-cost, affordable innovation solutions.

Reading: Reverse innovation

1 Learners read the summary, choose the correct words and compare answers in pairs.

Answers
1 developing
2 adapted
3 local population
4 availability of skilled workers

2 Ask learners to scan the text for the companies' names and underline them. Pair them to match the companies to the examples and then check answers.

Answers
1 PepsiCo
2 Mahindra & Mahindra
3 Deere & Company
4 Renault-Nissan
5 Renault-Nissan

3 Encourage learners to work individually to find the words and expressions, then pair or group them to check answers.

Answers
1 in a nutshell
2 minor tweaks
3 driver
4 no-frills
5 predominantly
6 mindset
7 frugal
8 on a par
9 came up with
10 know-how
11 unveiled
12 tap into

Output: Debate low-cost innovation solutions

Stage 1

Check understanding of *effectiveness* and *viability*. Is effectiveness the same as efficiency? Is innovation capable of growing in developing economies? Elicit what learners are going to do and then read the motion before turning to page 139 to read the arguments. Instruct learners to work individually to mark them for or against. They could compare their ideas in pairs.

Answers
Against: 1, 3, 5 For: 2, 4, 6

Stage 2

Put learners into groups of three or four. Assign them for or against roles and ask them to prepare for the debate in 10 minutes. You may wish to check understanding of *dismantle the arguments*.

Stage 3

Bring the learners together as two teams and hold a debate on the motion. Take a vote on the motion after all the arguments have been discussed. Alternatively, you could pair learners for and against the motion to hold a debate and then take a vote.

9.2 Practice: GE Healthcare – low-cost reverse innovation in practice

Profile: GE Healthcare

Introduction

1 Ask learners to scan the profile and elicit the countries where GE has a presence. Pair learners to discuss the question. Encourage them to take notes on healthcare needs in developed and developing countries. Elicit a few of their ideas on the board in two columns.

2 Discuss the question as a whole class.

3 & 4 Learners rank the top three influencing drivers individually, and then decide on a collaborative ranking decision in pairs. Give the answers and elicit which pairs were correct.

Answers
The top three factors in order are: e, b, d
Developing countries would score highest on c, d, e and possibly b. They would score lowest on factors a and f.

Listening 1: GE Healthcare in China 2.09

1 Discuss possible uses of the two machines: blood clots, damage to the heart muscle, large blood vessel complications. Then elicit how learners think the machines are used in China and the USA.

2 Learners predict possible answers, and then listen. Elicit their answers.

Answers
1 It costs $15,000 in China compared to $350,000 in the USA for premium models.
2 The first advantage is that it is portable so it can be taken to the patients. This is particularly important in remote villages in rural China, as ultrasound machines are normally located in hospitals and they don't have hospitals in these areas. The second advantage is its ultra low cost, which makes it affordable for customers.
3 $300 million
4 It's used in highway accidents.

Audio script
Five years ago, GE pioneered an ultra-low-cost, portable ultrasound machine in China which cost fifteen thousand dollars; contrast that with the premium ultrasound machines that are sold in the US for three hundred and fifty thousand dollars. Where do you need a portable machine in China? Ninety percent of China is in rural China. In rural China you don't have hospitals, so you can't ask the patient to go to the hospital – the hospital has to come to the patient. That means that the machine has to be portable. You can put it in your backpack and go to these remote villages. It has to be ultra-low-cost because of customer affordability. The low-cost, affordable ultrasound machine which was originally innovated for the Chinese market is now creating market for General Electric all over the world including the United States. In fact, the portable ultrasound machine today, five years later, is a three hundred million-dollar global business for GE.
Let me just describe one application of this in the US. Imagine there is an accident on a highway; an ambulance is going there. You can't put the big three hundred and fifty thousand-dollar machine in an ambulance, but you can put the portable ultrasound machine – which looks like a laptop computer – in an ambulance. This is the kind of new market innovation from poor countries that can be re-created in rich countries.

Listening 2: GE Healthcare global strategy 2.10

1 Ask learners to predict possible answers. You may wish to check what learners understand by *outmoded*. Learners listen and then check their answers in pairs. Elicit their answers as feedback.

Answers
1 Because global recession has shifted economic growth from developed to developing countries.
2 US, Western Europe, Japan, rest of the world
3 BRIC (Brazil, Russia, India and China), resource-rich countries (Middle East, Canada, Australia), rest of the world
4 The idea that the world population is divided into two parts – 2 billion who can afford to buy products made by companies. and 5 billion who are 'left' to governments, NGOs and charities.

Audio script
You may wonder how come reverse innovation has become such an important strategic priority for companies today. It is really because of the great recession which has fundamentally reset this world. And one way it has reset the world is growth has shifted from developed countries to developing countries. There was a time, fifteen years ago, when General Electric used to prepare its global strategy. It used to have a strategy for the US, for Western Europe and for Japan and then a strategy for the rest of the world. Today, when GE prepares its global strategy, it has a strategy for the so called BRIC

countries: Brazil, Russia, India, China. And resource-rich countries like the Middle East, Canada, Australia. And the rest of the world. And 'the rest of the world' includes the US, Western Europe and Japan. That is the kind of fundamental change we are seeing.
Multinationals had taken the total population of this world of seven billion and divided them into two. There are two billion rich customers who can afford to buy the products we make in the US, and the five billion poor we have left for charity to take care of, government to take care of, NGOs to take care of. That's an outmoded way of thinking. We need to bring the five billion poor into the consumer base. And they cannot consume the same products the two billion rich are consuming.

Critical analysis

Pair or group learners into threes to discuss the pros and cons of the statement. Encourage them to visualise a 'non-consumer' and discuss for a few minutes what it would take to achieve the objective of making them consumers. Alternatively, you could divide the class into two and ask them to prepare arguments for and against the statement and then pair them to debate it.

Suggested answer
Turning non-consumers into consumers is desirable as it is a form of inclusion and a moral imperative. The benefits of innovation and technology are multiple and wide-reaching and should be shared by the majority of the world's population who are excluded without addressing issues of affordability. The examples given of Tata and Aakash show that it is realistic. The argument against turning non-consumers into consumers is largely linked to environmental issues. What would happen to the level of carbon emissions, for example, if all the people riding bicycles and mopeds in the developing world started driving cars?

Transferable skill: Keeping a listener's attention

1 Discuss what learners understand by holding 'an imaginary conversation', e.g. visualising the conversation, asking questions to yourself, talking to a mirror, a cuddly toy or a pet, and why they think this an effective way of involving the audience. Ask them to match the two parts and elicit their answers.

Answers
1 b 2 a

2 Ask learners to underline the language for imaginary conversations. Elicit their answers.

Answers
Underlined language:
You may wonder how come; Imagine …; Let me just …;

3 Discuss whether the language from exercise 2 and the examples are a form of *rhetorical* questioning, i.e. questions asked for effect, where an answer isn't expected. In small classes, ask learners to prepare the short case individually and then to present it to the class. In larger classes, learners can practise with each other while you monitor.

Reading: Disrupting international business strategy

1 Check understanding of the phrases. Ask learners to put them into the text and elicit their answers. You could point out that the text is written in American English and therefore uses 'z' spellings for *glocalization*, etc.

Answers
1 substantially lower costs
2 emerging economies
3 pioneering new uses
4 glocalization approach
5 global scale
6 local customization
7 rapid development
8 slowing growth

2 Ask learners to mark the statements true or false and then check their answers in pairs. Learners could change the false statements into true ones as feedback.

Answers
1 False (it was developed for rural China)
2 True
3 False (companies develop products at home and then distribute them worldwide)
4 False (countries like China and India are developing rapidly and wealth nations are growing more slowly)

Language focus: Marketing of innovation

1 Learners work individually to fill in the gaps. Elicit their answers. You could elicit the forms of *glocalisation* before asking them to do the exercise.

Answers
1 global, local
2 global

2 Discuss the question as a whole class or in small groups. In large classes, group learners to discuss the question, and elicit their conclusions from a member of each.

3 Brainstorm some possible collocations with each word as a whole class, e.g. *apple – core*, *price – cut*, *multiple – units*, *enhanced – capabilities*, *wide – range*, *appropriate – strategy*, *internet – provider*, *initial – thought*. Learners put the words in the gaps and check answers in pairs. Elicit their answers.

Answers
1 wide
2 initial
3 multiple
4 appropriate
5 price
6 internet
7 core
8 enhanced

Output: Developing a marketing innovation strategy

Stage 1

Elicit which countries learners consider *rich* and *industrialised* and why. You could then ask them if they know any of those countries well. Then, ask learners if they have ever seen or ridden in a tuk-tuk, then tell them to read the profile of the tuk-tuk and elicit its advantages and disadvantages.

Put learners into groups of three or four and ask them to discuss the market for tuk-tuks in a developed country of their choice and to complete the summary table.

Stage 2

Learners discuss a possible marketing strategy for one of the target groups, completing the table in the process for about 15 minutes. You may wish to review the 4 Ps of marketing (product, price, place, promotion) with reference to possible questions about tuk-tuks with books closed before they do the exercise.

Stage 3

Re-group learners to make their market strategy presentations to each other. As a follow-up, ask them to decide on the best marketing strategy they hear in their groups and elicit it from each group to finish the exercise.

9.3 Skills: Dealing with criticism

Introduction

1, 2 & 3 Write *criticism* on the board and elicit possible synonyms, e.g. *comment, judgement, review*. Pair learners to discuss the three questions. You may wish to check their understanding of direct and indirect criticism before they do the exercise. You could ask them to rank the types of criticism, and find out which type upsets them the most and the least, or re-pair them to report back on their discussions.

Language focus: Recognising and reacting to criticism 2.11

1 Briefly elicit what learners understand by positive and negative, direct and indirect criticism, and then ask them to match the types to the meanings. Elicit their answers.

> ***Answers***
> 1 constructive
> 2 indirect
> 3 negative
> 4 direct

2 Learners listen to 2.11 and follow the extracts on page 88. Elicit what form of criticism is exemplified by each.

> ***Answers***
> Extract A = direct and negative
> Extract B = indirect and constructive

3 Ask learners to underline the language that helped them decide and elicit their ideas.

> ***Suggested answers***
> In Extract A, all of the questions starting with *Why* tell us that the manager is being direct. As he doesn't give the employee a chance to answer the questions we can also sense that he is being negative. He also finishes with an insult, which is clearly negative.
> In Extract B, the manager is indirect in that she starts with a question to find out the reason for the problem, rather than a criticism. She also offers advice on how to resolve the problem, which is constructive in that it helps the employee.

4 Learners work individually to match tips to the language, then compare in pairs. Elicit their answers.

> ***Answers***
> a 3 b 8 c 4 d 2 e 1 f 5 g 6 h 7

5 Pair learners to discuss their responses to the criticism. Re-pair them to report back on their discussions. You could elicit one or two of their responses for each.

6 Play 2.12 and elicit which strategy the speaker is using for each criticism. You may wish to play the recording a second time, pausing after each example to elicit the speaker's strategy.

> ***Answers***
> 1 d 2 e 3 g 4 b 5 c

> ***Audio script***
>
> 1
> **Speaker A:** I have no idea why you didn't consult me before agreeing to the contract.
> **Speaker B:** The reason I did it was because they wanted a decision today and I didn't want to lose the contract.
>
> 2
> **Speaker A:** Your mistake has cost us an absolute fortune.
> **Speaker B:** I know I've made a mistake and I'll be more careful in future.
>
> 3
> **Speaker A:** That is the stupidest idea that I've ever heard.
> **Speaker B:** I'm not prepared to accept that.
>
> 4
> **Speaker A:** I can't believe it. I never had these problems with my old supplier.
> **Speaker B:** I hear what you're saying and understand the problem.
>
> 5
> **Speaker A:** It's all your fault. What are you going to do about it?
> **Speaker B:** Let me have a think and I'll get back to you.

Listening: Discussing the results of an exhibition 2.13

1 Learners read through the questions, predict possible answers then listen to check them.

Answers
1 Just over £2,000.
2 Because advertising alone doesn't work.
3 Because they haven't had the resources.
4 They also had to send over magazines, which cost £1,000.
5 Because they made some good contacts there.
6 Because it can take between 18 months and 2 years before you see the results.

Audio script
Sally: What feedback have we had? How worthwhile has it been? It says here you spent just over two thousand pounds. What have we got for our money?
Mark: We got quite a few leads. I mean, the leads followed up haven't produced anything in the way of actual sales.
Sally: So.
Mark: So, you know, you could argue there's not been a return yet.
Sally: OK.
Mark: This was really the first year that we've entered into the marketplace and started to push the product. Over a period of time it will come, but I don't think advertising on its own is ever going to be the answer, is it? I think you've got to follow up with attending these exhibitions, with mailshots and trying to contact the customers as a result, which we just haven't had the resources to. But just as a straight answer to what we've done up to now I can say no, we haven't had a return on our two thousand pounds.
Sally: You haven't sold one subscription?
Mark: No.
Sally: I don't know what that exhibition cost you but it probably cost a lot more than two thousand pounds, because I know it cost us nearly a thousand pounds just to get the magazines over there. So our bill was probably nearly three and a half to four thousand pounds.
Mark: Yeah.
Sally: Just for that one exhibition. And it's like anything else. I think everybody at the exhibition said 'Yeah, it's been a good exhibition, this. We've got a half a dozen good names.' And you will probably not see any business from that exhibition for maybe eighteen months, two years.
Mark: No.
Sally: I think exhibitions are very expensive, but there again it's getting in front of the people. And that's the thing, isn't it?

2 Ask learners to take some notes for each question. Play 2.13 again and pair them to discuss their answers. Elicit one or two of their ideas for each question.

Suggested answers
1 The way that she questions Mark is direct, but she frames her criticism in the form of questions that are indirect in order to try and find out what the problem is.
2 It seems to be effective – she gets the information that she wants from Mark and then uses the information constructively.
3 He deals well with the criticism. He does not get defensive; he gives reasons for the lack of results and looks at ways that they can gain positives from the lack of sales.
4 It ends on a positive note, with Sally looking at the positives that can come out of the exhibition.

Critical analysis

Pair learners to discuss the question. Elicit their ideas. You could extend the analysis by asking them to discuss which type of management style might be more constructive and which might be more negative, i.e. transformational and transactional management style. You could also ask them to discuss which critical style they prefer and why.

Output: Making and taking criticism

Stage 1

Pair learners and refer Student A to page 144. Student B's information is on page 89. Check understanding of the task. In the case of an extra student, ask them to play the role of an employee. Give them 10 minutes for each role play.

Stage 2

Learners role play the situation between the manager and the employee, where the manager is direct.

Stage 3

Ask learners to change roles, where the manager is more indirect and constructive. If you have an extra student, you could pair with them or have a 'panel' management discussion.

Stage 4

Group learners to discuss the outcomes of the role plays for 10 minutes as a round-up. Elicit their thoughts on which was the most successful style of criticism.

Worksheet 9 (See page 136)

Improve your knowledge of employee appraisal

Level **C1 +**

Time **55–60 minutes**

1 Lead-in (10 minutes)

Pair learners to discuss the questions.

Suggested answers

1 Depends on individual learners.
2 To judge the merits, good or otherwise, of a film or a play.
3 Negative language can result in defensive behaviour; positive language usually pacifies.
4 Most people would react defensively and emotion could take over.
5 The word *feedback* does not convey whether it is positive or negative, while constructive criticism is intended to be helpful.

2 Forms of *critic* (10 minutes)

Learners fill in the gaps and then check their answers in pairs.

Answers

1 critically
2 critical
3 critique
4 uncritical
5 critic
6 criticism
7 uncritically
8 criticise

3 Linguistic reactions (10 minutes)

Pair learners to discuss the questions or discuss them in smaller classes. You could re-pair to report back or elicit one or two comments.

Suggested answers

1 Feel threatened – likely to plea for the job or say go ahead – depending on employee's situation.
2 Likely to thank the critic and ask for ways for improvement.
3 Feel threatened – likely to say sorry or become defensive depending on situation.
4 Likely to thank the critic and offer to continue the present behaviour.
5 Likely to react with astonishment in the age of the smartphone, social media marketing, etc.

4 Employee appraisal categories (10 minutes)

1 Learners match the appraisal competencies to their content, then check in pairs.

Answers

Competency	Content
Team working	cooperation across departments to achieve shared goals
Customer service	delivery of appropriate and high quality services
Flexibility	ability to adapt to a changing working environment
Self-awareness	understanding of one's emotions and their impact on others
Organisational skills	ability to prioritise and achieve deadlines
Financial compliance	achievement of expected monetary targets
Overall performance	rating of the employee's work as a whole
Intercultural competence	consideration for a variety of beliefs and traditions
Mentoring	advising and monitoring colleagues to realise their full potential
Entrepreneurship	identifying or creating opportunities and maximising them

2 Discuss the question as a whole class. You could ask them to design an employee appraisal form as an extra activity.

5 Employee appraisal role play (20 minutes)

Learners prepare in pairs for the role play. Give each pair their role cards, line manager and employee. In cases of odd numbers, the odd one could help conduct a panel appraisal. Allow some time for preparation of what they would like to say.

As an extra activity, learners could role play the situation again, but this time the line manager could use inappropriate language and the employee could act defensively.

10 Design and invention

Overview of the unit

10.1 Theory: Design in business

> 'Sometimes when you innovate, you make mistakes. It is best to admit them quickly, and get on with improving your other innovations.'
>
> *Steve Jobs*

Innovation Design Engineering (IDE) is the term given to creating new industrial products such as medical equipment or consumer products in different ways that include experimental exploration, market-focused new product prototypes, improvement to existing products, products driven by new business models, and commercial planning. IDE can provide radical and revolutionary solutions, starting with the development of the product concept, through the design process, prototyping, to production. It utilises a wide range of design skills, e.g. innovation-focused thinking, industrial design techniques, manufacturing, mechanical engineering, design research, user-centred design, and sustainability.

In modern manufacturing, everything supporting a product proposition can be seen as under the influence of a designer. Industrial design is where the usability of products is improved and people have more space to innovate, visualise, form or expand on ideas. Design engineering explores engineering constraints and workability, exploits creativity and transforms ideas into something end-users will want to purchase.

10.2 Practice: Dyson – a design-led company

Profile: Dyson

James Dyson is a British industrial designer and founder of the Dyson company, which has its headquarters and a research and development centre in England. Its production facility is based in Malaysia.

He is best known as the inventor of the Dual Cycle bagless vacuum cleaner, but the company has also had success with the Dyson Airblade™, a fast hand dryer, often seen in public lavatories, the Dyson Airmultiplier™, a fan without external blades, and the Ballbarrow, a modified version of the wheelbarrow using a ball instead of a wheel. Not all of Dyson's inventions have been a commercial success. A washing machine with two rotating drums, moving in opposite directions, was launched, but has since been withdrawn due to a lack of commercial viability.

James Dyson set up the James Dyson Foundation in 2002. The organisation aims to inspire young people to study engineering, to encourage students to be inventive and make mistakes, and to support design and engineering through a variety of educational projects. In addition, the James Dyson Award celebrates students' work in product design, industrial design and engineering.

10.3 Skills: Communicating negative information in a positive light

Negative news and information may not be at all easy to deliver, but it is often necessary and should be done clearly and concisely. If, as a manager, you are telling someone they have been made redundant, or providing constructive criticism on a subordinate's poor job performance, how you choose to deliver the message can influence the response to it.

Communicating negative information has to be handled delicately to counterbalance the demotivating impact of the message. It also requires a greater cultural sensitivity to the issues that surround reprimanding people of different nationalities where the word *no* is rarely said directly, e.g. Japan.

Negative language includes the word *not*, e.g. *mustn't*, *can't* or *shouldn't*, and implies what is impossible to do, assigns blame and finds scapegoats for problems. Positive language suggests alternatives and possible solutions to problems, and has a helpful and encouraging tone.

10.1 Theory: Design in business

Introduction

1 & 2 Pair or group learners to discuss the questions. Encourage them to discuss what makes a well and badly designed product. You may want to extend the discussion and elicit why the floppy disc was replaced by the CD, the CD by the USB stick and the USB stick by cloud computing, i.e. the wish to reduce the weight of a computer by removing various drives.

Listening 1: Design and people (2.14)

1 Ask learners to predict possible answers to the questions. then play 2.14 and feed back.

Answers
1 Designers and engineers
2 Apple and the iPod

Audio script

Interviewer: When you talk about design, you mention 'people' again and again. Why is that?

Dr Clare Brass: Well, designers are people-focused. It's a people-centred activity. And I think this is what sets it apart from many other disciplines. I think there are many disciplines that could be said to be problem-solving disciplines, but design has an almost natural tendency to start with the user, start with a person. So when engineers solve a problem, they start with a technical problem which they aim to solve. However, when a designer starts to address a problem, they often worry less about how to solve it, and they think more about who they're solving it for and then they worry about solving the technical aspects later on. Take Apple, for example. There is nothing quite like Apple for having really taken design thinking and created successful products on the market. There are plenty of mp3 players on the market, they all basically use a similar technology, but what Apple have been able to do with the iPod is create a delightfulness through that interaction with the product. In this case, design provides the interface which allows a person to access a whole system behind the product, in a way which is both functional, but also delightful.

2 Learners make more detailed notes on a second listening. Elicit their ideas.

Answers

1 Designers start with the people who use the product and try to understand their behaviour first. Engineers start with a technical problem and try to solve it.
2 Apple have created a 'delightfulness' through interaction with the product. Users find it delightful but it still has good functionality too.

Listening 2: New ways of thinking 2.15

1 Ask learners to predict both the answers within the table and the true and false statements in exercise 2. Play 2.15 for learners to complete the table and then check in pairs.

Answers

1 toaster
2 toasting
3 noun
4 verb
5 object
6 surrounding, object

Audio script

Interviewer: There's an old business saying: 'If you do what you've always done, you'll get what you've always got.' How does design help business people break out of this way of thinking?

Dr Clare Brass: Well, I think the key here is about not focusing on an object. So, if you set out to design a toaster, for example, you'll get a toaster. So you might have it in an infinite number of different colours, or you might have buttons that look different, but basically you'll get a toaster. So the way we train Innovation Design Engineering students, and the way that many designers work, is not to look at the design as a noun, but to look at design as a verb. So you might end up with something completely different – because you no longer are constraining yourself to look at the object. You're looking at everything that's surrounding the object. So, if we just stick with a very simple example of toast, if you're designing toasting then you might take into consideration the whole system around toasting, everything else, all the other aspects that might come into play. So you might be thinking about how do you spread butter on toast, or how do you slice the bread. Or you might be thinking about how do you open the bag of sliced bread, or where do you keep the bag of sliced bread. So you begin to think about all the things that are connected with toasting, and the design trick is to join them up according to the user's need.

Interviewer: Right. And how do you find out about the user's need?

Dr Clare Brass: Well, the only way you can really find out about user's needs is by going and finding users. So, if you want to innovate, what you need to do is go and look people in the eyes and talk to them. When you really go out and talk to people it brings your ideas to life. And what you notice is there are lots of things people do which we all know about, we've seen them before, but we've never really noticed, we've never really looked properly. And those insights can lead to you doing something in a different way.

2 Learners listen again if necessary and decide whether the statements are true or false. Discuss their answers in whole class and encourage them to give reasons for their answers.

Answers

1 False (you have to talk to them)
2 True
3 True

Critical analysis

Ask learners if they have heard of Henry Ford and Steve Jobs and discuss why they are seen as successful businessmen. Put learners into pairs or groups of three or four to discuss the questions. You could re-pair or regroup them to report back on their discussions, or elicit their answers.

Suggested answers

1 The quotes suggest that speaking to potential users is a waste of time as they don't know what they want.
2 Innovators like the people Dr Clare Brass talks about are improving on an existing product, so users have an idea of what they want from the product in the future. Inventors are coming up with a completely new product, so people are less likely to know what they want until they see it.
3 They should ask questions about their existing problems and try to solve them rather than ask questions about what they want.

Language focus: Noun–noun partnerships with 'design'

1 Learners work individually to find the mistakes and correct them. Pair them to check answers. You could warn them before they do the exercise that the mistakes are not only in the forms of *design*.

Answers

1 She is responsible for all types of **design** work for our company.
2 Her main responsibility is **(for designing / to design/ designing)** new products. (*or* Her main responsibility is **new product design.)**
3 She is responsible for the **company's product** design department.
4 The shopping malls sell lots of very cheap **designer** clothes. (*or* The shopping malls sell lots of very **cheaply** designed clothes.)
5 The whole house has used one **overall** design and colour scheme.
6 She will be the core member of the **design** team.
7 The restaurant's **design** reflects aspects of a country's culture.

2 Elicit the compounds with *design* as a whole class.

> ***Answers***
> 1 design work
> 2 (new) product design
> 3 product design / design department
> 6 design team

3 Pair learners to do the exercise. Re-pair them to check answers before giving feedback. You could elicit any other combinations they know with *design* to round up, e.g. *designer teeth*, *designer drug*, *interior designer*.

> ***Answers***
> 1 design proposal
> 2 software design
> 3 design company
> 4 design thinking
> 5 design trick
> 6 design profession
> 7 design brief
> 8 design department

Output: Designing something to solve an everyday problem

Stage 1 – problems/inspirations

Ask learners to read the introduction and elicit the task in their own words. Put them into small groups. Encourage them to discuss experience of any of the problems, before selecting one to concentrate on. You may wish to check understanding of *frustrating*, *runaway*, *furious*, *get rid of*.

Stage 2 – designing a solution

Keeping learners in their groups, ask them to design a solution to the problem they selected, making a sketch. You could regroup learners to discuss and comment on each other's designs to round off the exercise.

10.2 Practice: Dyson – a design-led company

Profile: Dyson

Introduction

1 Briefly discuss what Dyson means in the quotation, or ask them to rewrite it and elicit a few ideas. Ask learners to read the profile, before comparing their ideas in pairs. You may wish to elicit one or two ideas, e.g. *People like things that are familiar and that they don't have to learn how to use.*

2 Elicit a few electrical household products, e.g. *kettle*, *fridge*, *vacuum cleaner*, before asking learners to choose three factors that would influence their buying decision. Pair them to compare their ideas and why they chose the factors.

Reading: The Dyson story

1 Check comprehension of the words in the box. Ask learners to work individually to match the titles to the text, and then compare their answers in pairs. Encourage them to discuss why they chose their answer.

> ***Answers***
> 1 Against the odds
> 2 Research and development
> 3 A cautionary tale

2 Learners find the words and phrases to match. Elicit their answers. In smaller groups, give one or two questions to each individual, for them to explain the answers in feedback.

> ***Answers***
> 1 prototypes
> 2 determination
> 3 just round the corner
> 4 the lifeblood
> 5 once in a while
> 6 eclectic pastimes
> 7 assign the patent (*assigned* in the text)
> 8 majority shareholders

3 Learners answer the questions before comparing their answers in pairs. Take feedback.

> ***Answers***
> 1 determination and hard work
> 2 eclectic engineering pastimes
> 5 He lost control of the company and hence his control over his inventions.

4 Discuss the question as a whole class.

> ***Suggested answer***
> The writing style is quite an informal, anecdotal style that tells a set of stories of the company's history and founder. Examples of informal language include *a varied bunch*, *just around the corner*, *James* (not *James Dyson*). The style communicates a company culture that is the opposite of a big hierarchical corporation.

5 Pair or group learners to brainstorm adjectives. Re-pair or regroup for them to report back. You may wish to elicit one from each pair or group.

> ***Suggested answer***
> young, dynamic, entrepreneurial, diverse, tolerant, fun, design-focused, creative, determined

Language focus: Describing products using multiple adjectives and analogies

1 Ask learners to put the adjectives in order, then compare in pairs. Then give the answer.

> ***Answer***
> a beautiful painted large square eighteenth-century red Chinese wooden box

2 Ask learners to put the adjective type in order using the example, before comparing in pairs and giving the answer. Emphasise that it is highly unusual for a native speaker to use this many adjectives in speech.

> ***Answer***
> opinion / observation / size / shape / age / colour / origin / material / noun

3 Pair learners to put the adjectives in the correct position, before re-pairing them to compare their answers. Elicit their ideas on the board and correct or peer-correct as appropriate.

> ***Answers***
> 1 a huge range of products
> 2 beautiful sweet-smelling cosmetic products
> 3 an inefficient old imported product
> 4 great American paper products
> 5 exciting innovative European products
> 6 a fantastic innovative product

4 Speculate on reasons for the preferable version as a whole class. Accept reasonable answers before giving the answer or referring them to the answer key.

> ***Answers***
> Because it offers an immediately accessible everyday image to demonstrate a complex technical process.

5 Pair learners to work out the meaning, then re-pair them to compare answers. Elicit their ideas.

> ***Answers***
> 1 People come in and leave the company all of the time.
> 2 She feels as if she is in the wrong place. / The job doesn't suit her at all.
> 3 If you talk to her boss, you won't get a response.
> 4 If the product is good, you should have no problem in selling it.

6 Ask learners to work individually to create a product analogy. They could compare in pairs or work in small groups to say the analogy for others to guess the product.

Listening: James Dyson talks about design and invention

2.16

1 Books closed. Tell learners to listen to an interview with James Dyson in order to invent a title for it. Elicit a few of their ideas.

> ***Answers***
> The original title of this interview was 'Failure'.

> ***Audio script***
> **James Dyson:** There's a myth about inventors that all you need is one good idea and you'll make your fortune. But the fact of the matter is you don't have ideas like that. You start with a problem that you're having to solve and you start building prototypes, hundreds of them, perhaps even thousands of them. And very often the original idea or the original problem doesn't look anything like the final solution. So the important thing is this journey from prototype to prototype and during that process, of course, you get hundreds or thousands of failures. And the failure is the starting point because when something fails you understand why it fails, and then you start to think of ideas as to ways to overcome that failure. I mean, the cyclones for my vacuum cleaner took over 5,000 prototypes. That's 5,000 failures before I cracked it. So the moral of the tale is keep on failing. It works.

2 Learners read the questions, listen again and then compare in pairs. Elicit the answers.

> ***Answers***
> 1 They have one good idea which will make a fortune.
> 2 Inventors will benefit from understanding why something fails and then think of ways of overcoming this failure.
> 3 It refers to the number of prototypes and the number of failures before his vacuum cleaner worked.

Intercultural analysis

Pair or group learners appropriately to discuss attitudes to failure. You may want to ask them to distinguish between the organisation they work for/study in, their country and, if you feel it is not too personal, they could discuss attitudes across generations of their family.

Transferable skills: Thinking differently

1 You may wish to discuss what *thinking outside the box* means before asking learners to rank how likely they would be to use the lateral thinking techniques.

2 Pair learners to compare answers. Encourage them to discuss why they would or wouldn't use the techniques.

Output: Explaining unusual inventions to potential investors

Briefly brainstorm any unusual product inventions learners may have bought or know about.

Stage 1

Put learners into two groups of roughly equal number, A and B. Refer Group A to page 140 and Group B to page 144.

Stage 2

Check understanding of the task and elicit that they will make a presentation that answers the questions, adding any extra ideas they deem appropriate. They then practise their presentation. Encourage them to involve all the people.

Stage 3

Make new groups, putting one or two members together of the groups from the previous stage to make their presentations. Encourage them to discuss the commercial viability for five minutes, before eliciting which product would be most viable in the opinion of the groups.

10.3 Skills: Communicating negative information in a positive light

Introduction

1 In pairs, learners discuss the questions. You could ask them to rank the statements in order of difficulty and elicit their ideas. You may also want to check their understanding of *key supplier* (important provider of materials you need) and *lay off* (stop employing because there is not enough work) before they do the exercise.

2 Learners discuss how to present the information positively. Encourage learners to think in terms of the response of the receiver. You could re-pair them to practise saying how to put over the message. You could ask them to communicate one or two statements negatively and compare responses.

> ***Suggested answers***
> It is important to communicate the information clearly, while at the same time protecting the relationship / keeping the goodwill of the recipient. Therefore framing the message is very important. This means that you prepare the listeners for the message before they hear it. For example:
> 1 We are now looking for a new supplier, as ABC suppliers will no longer be working with us. This obviously provides new challenges as well as opportunities …
> 2 As you know, company profits have been down for several quarters now, and we are receiving increasing competition from X and Y … obviously if things continue like this, there is a chance that the company could find itself in real trouble …
> 3 Our sales for the past six months were very good, but we have had a blip in the last period. I'm sure we are all desperate to rectify this, so this is what I suggest …
> 4 Given the present economic situation – and the drop in sales we have suffered as a result – rather than lay people off, the board has decided that a reduction in staff salaries is the most effective way to guarantee the survival of the company. Thankfully this will be only for six months …
> 5 In line with the company policy of rewarding the best performers, the top sales person will now receive an extra 5 days off a year. This does mean however that reducing the standard number of holidays across the board is necessary…

3 Briefly discuss the question as a whole class. You could extend the discussion by asking them if it is better to receive such information face-to-face, over the telephone, or by email.

Language focus 1: Understand how euphemisms provide a more positive alternative

1 Learners match the real meaning to the euphemism, and then compare answers in pairs. You could brainstorm which words your class would find unpleasant or offensive in a business context before they do the exercise, e.g. comments based on body size, race or hair colour.

> ***Answers***
> 1 B 2 A 3 A 4 C 5 C 6 B

2 Ask learners to predict meaning and elicit a few of their ideas for each.

> ***Answers***
> 1 there is an insufficient number of staff in the department
> 2 we are facing some real difficulties
> 3 it will be hard to attract these customers (back)

3 Learners underline the euphemisms in the extract. Elicit their answers.

> ***Answers***
> 1 a really complex set of customers
> 2 we've got some real challenges
> 3 focus in on

Listening 1: Talking about the customers 2.17

1 Ask learners to predict possible answers, play 2.17 and elicit them. In weaker classes, you may wish to point out there are two answers to the question.

> ***Answers***
> 1 and 3

> ***Audio script***
> **Sales director:** There's an astonishing number of businesses out there which used to be our customers and have churned. That may have been because they didn't pay. They may have churned because they chose to, but there's an opportunity there perhaps to go back in and reconnect with them, because the network will be on their doorstep so there'll be no connection problems, and there must be some of those thousands of churned customers who might want to reconsider us again. You know, they will be tough doors to knock on but they might want to come back to us … And of course, existing customers are an easier win. Teamwork, as I said – we aren't going to achieve this on our own, no one individual is going to make that target next year, and we all need time in front of the customer.

2 Elicit the answers if possible or ask learners if they want to listen again to check their answers.

> ***Answers***
> 1 and 3

3 Ask learners if they want to listen again. Elicit the message about teamwork.

> ***Answer***
> Without teamwork, there is little chance the company can reach these sales targets.

Listening 2: Talking about marketing support 2.18

1 Learners read the questions. Elicit possible answers for each, play 2.18 and check answers in pairs. Learners may need to listen two or three times before you give them the answers. Alternatively, take questions 1 and 2 together, then concentrate on questions 3 and 4.

Answers
1 He hopes that they are going to be more proactive in finding new customers.
2 Some of the marketing workforce have been laid off, so they are now short of staff. The euphemism he uses is *thin on the ground*.
3 b and c
4 It seems to be in financial difficulty, as he mentions a *strange environment*, *a lack of capital* and the fact they have lost staff.

Audio script
Sales director: In terms of support for the sales guys, we'll be helping them as much as we can. So we're arming the guys with the capability, hopefully to go out there and up their activity levels. We've got to get out there in front of the customer. We're expecting support from Marketing. I was talking to someone in Marketing the other day; they've had to cut people too. So they're thin on the ground but we're looking for their support this coming year with specific product focus. Front Line is the tool that we're going to use for monitoring all sales activity and sales opportunities. It's crucial that all the guys understand Front Line. Everyone uses Front Line in one way or another, and that will be a key tool for us in the coming year.
But the point is – can we go along and do what we did this year, next year? I think you probably all know the answer.
So we've got to make some step changes, and some of the challenges we're facing today are how to grow the business more quickly in a very strange environment, with a lack of capital, with fewer people. Everyone's lost people, so it's a huge challenge for us all.

2 Pair learners to discuss the questions. You may wish to re-pair them to report back.

Language focus 2: Making excuses

1 Elicit a synonym for the noun *excuse*, e.g. *apology*, *evasion*, *justification*, and tell learners to match the type to the example and check their answers in pairs before feedback. You could discuss whether learners have any other examples of excuses they have heard that fit the types.

Answers
1 f 2 e 3 c 4 a 5 d 6 b

2 Briefly discuss the question as a whole class. Alternatively in larger classes, put learners in groups of three or four to discuss the question and come up with an excuse to fire somebody. Elicit their ideas.

Critical analysis

Put learners into groups of three or four to discuss the question, then report back in whole class.

Suggested answer
Euphemisms can be a useful way to make bad news sound less negative, or to lessen the reaction to bad news, and in this way they can be useful for both staff and managers.
However, euphemisms can also sound dishonest sometimes, and may give the impression that the staff member is untrustworthy or the manager is out of touch. Similarly, excuses can make a speaker appear irresponsible or dishonest.
You have to be especially careful using euphemisms and excuses to people from other companies, as you don't necessarily know the culture of their company. If you appear dishonest, the whole company could lose its reputation.

Output: Communicating negative information

Stage 1

Group learners to discuss the scenarios. You may wish to check understanding of *quit* and *a lack of* by brainstorming collocations, e.g. *quit a job*, *quit smoking*, *quit while you're ahead*; *a lack of money*, *a lack of space*, *a lack of energy*.

Stage 2

Learners role play a situation in their groups. In larger classes you could specify they choose situation one or four where they make an announcement to a larger group of people (played by the rest of your class). Discuss with the class how they felt after each presentation. Smaller classes could role play all situations in pairs or small groups.

You may want to watch Sequence 5 on the DVD to find out more about Design, technology and innovation or ask learners to watch it for homework. There is an accompanying worksheet on page 155.

Worksheet 10 (See page 138)

Improve your knowledge of new business models in newspaper publishing

Level **C1 +**

Time **55–60 minutes**

1 Lead-in (10 minutes)

Pair learners to discuss the questions. Elicit a few of their answers as feedback.

Suggested answers
1 This depends on age range of class. Younger learners perhaps never buy a printed edition.
2 Definitely: many newspapers are closing, and all are having to innovate new business models.
3 Brand loyalty plays a role here; also people are more likely to pay for specialist information.
4 This is well documented – many people will browse a newspaper online before starting their working day ('snack information' refers to the habit of reading snippets of information rather than whole articles.
5 Not necessarily – both headlines and pictures play a role in grabbing attention.

2 Word collocations with *printed, media* and *computer* (10 minutes)

Ask learners to match the words and then compare answers in pairs. You could elicit which words are joined by hyphens, or example usage of new words, to extend the exercise.

Answers
Printed copy, printed edition, printed matter, printed version, printed word
Mass media, media mogul, multi-media, media hype, new media
Computer-animated, computer-based, computer-designed, computer-generated, computer graphics

3 Newspaper business models (15 minutes)

1 Discuss the question as a whole class.

Suggested answers
Traditional: something relevant to older people, uses dated or old-fashioned technology
Pay wall: something cannot be entered without paying
Metered pay wall: you have a set limit before you have to pay to enter something
Mobile services: something is available only on mobile devices
Joint digital/print: a combination of new and older technologies
Online not-for-profit: something free to use on the Internet, but it has to cover running costs

2 Pair learners to match the type of newspaper model to its positive and negative characteristics. Encourage them to think in terms of the reader and the advertiser. You could ask if learners know of any other successful business models, e.g. free press aimed at commuters.

Answers

Model	Positive characteristics	Negative characteristics
Traditional	audience easy to reach, employ professionals, cheap to produce	younger readers and advertisers have shifted to a new media
Pay wall	access is restricted, advertising is more targeted and valuable	most customers are unwilling to pay for general news content
Metered pay wall	casual reader is not deterred, a limited number of stories are free	some people will read what is allowed and will not visit again
Mobile services	readers may be more prepared to pay for content on smart devices	app market is not developed enough to replace print revenue as yet
Joint digital/print	subscribers get access to all digital content, allows reader to choose	people will take more time to move away from printed copy to new media
Online not-for-profit	not dependent on print advertising or physical printing press	reliant on donations, grants and corporate sponsorship of specific issues

4 Declining revenue problem (25 minutes)

Group learners and tell them they are going to role play a meeting where they will discuss the declining revenues of a newspaper. Encourage them to use the stimulus points plus their own experience of buying information to present a new business model for the paper. You could take a vote on the best solution and discuss why it is applicable.

Writing 5: Writing for meetings – notes, minutes and agenda

Overview of the unit

An effective meeting serves a purpose that adds value and an outcome is achieved and accomplished within an allotted time frame. With a clear objective decided, everything that happens before, during and after the meeting, e.g. the contents, the participants, the timing, should move towards this goal.

The agenda ensures the meeting will cover what it is intended to cover and keeps the meeting on time and on track. It shows priorities, participants, sequence, timing, date, time and place. It should be distributed before the meeting, to enable feedback from the participants.

The terms *notes* and *minutes* are sometimes used interchangeably, as both are records of what was achieved, and who is responsible for taking the action that was decided. However, they are not the same. Each individual may take different notes and they are written during a meeting. *Minutes* are a formal legal document and are agreed by everybody present. They are written up soon after the meeting and should have headings so that readers can scan them for information. They should also include when the meeting took place, who attended, who did not attend, what was discussed, what was decided, what actions were agreed upon, a copy of any hand-outs, and if there will be a follow-up meeting.

Introduction

1 Ask learners to complete the sentences individually and then feed back in whole class.

> ***Answers***
> 1 minutes, are, after
> 2 agenda, is, before

2 Ask learners to scan the list for items they think would not be in minutes. Elicit their ideas.

> ***Answers***
> It's not usual practice to include jokes, relationship-building discourse (small talk), private discussions or much background information in minutes and so there is no point in taking notes on these parts of the meeting.

Writing skill 1: Taking meeting notes and interpreting an agenda 2.19

1 Focus attention on the questions and elicit what the learners are *scan reading for*, i.e. time, place, name of a person or group of people, direct them to the agenda and elicit their answers. As a round-up, discuss as a whole class what each agenda point means.

> ***Answers***
> 1 The meeting is at 10 am on 28 May. It will be held in Room S224 in the Stamford Building.
> 2 The minutes have been circulated to the following people: Dave Sinclair, Peter Chen, Paula Summers, Emile Lahar, Elizabeth Willis. They are all part of the SB Technical Assistance Team.
> 3 Point 1 refers to apologies received in advance of the meeting from any person invited who is not able to attend.
> Point 2 refers to regular minutes from regular meetings (monthly or weekly, for example); it is common to approve (or amend) draft minutes that were circulated after the previous meeting.
> Point 3 refers to any issues that are *arising* (coming out) from the previous meeting that still need discussing.
> Point 9 is a common acronym that stands for *any other business*. It refers to 'any other issues not on the agenda that people would like to raise or discuss'.

2 Tell learners to listen and take notes, play 2.19, and then check answers in pairs. (They will compare these with the draft minutes in exercise 4.)

> ***Answers***
> Paula absent – Paris trade fair
> Minutes OK
> Didn't discuss liaison/IT + equip survey – done (already).
> 'User-First' – circulate minutes (DS)

> ***Audio script***
> **David Sinclair:** Let's press on quickly because I'm sure we've all got plenty of other things to get on with. Apologies for absence. I have apologies from Paula Summers, who apparently is in Paris sightseeing for a week. That's a joke, by the way. Paula's setting up our stand at the Trade Fair over there. Any other apologies?
> **Elizabeth Willis:** I don't know about the Health and Safety people?
> **Emile Lahar:** Are we expecting them?
> **David Sinclair:** No, they're not coming in on this one. Shall we press on with the next item? Everyone OK about those minutes? OK. Any matters arising? Peter.
> **Peter Chen:** Can I make a suggestion? Well, it crossed my mind that a few of the headings on this agenda here are actually duplicated by the 'User-First' interdepartmental meeting we had with IT and Estates Management last week, which covered some of these things, so do we want to cover them again in this meeting?
> **Elizabeth Willis:** You're right, 'Liaison with IT' and 'Equipment survey' were definitely covered.
> **David Sinclair:** OK, if everyone's in agreement let's bin these two. I followed an entirely conventional format for the agenda here. So, where was I? Right, yes, we're going to jump all the way to item 6.
> **Elizabeth Willis:** Can we just come back to matters arising coming out of those 'User-First' meetings a moment? I think we ought to circulate the minutes of those meetings to the whole group.

David Sinclair: Good, yes. They've been done; they haven't been circulated, but they're available. But if everybody would like them? Who would like them? Well, I can get them. I'll get on to that. So ...

5 Pair learners to compare their note-taking style. You may wish to elicit other examples of the conventions listed.

6 Learners listen again, before comparing their notes to the draft minutes. You could check whether anyone missed anything.

Language focus: Structure and style of meeting minutes

1 Pair learners to compare the draft minutes and the guidelines. You could ask them to underline examples of where the guidelines are used, before re-pairing them to compare answers. Elicit their ideas as feedback.

Answers
Points covered:
1 Numbering follows the agenda points with points within those sections numbered as 1.1, 2.1, etc.
2 **Action:** DS to circulate ...
3 DS to ...
4 Paula Summers; DS (David Sinclair)
5 DS to circulate
6 Points 1.1, 3.1, 4.1 do this
7 Not covered. In many organisations it is common practice to highlight agreements in bold and sometimes also in capitals within the minutes, e.g. **AGREED.**
8 Paula Summers in Paris setting up (the) trade fair stand; (It was) Agreed; ... for SB Technical team to have (the minutes) of ...; DS to circulate (the) 'User First' meeting minutes; (it was) Decided to ...
9 Use of passive: Agreed it would be useful; Decided to delete ...; none of the note-taking forms in exercise 5 is used here.

2 Pair learners to discuss the question and then elicit two or three answers.

Answers
The minutes of a meeting are always written as a formal document, even if the meeting was quite informal, as this will be the official record of what was said at the meeting. These minutes can be circulated to people not at the meeting, including bosses, and can be made public.

3 Tell learners to take notes on the four extracts as they listen to 2.20, write them up as formal minutes and compare their answers in pairs. Elicit the action points as feedback. You could ask learners to rewrite the example in note form before doing this exercise.

Suggested answers
2 **Action:** AG to request Marketing Dept. to provide revised sales figures for last month.
3 **Action:** SK to distribute copies of course outlines for Engineering and Design (the two 'course areas' discussed need to be specified).
4 **Action:** Agreed to do large-scale mailing to all our clients in Spain, Italy and France.

Audio script
1 **Dina Ahmed:** OK, I'll investigate the incident about that injury the other day when that guy from the bank tripped over the PC leads in Caroline's office.
2 **Alfonso Garcia:** No problem, I'll ask the guys in marketing to give us the revised sales figures for last month.
3 **Steve Knox:** If that's what everyone wants, I can send round copies of the course outlines for those two areas.
4 **Magda Zboina:** OK, let's do it. Let's get that leaflet going out in a mega mailing to all our clients in Spain, Italy and France.

Output: Produce an agenda, notes and minutes of issues affecting your workplace

Stage 1

Group learners to draw up an agenda. In one-to-one classes, you could use the opportunity to discuss the organisation of your course. You may like to brainstorm more possible problems before moving onto the next stage.

Stage 2

Put groups together of roughly equal size to discuss one item on their agendas in the time limit. The listening group should take notes, including any action points, while the speaking group discuss.

Stage 3

Split the groups into their original make-up to write up the draft minutes to pass them on. You might like to set a time limit for the writing of 10–15 minutes. As a follow-on activity, you could ask for two or three comments on the level of formality used in the minutes.

Progress test 2 (See page 122)

Answers
Grammar 1
1 By 2 of whom 3 and thus 4 whether 5 adding that
6 as 7 while 8 but 9 saying 10 although

Grammar 2
1 That supermarket stocks a wide range of fresh local produce.
2 a beautiful, hand-painted, wooden box
3 some lovely, colourful, sweet-smelling cosmetics
4 The paperback is portable, compact and almost indestructible.
5 The 3D printer is a fantastic revolutionary invention.

Vocabulary 1
1 designer 2 Designer 3 designed 4 design 5 designed

Vocabulary 2
1 self-belief 2 inspire 3 passionate 4 energy
5 dictatorial 6 charisma 7 persuasion 8 visionary
9 consistency 10 motivated

Vocabulary 3
1 provider 2 downsizing 3 reintegrate activities
4 Just-in-time 5 shortfall in inventory 6 switch providers
7 renegotiate 8 core business 9 Logistics
10 back office

Writing
Allow 2 marks each for task achievement, organisation, grammar, vocabulary and coherence.

11 The economic environment

Overview of the unit

11.1 Theory: Government influence on the economic environment

> 'I have long believed taxpayers make better use of their money than the government ever could.'
>
> *Kay Bailey Hutchinson*

Ideally, with regards to a national economy, a government's role is to preside over the overall rate of economic activity, maintain a steady growth pattern, operate at close to full employment and ensure price stability.

This role of government in the economic sphere stems from the works of John Maynard Keynes in the 1930s. He argued that government could influence economic activity through interest rate policy to affect the level of consumption, tax policy to redistribute money to and from the treasury, and government spending to generate demand via the multiplier effect. Interest rates could be manipulated through the central bank and taxes through parliament. In the 1980s, a lower tax policy was used in the developed world to spur entrepreneurship and increase national savings and investment, because high taxes logically pushed capital to move to more profitable areas. In the 2000s some central banks were allowed to set interest rates independently according to the general borrowing needs of business and private consumers. Many governments maintained a budget deficit, through a constant flow of treasury bills, to encourage lower interest rates. It was hoped that this would lead to increased investment and job creation in the private sector and would fund spending on education, healthcare and infrastructure, and provide an impetus to technological change and innovation, instead of increasing taxes significantly, in the public sector.

Recent economic thinking maintains that the speed of the modern global flow of capital, goods and people across borders now makes a government's interest rate and spending policy only marginally effective in affecting the national economic environment. This is because there is no longer one dominant economy influencing the global money flow and because of the ease of locating high-tech facilities and factories, in places with a suitable workforce, compared to Keynes's time.

11.2 Practice: Managing economic and financial risk – Unilever

Profile: Unilever

Unilever is an Anglo-Dutch multinational that can trace its roots as far back as the 1870s when Jurgens and Van den Bergh produced the first margarine and Lever Brothers produced a soap called Sunlight. Unilever was officially born when the Margarine Union and Lever Brothers amalgamated. Over the years, Unilever has acquired or launched some extremely iconic brands in the food, drink, cosmetics and soap powder markets such as Dove, Marmite, Omo, Sunsilk, PG Tips and Lipton teas. In addition to acquisitions and mergers, Unilever's financial results are affected by a vast range of factors including general economic, political and social conditions, competitors' pricing strategy, access to credit, the security of supply of raw materials, fluctuations in commodity prices, the ability of its staff to maintain and manage customer and supplier relationships, reputational risks, and environmental risk.
The company has recently made a decision to set up a sustainable agricultural programme due to environmental and customer concerns about the food chain. In response to this customer feedback, it has committed to source all its tea from sustainable and ethical sources.

11.3 Skills: Presenting charts and statistics

Many technological tools are now available to help visualise numerical information, but the focus of a presentation of facts and figures must always be on the content and the message of the chart and not on the technology itself.

A visual presentation of data should make the main findings easy to spot and understand. Statistics are best understood as a chart because data is easily displayed and can be compared, because shares of the whole are outlined and because trends and relationships can be identified. This visualisation can be done through bar, pie and line charts, scatter plots and population pyramids, all of which have advantages and disadvantages. For example, a bar chart is good for comparison, a pie chart can show a relationship to a whole category, and a line chart is good for showing statistics over time.

Chart title, use of gridlines and labelling must be considered carefully as plain language is faster to read, gets the message across clearer and is more likely to hold the audience's attention.

Charts are not ideal for presenting statistics when there are too few or many variables and too much or too little variation in the numerical value of variables.

11.1 Theory: Government influence on the economic environment

Introduction

1 Discuss the quote as a whole class. You could check learners' understanding of *subsidise*, i.e. support with a *subsidy*, a form of government spending designed to protect strategically important industries such as agriculture from price instability and used to foster technological development.

> ***Suggested answer***
> 2 Government spending is financed by tax, which is an essential means of paying for public services that benefit the whole community, ranging from schools and hospitals to building roads and crime prevention. If taxes are too low, then public services will be cut back which negatively impacts on the whole community. Government intervention in the economy is designed to help business and can take many forms, such as offering financial incentives to companies to locate their operations in regions of high unemployment, or it can act to stop creations of monopolies that are not in the interests of consumers.

2 If learners are interested, you could tell them that the quote comes from *Hamlet*. Write up *borrow* and *lend* and elicit a phrase meaning the same for each, e.g. *take and return*; *give for an amount of time or a price*. You could also elicit forms, e.g. *borrow from* and *lend to*. Pair learners to discuss the questions, before re-pairing them to report back. You could also discuss the questions as whole-class feedback, as attitudes towards usury may stimulate discussion on the rise of Islamic banking.

> ***Suggested answer***
> 1 Lenders risk not having their loans repaid and losing their money. Borrowers risk not being able to repay the loan or even afford to pay the interest rates charged by lenders. If they don't repay their loans, then the lenders can repossess what they own (their house, their cars, their businesses). On a personal level, lending money to friends who then do not repay you can lead to broken friendships. (In *Hamlet*, the character Polonius gives this advice to his son Laertes who is about to leave home for the first time.)
> 2 If nobody borrowed or lent money, then the whole financial system as we know it would collapse. The banking sector would cease to exist. Individuals, for example, would have to save for a very long time to buy a house if there were no mortgages available. Most businesses are unable to fund investment from their own resources (retained profits) and so if they could not borrow, levels of investment would fall dramatically, leading to widespread unemployment. Governments need to borrow money when their expenditure exceeds their income, so if they were unable to borrow, they would need to raise taxes (to increase income) or cut spending. Some people think this is a good financial discipline, although others would disagree.

Language focus 1: Financial and economic word partnerships

1 Pair learners to calculate to increase in cost and discuss changes in lifestyle. Elicit the answer and their ideas. You could introduce one or two budgetary idioms, e.g. *tighten one's belt, live from hand to mouth*.

> ***Suggested answer***
> They would have to cut expenses on such things as eating out, and they would need to shop around more for better deals on things like car insurance. If they couldn't cut expenses, they might have to use their savings to pay their living expenses.

2 Learners mark the government policies individually, and then check answers in pairs. As feedback, you could discuss how quickly a government can implement each policy.

> ***Answers***
> 1 S
> 2 SD
> 3 SD
> 4 S
> 5 SD
> 6 S

3 Group learners in threes or fours, in different nationalities if possible, to discuss the questions. In a monolingual class, you could ask them to discuss what they would do for different countries.

4 Pair learners to match the words. Re-pair them to check answers.

> ***Answers***
> 1 e 2 c 3 b 4 a 5 d

5 Group learners to check understanding of the differences in meaning. In one-to-one classes, you could ask the student to look up in a dictionary a definition of any terms they are unsure about.

6 Learners complete the gaps individually and then check their answers in pairs. Elicit their answers.

> ***Answers***
> 1 tax revenue
> 2 financial crisis
> 3 economic recovery
> 4 stable currency
> 5 government intervention

Listening 1: Government and central bank objectives

2.21

1 Ask learners to predict what the speaker's job description might entail. They then predict answers to the questions and listen to check their ideas.

> ***Answers***
> 1 For the welfare of their citizens
> 2 Poor people want higher taxes and spending, rich people want the opposite.
> 3 To create a stable financial and economic environment
> 4 A stable currency that people have trust in

Audio script
Interviewer: Why do governments seek to manage their economies, and what are they trying to achieve?
Dr Tatiana Damjanovic: Well, usually governments try to achieve the welfare of their citizens through an appropriate mix of taxation and spending that is broadly acceptable to the people living in that country. In general, the poor will be in favour of higher taxation and higher spending and the rich in favour of far less taxation and spending.
Interviewer: What are the main tools that governments and central banks can use to effect changes in the economy? And how do they work in theory?
Dr Tatiana Damjanovic: The purpose of the central banks and the purpose of the government can be different. In general though, the objective of the central bank is to ensure a stable economic and financial environment. The basis of this involves issuing and maintaining a stable national currency that people have trust in; a currency that holds its value and can be used as a reliable means of payment for goods and services.

2 Discuss the question as a whole class. You could extend the discussion by asking them if they agree about what she says is the role of the central bank.

Listening 2: The impact of government spending 2.22

1 Pair learners to predict possible answers before they listen. Elicit their ideas.

Answers
1 Lower corporation tax collected (business losses), less income tax collected (unemployment) and less VAT collected (people spend less).
2 Governments don't have enough revenue to meet their expenditure programmes.
3 Unemployed people need benefits, businesses need government orders and it's a way to stimulate the economy that is slowing down too much.

Audio script
Interviewer: In a time of economic crisis, some economists recommend government spending should be cut, whilst others say it should be increased. Which approach do you favour personally?
Dr Tatiana Damjanovic: In times of crisis, governments usually collect lower revenue because there are businesses that make losses and so governments cannot collect so much corporate tax. People become unemployed, so governments cannot collect so much income tax. And because people are unemployed they spend less, so VAT collection is also lower. So in times of crisis, government revenues fall, sometimes significantly. So this is why governments actually do not have enough resources to pay for their expenditure programmes, and it's why some people think that governments should reduce expenditure in times of crisis.
Interviewer: OK.
Dr Tatiana Damjanovic: However, government expenditure in times of crisis has a much higher value than in time of prosperity. It's really a time when people require their unemployment benefits for example, and business is more dependent on government orders for their goods and services. It's a way for the government to stimulate the economy that is slowing down too much.

2 Group learners in threes to discuss the question. Alternatively, if your class is roughly split on the role of government in an economic crisis, hold a debate on the issue.

Listening 3: Taxation 2.23

1 Tell learners to listen and tick what is mentioned.

Answers
Tax rates, tax evasion, tax collection

Audio script
Interviewer: How effective is government economic management in different countries in the world?
Dr Tatiana Damjanovic: There are definitely huge differences in fiscal policies. There are different levels of taxation. For example, income tax can be more than sixty percent in some Scandinavian countries, and it can be zero percent in countries such as the United Arab Emirates. In Russia it's thirteen percent. VAT also varies considerably between one country and another, in most of Europe it's about twenty percent but in Korea, for example, it's very low – around ten percent.
Interviewer: What do you think are the main reasons for this?
Dr Tatiana Damjanovic: It's relatively easy for the Arab Emirates, because their governments have such large oil revenues that they don't need to collect taxes. In Scandinavian countries I think they actually are able to tax so much because tax discipline is very good. So there's no issue about tax evasion – the issue in Sweden is much smaller than in India, for example, or in Russia. Actually, there are some empirical studies which say that higher levels of taxation result in higher levels of tax evasion. It's partly why Russia has such low income tax, because even if they try to charge higher tax rates ...
Interviewer: ... people will declare lower and get away with it.
Dr Tatiana Damjanovic: Exactly.

2 Learners listen again to find what the numbers refer to. You could ask them if they need to listen again or refer them to the audio script and scan for the numbers before eliciting the answers.

Answers
1 a income tax in Scandinavia
b income tax in the UAE
c income tax in Russia
d VAT rate in most of Europe
e VAT rate in Korea
2 The UAE has large oil revenues, Scandinavia has good tax discipline, Russia aims to minimise tax evasion.

3 Discuss the quote as a whole class. You could also discuss whether tax evasion is a national 'sport' in their countries or brainstorm other collocations with *tax*, e.g. *tax haven*, *tax avoidance*, *tax-deductible*.

Answers
The quote refers to the issue of tax evasion and people inventing numbers when completing their tax returns, i.e. they declare far less than they actually earn.

Critical analysis

Pair or group learners appropriately to discuss the question. Encourage them to think about the size of the characters/images, the position of the characters/images, how the speech bubbles affect timing, etc. to criticise government policy. You could ask them to write alternative speech bubbles as a follow-on activity.

Suggested answer
The cartoon shows a very fat man representing an over-inflated economy. In other words, the government has made the mistake of over-stimulating the economy (cutting interest rates too low, cutting taxes too much, spending and borrowing too much) with the result that economic growth is unsustainable and the economy is now moving into recession, as shown by the man falling. 'Uncle Sam', who represents the government of the USA, is attempting to provide a 'soft landing' for the economy by providing a 'stimulus package' as a cushion to soften the inevitable hardships of recession. The small size of the cushion suggests that government action here will have no effect.

Language focus 2: Verb patterns in finance

1 Learners work individually before comparing their answers in pairs. Elicit the answers and clear up any misunderstanding of the terms *transitive verb* and *intransitive verb.*

Answers
1 cut
2 fall
3 move (moving)

2 Learners look at the sentences. Elicit those that cannot be written in the passive form, and then ask them to write the new sentences. Elicit their answers on the board to check the correct form.

Answers
1 Spending in the public sector will be reduced. / Spending will be reduced in the public sector.
2 not possible
3 Taxes will be cut.
4 not possible

3 Briefly elicit the answer.

Answer
intransitive

4 Pair learners to decide on the type of verb. Then check their answers.

Answers
1 intransitive
2 transitive
3 intransitive
4 both
5 both
6 intransitive

5 Learners correct the sentences. Elicit their answers as feedback.

Suggested answers
1 She was able to raise turnover by 5%.
2 TV sales will rise by 10%.
3 The deficit has disappeared. / The government has made the deficit disappear.
4 The economy has been impacted (on) because of falling exports. / Falling exports have impacted (on) the country's economy.
5 The company's assets will be frozen if he doesn't pay the bill. / They will freeze the company's assets if he doesn't pay the bill.
6 The company had to cut its prices due to the recession.

Output: Assess impact of government and central bank action on a family household

Stage 1

Learners read the introduction. Elicit the task, i.e. there will be a change in fiscal and monetary policy and they are going to advise an 'average' family on their changed conditions in life.

Group learners in fours or fives to read the summary and discuss possible effects of the action. Point out that the monetary values are for visualisation purposes and do not represent a real country.

Stage 2

Refer learners to the profile of the family on page 140 to discuss the points. They could address one of the four categories in smaller groups and tell each other their ideas in stage 3.

Stage 3

Bring two groups together to compare their ideas and agree collaboratively on their advice. Alternatively you could set up a role play between financial advisors and the family with the two groups together.

11.2 Practice: Managing economic and financial risk – Unilever

Profile: Unilever

Introduction

Group learners in threes or fours to discuss the questions for 5 minutes. Elicit the risks identified and ways of reducing or avoiding each one.

Re-group learners to discuss question 3. Alternatively, as a whole class, elicit if any of your learners have heard of Unilever and any of its brands. Then predict the types of risks the company might face bringing its products to market.

Suggested answer
3 They face higher levels of economic, political and environmental risk and volatility due to their exposure to developing and emerging markets, where they do over 50% of their business. They also face foreign exchange rate risk as they earn their money in local currency but will need to pay for supplies in international traded currencies such as the euro or US dollar. The other main risk is to its supply of raw materials, which can change sharply in price.

Language focus 1: Economic and financial terms and phrases

1 Ask learners to work individually to scan the table to match the definitions. Then pair them to check answers. Elicit answers as a whole class as feedback.

> ***Answers***
> a fluctuate
> b net cash flow
> c adverse
> d viability
> e contingency plans
> f model
> g exposure
> h shortfall
> i floating rate

2 Learners individually match the risks to the strategies before checking.

> ***Answers***
> 1 d 2 e 3 b 4 c 5 f 6 a

3 Group learners appropriately to discuss the questions. Elicit one or two of their ideas as feedback after 5–10 minutes. You could also discuss whether end users respond to variables other than price, e.g. fair trade, sustainable resources.

> ***Suggested answer***
> Customers will increase consumption if Unilever increases brand promotion and it enters new markets. If economic conditions in existing markets improve (e.g. unemployment falls, wages rise), it will give customers more spending power. If commodity prices fall, Unilever may pass the savings on to customers, which will also increase consumption.
> If the opposite conditions exist, consumption will decrease.

Reading: Unilever outlook and risks

1 Elicit the source of the reading and whether any learner has ever read a company report. You could also discuss why companies publish these documents, e.g. to inform shareholders of proposed actions. Learners skim each paragraph of the text to gather the main idea before adding a subheading. You could elicit reasons for their choice, e.g. 1: consumers unwilling to purchase, 2: constrained access to credit.

> ***Answers***
> 1 a 2 d 3 e 4 f 5 c 6 b

2 Pair learners to answer the questions and then put them in small groups to compare answers.

> ***Answers***
> 1 adverse economic conditions
> 2 It has a broad brand portfolio and geographic reach (in many different countries) so it is not dependent on only one or two brands, or one or two specific local country markets.
> 3 They have constrained access to credit. (They can no longer get sufficient loans, etc. from the banks to finance their needs.)
> 4 It has strategies in place to source materials from alternative suppliers or use substitute materials.
> 5 It gives the company continued access to global debt markets. (It can issue bonds at a reasonable interest rate which will still be attractive to investors who will still want to buy them.)

3 Brainstorm the question as a whole class and emphasise the risk to large companies.

> ***Suggested answer***
> Other risks could include unforeseen risks such as a company being a victim of a cyber attack where it loses key data. Companies operating in parts of the world with unstable governments are exposed to political risk and their operation can be at risk of civil disorder in those countries.

4 Pair learners to brainstorm risks that may affect small businesses, i.e. businesses with few employees, often family-run. Elicit their ideas.

> ***Suggested answer***
> Many small businesses are very dependent on their owners – any serious, long-term illness that affects them will seriously affect the company. Also, cash flow problems: if a customer does not pay it may have a bigger impact than it does on a larger company, as smaller companies may find it more difficult to obtain credit.

Language focus 2: Financial terms

1 Refer learners to the glossary and ask them to fill the gaps with the appropriate words. Let them check answers in pairs.

> ***Answers***
> 1 impair
> 2 balance sheet value
> 3 credit rating
> 4 intangible assets

2 Group learners in threes or fours to discuss the scenarios. In smaller groups you may want to choose one that would interest your group.

> ***Suggested answers***
> 1 If Unilever sets its credit limits too low, it could discourage its customers from buying from it. These customers might then decide not to stock Unilever products and instead buy more from competitors. If Unilever sets the credit limit for its suppliers too high, the company exposes itself to a higher risk of customer default.
> 2 If the company's credit rating was cut, it would find it more difficult to raise money (selling its bonds) in the debt market to investors. Investors would view Unilever as a higher-risk company and would therefore demand a higher level of interest on the bonds it offers for sale in the debt markets. If the company did not offer higher levels of interest on its bonds, investors would be unlikely to buy them.

Output: Advising a company on managing risk

Stage 1

Discuss the role of financial consultants (or small business advisors, if learners are more familiar with this term), i.e. to provide secure analysis of risks to a firm's financial situation.

Group them into threes or fours and refer them to the profile on page 105. Give them about 10 minutes to read through and complete the tasks. You could help with the financial section and check understanding of financial terms, e.g. *overdraft*, *fixed interest*, *secured loan*. You could also check *in the red* and its opposite *in the black*.

Stage 2

Bring two groups together to form one to agree on a collaborative set of action points.

11.3 Skills: Presenting charts and statistics

Introduction

1 Learners choose an option for each question.

2 Pair learners to compare answers and discuss the question. Elicit ways of improving as feedback.

Listening: Analyse a chart and slide presentation 2.24

1 Briefly elicit what a *webinar* is (an online discussion or meeting) and what *auto* is short for (automobile). Refer learners to the chart and discuss what is most noticeable at first glance. Ask learners to answer the questions and then compare answers in pairs.

2 Play 2.24 to check answers. Discuss the follow-up question as a whole class.

> ***Answers***
> 1 Different markets (emerging, evolving, established)
> 2 The percentage of new car purchasers who give this reason for buying a new car
> 3 To highlight the most important points (the key data)
> 4 The present tense is used for describing facts
> 5 c

> ***Audio script***
> **Josh Crandall:** So, let's begin by looking at what the trigger points are or the triggers are that force people to purchase a new car. In established markets it shouldn't be much of a surprise that the primary reason that people are purchasing a new car is that their former vehicle is no longer functional. And that's the main, the primary, trigger for twenty-three percent of respondents from the established markets.
> Whereas in emerging markets we find that people didn't previously own a vehicle. So, these data confirm what we would expect to see in emerging markets versus the established markets.
> In the evolving markets, the yellow bars, we see that the desire for a second car as well as a change in circumstances are driving … twenty-seven percent of the purchases of new cars in these markets. And what we mean by changing circumstance …

3 Pair learners to discuss the question. Elicit what they found most surprising.

4 Put learners into threes to discuss the question. Elicit when each type of chart is best to visualise numerical data.

> ***Answers***
> Line graphs are best used to show changing numbers (e.g. sales figures) over a period of time. The information presented here is a 'snapshot' in time – it's not a period of time. Pie charts would work well to show figures for <u>one</u> market (established or evolving or emerging) but would not allow people to compare these markets easily. A table of statistics containing a lot of numbers is best used in an Appendix of a written report; in a presentation it is difficult for the audience to understand the data and make comparisons 'at a glance' which is essential in this slide presentation.

Language focus: Structuring and describing a chart 2.25

1 Pair learners to discuss the questions and write appropriate endings to the prompts. They then compare ideas with another pair.

> ***Suggested answers***
> 1 Now let's look at where people go to find information to buy a new car.
> 2 So, what is the first source of information people go to when considering buying a new car?
> 3 As you can see, the Internet is by far the most important source of information for new car purchasers. / When we compare the use of the Internet to other media it's pretty striking.
> 4 Finally, it's interesting to note how many people in emerging markets use friends and family contacts as a major source of information.

2 Learners listen to compare their ideas with the presenter. Elicit any major differences.

> ***Audio script***
> Now, what's the first source of information people use to research different brands of car? Where do you go first? And it is surprising to me to see the strength of the Internet here. Forty-seven percent of all new car buyers surveyed said that they use the Internet first for their auto research. This is significantly higher than auto dealerships, and other traditional media sources really fall off the cliff. So, when we compare the use of the Internet to other media, it's pretty striking. Given the difference we can't really make these comparisons by point differences, but we have to look at this in terms of multiples. So, the Internet is eight times more popular as the first means of research than car magazines and brochures; twelve times more popular than newspapers; and twenty-four times more popular than TV as the first 'go to source' for research in the auto purchase process. Finally, it is interesting to note the reliance on friends and family in emerging markets – it is actually comparable to the use of dealerships, and as the auto industry matures in these markets it will be important to monitor how this trend evolves over time.

3 Learners predict the order and compare in pairs.

> ***Answers***
> b, d, a, c

4 Learners listen while reading the audio script and mark the breaks. As a follow-up, you could discuss if any experienced presenters in your group have followed this order.

> ***Answers***
> [Part 1] Now, ... Where do you go first? //
> [Part 2] And it is surprising ... it's pretty striking. //
> [Part 3] Given the difference ... in the auto purchase process. //
> [Part 4] Finally, ... evolves over time.

5 Pair learners to discuss and fill in the gaps. Elicit their answers.

> ***Answers***
> 1 second most
> 2 Hardly anyone
> 3 twice as many

Transferable skill: Highlighting key data in a chart

1 Discuss these questions as a whole class and ask learners to mark their charts individually.

2 Refer learners to the presenter's chart on page 140 to compare with theirs. Ask them to discuss the questions before eliciting their ideas.

> ***Answers***
> 1 It's very effective. The secondary point is highlighted with a green circle to show clearly that the data refers to emerging markets. Numerical comparison in the form of multiples is clearly shown with red dotted lines, which really emphasises the message the presenter wants to convey.
> 2 Highlighting the data during the presentation adds a more dramatic effect and keeps audience attention focused on the data you want to show at the time you want to show it. You can reveal these data highlights in stages. Having the data highlighted at the beginning of the slide is helpful to more inexperienced presenters as it is a useful support and reminder to mention these points.

Output: Represent data on a chart and present it on a slide

Stage 1

Tell learners to draw up a pie chart for their personal Internet usage.

Stage 2

Group learners into threes or fours to create a single bar chart using the ones they have looked at as an example. All members of the group should practise giving the presentation.

Stage 3

Make larger groups or alternatively mix groups up in larger classes to present their data to each other, making notes in order to give feedback.

Worksheet 11 (See page 139)

Improve your knowledge of taxation

Level **C1 +**

Timing **55–60 minutes**

1 Lead-in (10 minutes)

Pair learners to discuss the questions. Elicit a few of their answers as feedback.

Suggested answers

1 Direct taxes are generally levied according to the financial circumstances of the payee, e.g. income tax. Indirect taxes are levied on transactions that take no account of the ability to pay of the payee, e.g. sales tax. The definition can vary in different tax jurisdictions, e.g. US constitutional law.
2 An excise duty is an extra indirect tax levied on specific goods, often for public health purposes, e.g. petrol, alcohol and tobacco.
3 Tax-exempt goods and services are considered taxable, but are zero-rated for social reasons, e.g. basic groceries, agricultural products, medical prescriptions, children's clothes, etc.
4 Depends on individual learners' beliefs. The concept was very popular in the 1980s, as tax cuts are believed to increase entrepreneurial activity and create new employment. Hence money from tax cuts 'trickles down' from the top earners to the lower earners.
5 This depends on learners' origin. In the USA, state and local government are funded from a locally imposed sales tax, turnpike tariffs and federal grants. In the UK, local government is funded by a council tax levied on the size of a property and central government grants

2 Collocations with *tax* (15 minutes)

1 Pair learners to match the words that collate with *tax* and their definitions. Re-pair them to check their answers.

Answers

loophole: a mistake in the law which allows the chance to avoid tax
haven: a place where people pay less tax than their own country
avoidance: reduction, by legal methods, of the amount of tax paid
evasion: illegal ways of paying less tax than you should
deductible: can be subtracted from the total taxable amount
office: the national authority to make and deal with tax decisions
liability: an amount of tax that a person or business must pay
exile: a person who moves to a place where taxes are lower
rate: the percentage of an amount or value that has to be paid in tax
declaration: the income information that is given to the tax authorities each year
relief: a system that allows a person not to pay tax on some of their income
refund: money returned after an overpayment of tax is calculated

2 Discuss the question as a whole class.

Suggested answers

tax jurisdiction, tax holiday, taxpayer, tax shelter

3 Types of tax (10 minutes)

Pair learners to match the types of tax to when they are levied. You could extend by discussing as a whole group if these types of taxes are levied in their countries.

Answers

Income tax		on people's earnings, salary or wages
Sales tax		when people buy goods or services
Inheritance tax		on money or property received from a relative who has died
Wealth tax	is levied	on personal property and financial assets above a particular level
Corporation tax		by government on businesses' profits
Road tax		on a vehicle before being allowed to drive it legally
Capital gains tax		on profits made from selling something you own
Value added tax		at each stage of production on the worth of the product at that stage

4 Limiting tax liabilities (20 minutes)

1 Pair learners to discuss how they would present the information on a slide. You could ask them to generate it on a computer to see if their ideas were correct.

2 Bring two pairs together to form small groups. Ask them to compare their ideas, do a rough sketch of a presentation slide and then present the information to the class.

Suggested answer

The best way of presenting this in visual form is a bar chart as it allows easier comparison. However, some of these variables are quite close, so a table may actually be the best way of presenting for an audience to compare on a slide.

12 International trade

Overview of the unit

12.1 Theory: Free trade or protectionism?

> 'Peace is the natural effect of trade.'
>
> *Charles de Montesquieu*

Free trade refers to the openness of the exchange of goods, services and information within, between and among groups of individual nations with few or no restrictions on market entry. *Protectionism* refers to increasing the market share of domestic companies and domestic employment through restrictions on foreign-made goods and services. Free traders believe there is a division of labour across borders, as well as within them, and treat foreign-produced goods no differently from domestically produced ones. Individual countries, and regions within countries, are free to trade with goods where they have comparative advantage, i.e. they can produce them relatively more cheaply and efficiently than other countries.

Employment is both lost in the importing country and created in the exporting country, but because all countries should increase both imports and exports, the effects on overall unemployment may balance out to some extent. Free traders also believe that as a consequence of unrestricted trade, producers of goods and suppliers of services increase their output, prices of goods and services are reduced and consumers benefit.

Protectionism often aims both to save domestic businesses and to nurture nascent ones. Domestic employment and manufacturers are expected to benefit through tools including the outright banning of trade, levying higher taxes on imported goods, and imposing import quotas. Those in favour are usually very vocal in exploiting national prejudices and traditions. Interestingly, both free trade and protectionism are sometimes referred to as *fair trade.* Both aim to mitigate the effects of poverty, but differ in approach. Free traders believe an unrestricted market will lead to an optimal allocation of resources worldwide, while protectionists view a balanced and equitable trade exchange between the rich and poor nations as a just cause.

12.2 Practice: NAFTA and Mexico

Profile: NAFTA

The North American Free Trade Agreement came into force on 1 January 1994. All remaining import taxes and quotas were eliminated on 1 January 2008 to create the world's largest free trade area on the pretext that the liberalisation of trade stimulates economic growth.

The agreement's overall mandate is to increase cooperation in spheres that affect the security, prosperity and quality of life of the citizens of North America. Studies show that trade has increased significantly between the three countries of Mexico, Canada and the USA and there has been a growth of agricultural trade, manufacturing output and investment in infrastructure. Some argue that there has also been a rise in wages, and an increase in employment opportunities, in the export industries where there have been high levels of investment within NAFTA.

For many, the agreement has generally facilitated the generation of greater export opportunities for manufacturers, farmers and service providers in all three participating countries, while consumers now have greater choice at lower prices.

12.3 Skills: Managing meetings

Meetings are often required with both clients and colleagues and they have to be managed effectively, objectively and professionally so that the time in meetings is not wasted and everyone contributes equally.

It is essential that it is clear to all participants what is expected in terms of behaviour, and how breaches of these terms will be dealt with, so that a meeting runs constructively. Each participant must bear responsibility for keeping the meeting on topic, following the agenda, treating the meeting as an important part of work and aiding the whole group in accomplishing the meeting's purpose. The chairperson must use language subtlety to bring out shyer participants and to move the discussion on when a particular speaker dominates.

Conflict in meetings can be productive if skilfully managed and new ideas and constructive solutions are generated. However, a personal conflict that degenerates into innuendos and hostile tones of voice will not be constructive and they lead to a loss of attention and the non-achievement of the meeting's objectives.

12.1 Theory: Free trade or protectionism?

Introduction

1 Focus learners' attention on the picture. Discuss what the people might be demonstrating about. Check understanding of the phrases, and then ask learners to fill in the gaps before comparing answers in pairs. Elicit their answers.

Answers
1 d 2 a 3 c 4 b

2 Learners complete the quiz, refer to page 141 to calculate their score, and then compare in pairs. After they compare, you could ask them to rephrase the profile given, according to their views, giving reasons for their position.

Transferable skill: Improving speed-reading techniques

1 Books closed. Elicit what learners understand by *speed-reading* (skimming for the general idea, looking for the main arguments, reading main words). Ask them to skim the text and then compare answers in pairs. You could elicit the words in the text to support their answer, e.g. A: *not everyone ... take advantage*; B: *help development*; C: *disparity in income ... grew*; D: *all nations benefiting ... excels*; E: *results in ... being worse off*; F: *forcing cuts ...*

> ***Answers***
> pro-free trade = B, D
> anti-free trade = A, C, E, F

2 Discuss the idea of creating a 'map of the text' as a way of breaking a longer text down into manageable sections. Put learners into pairs or small groups and allocate each pair or group one paragraph of the text to discuss its meaning. Then ask them to summarise their paragraph using the sentence opener provided, pointing out they should use not more than four additional words. Take whole-class feedback.

> ***Suggested answers***
> A ... support richer countries.
> B ... help development.
> C ... does not work.
> D ... do best.
> E ... downside of trade liberalisation.
> F ... less developed countries.

Reading: Making globalisation work

1 Learners read the questions and predict the extract where the answer lies.

> ***Answers***
> 1 A 2 F 3 B 4 D 5 C 6 E

2 Learners then read the extracts to find the answers, and compare in pairs before feedback.

> ***Answers***
> 1 Because of the lack of infrastructure and ability to produce goods at expected quality levels
> 2 There will be less revenue gained from import tariffs.
> 3 The right measures and policies have to be adopted.
> 4 specialising in the area in which you excel
> 5 It would reduce the income gap between Mexico and the USA and reduce illegal immigration.
> 6 Unskilled workers have been hit the most.

3 Group learners in threes or fours to discuss their opinions. Elicit two or three opinions to round up.

Language focus: Emphasising key points through inversion 2.26–2.27

1 Discuss what learners understand by *inversion* or *inverting sentences* and what its purpose is. Elicit a few phrases that do this, e.g. *not only*, *only by*, to prepare them for the later exercises. Ask learners to rewrite the sentence and compare their answers in pairs. Then ask two or three to write their answer on the board for the class to check as feedback. The answer follows exercise 2.

2 Play 2.26 and ask learners to mark the pauses and stress in their sentences. These are marked in the audio script below. Pair them to say the sentence and discuss how persuasive they are.

> ***Answers and audio script***
> Not only does liberalisation require removing tariffs | – which are an important source of public revenue for less developed countries | – but to compete, | a country may have to lower other taxes as well.

3 Pair learners to underline the inversion language and then compare in pairs. Elicit their answers.

> ***Answers***
> 1 not only
> 2 had we
> 3 Under no circumstances can
> 4 Were
> 5 Such
> 6 At no time
> 7 Only by

4 Ask learners to reformulate the sentences. Tell the learners to wait for the answers. Alternatively, you could play 2.27 here if learners want to check answers immediately. Answers to exercises 4, 5 and 6 are all on 2.27 .

> ***Answers and audio script***
> 1 Only by working together can countries achieve true globalisation.
> 2 At no time has the reduction of inequality been a more pressing issue.
> 3 Under no circumstances should the free movement of people between countries be allowed.
> 4 Such is the power of multinational corporations that fair trade is not possible.
> 5 Not only do the most powerful countries always win, they also ensure that their corporations have unfair trading advantages.

5 Focus learners' attention on the example, elicit the task and then ask them to reformulate the sentences.

> ***Answers and audio script***
> 1 Were there no trade barriers, developing countries could become richer.
> 2 Were international trade agreements fairer, the global economy would be more stable.
> 3 Had the UK adopted the euro 14 months ago, it wouldn't be suffering from a grossly overvalued currency today.

6 Play 2.27 for learners to check answers. Ask them to mark where they think the pauses and word stress occur.

7 Learners listen again and repeat the sentences. Alternatively, they could check where they marked where the pauses and stress occur. Then in pairs, they say the sentences as persuasively as they can.

Output: Debate arguments for and against free trade

Stage 1

Write the statement on the board so that learners can focus on thinking of arguments for and against.

Stage 2

Divide the class in two groups and ask one group to concentrate on the arguments for and the other on the arguments against for 5 minutes. In larger classes you could have four groups.

Stage 3

Ask the groups to decide on a chair or 'speaker of the house' to direct the debate, before they conduct it according to the chair's role.

12.2 Practice: NAFTA and Mexico

Profile: NAFTA

Introduction

1 Write *controversial* on the board and elicit alternative phrases, e.g. *likely to cause argument, debate, discussion or dispute*. Ask learners to skim the profile and elicit two or three of their ideas on why NAFTA causes debate.

> ***Answers***
> Opinions are divided on what effect it has had on the economy. Has it created employment or unemployment and has it increased or decreased wage levels?

2 Pair or group learners to discuss their opinions. You could re-pair or regroup to report back.

Language focus: Terms of economic convergence and divergence

1 Check learners' understanding of the terms, e.g. elicit synonyms or alternative phrases for *integration* (coming together), *barrier* (gate), *regulatory* (checking whether something is working according to laws), *polarisation* (moving to opposite extremes). Ask them to fill the gaps in the sentences, then compare in pairs. Elicit their answers.

> ***Answers***
> 1 increased bilateral trade
> 2 income disparity
> 3 inward investment
> 4 regulatory cooperation
> 5 export-orientated economy
> 6 duty-free trade
> 7 removing trade barriers
> 8 compliance with
> 9 protectionist trade policies
> 10 growing polarisation
> 11 economic integration

2 Learners categorise the terms before feedback.

> ***Answers***
> Economic convergence: economic integration, removing trade barriers, regulatory cooperation, compliance with [an international trade treaty], duty-free trade, inward investment, export-orientated economy, increased bilateral trade
> Economic divergence: protectionist trade policies, income disparity, growing polarisation

3 Pair learners to discuss the question. Rephrase the question to *our country* or *country of study* depending on country of study. In multinational groups, pair learners from different countries to compare ideas before whole class feedback.

Listening 1: The role and purpose of NAFTA 2.28

1 Check learners understand the objectives, then play 2.28 and check answers. As a pre-listening exercise, you could ask them if they think the speaker will be in favour of NAFTA.

> ***Answers***
> He mentions: 2, 3, 4, 5 and 6.

> ***Audio script***
> **Interviewer:** Can you briefly explain what NAFTA is and what is the role and purpose of the NAFTA Office of Mexico in Canada?
> **Carlos Piñera:** Well, as you know, NAFTA is a free trade agreement signed by Mexico, Canada and the United States, which came into force in 1994 and became the largest free trade area in the world. NAFTA has principles and obligations to govern the exchange of goods and services, but its main objective is to generate a greater economic integration between the economies of North America, and to create jobs and improve the welfare of the population in North America. NAFTA has now fulfilled its objective of creating a duty-free trade zone, but there are other aspects that we still have to work on to ensure barriers to competition are removed. For instance, we need to have more regulatory cooperation such as more harmonised labelling of products, better integrated transport infrastructure, improved procedures at customs and so on.
> **Interviewer:** So, how does the NAFTA Office of Mexico in Canada fit into all this?
> **Carlos Piñera:** Well, we're responsible for the monitoring and compliance of the commitments we have to make under the NAFTA agreement and we are also responsible for the promotion of trade and investment between Mexico and Canada. Our office develops strategic information in order to identify business opportunities for Mexican companies in the Canadian market.

2 Learners read the questions and listen again to complete the gaps in question 1. Pair learners to discuss question 2. Discuss answers as a class.

> ***Answers***
> 1 a harmonised labelling
> b integrated transport
> c procedures, customs
> 2 Monitoring and compliance of commitments under the NAFTA agreement and promotion of trade and investment between Canada and Mexico.

Listening 2: Benefits of NAFTA to Mexico 2.29

1 Learners predict their answers and listen to check.

Answers
1 NAFTA makes Mexico attractive for inward investment.
2 NAFTA has forced Mexican companies to be competitive and opened up international markets for them.
3 five-fold, to $300 billion per annum
4 auto parts, automotive industry, space sector
5 Oil exports are now a much smaller percentage of total exports (from 70% to 15%). Manufactured goods as a percentage of total exports have increased dramatically (to 60%). Foreign trade is now a much higher percentage of GDP (up from 8% of GDP in 1992 to 60% of GDP now).

Audio script
Interviewer: What are the main opportunities that NAFTA provides to Mexico and Mexican companies?
Carlos Piñera: Let me tell you that before Mexico signed NAFTA in the early nineties, we were implementing a policy of openness and modernisation of our industry. And at that time NAFTA was conceived as an important tool to support this process, and make our industry more competitive. We also saw another possibility coming out of NAFTA, that Mexico would become more attractive for inward investment with the consequent generation of greater employment opportunities. NAFTA has also created more opportunities for Mexican companies by making them more competitive and encouraging them to expand into international markets. For instance, since NAFTA came into force, Mexican exports have increased five-fold to the US and Canada and now stand at almost three hundred billion dollars.
NAFTA also has made positive interventions in some industry sectors, for instance auto parts and the automotive industry, in order that Mexico participates actively in the supply chains, reducing costs and facilitating access to the latest technology in these sectors. We are also now implementing a policy deriving from the NAFTA agreement where we are also promoting the integration of the space sector, which is really important for us.
In general, though, NAFTA has been a modernising factor in the Mexican economy that has generated a structural change in the economy of Mexico. Let me give you some data to underline this point: in 1990 oil exports accounted for seventy percent of total exports – exports were totally dominated by oil. Today, oil exports represent only fifteen percent of the total, while the manufacturing sector is sixty percent of total exports. In terms of the foreign trade component of GDP, it was eight percent in 1992, but the latest figures that we have now show that it's shot up to sixty percent of GDP. These are dramatic changes that show how we have transformed our industry and made it more open and more export-orientated.

2 Pair or group learners appropriately to discuss the questions. Elicit a few of their ideas for the question about the future.

Listening 3: Defence of NAFTA 2.30

1 Ask learners to predict the details of problems. Play 2.30 to allow them check their predictions, then again for them to take notes on the speaker's defence. Pair them to check their answers to the whole exercise before feedback.

Answers
2 Problem: Some segments are not exporting well and are not efficient.
Defence: He points out that other segments <u>are</u> exporting well and <u>are</u> efficient.
3 Problem: Some segments are not interested in exporting and are having problems adapting to new technologies
Defence: These sectors were initially protected under NAFTA ('protected' in terms of import tariffs remaining in place, for a limited period of time).
4 Problem: The USA is a big producer of corn, creating politically sensitive competition for Mexican farmers.
Defence: There was a long period of protection for Mexican farmers up until 2008. Mexican farmers now better off than before NAFTA.
5 Problem: Campaigners say that NAFTA is a threat to local economies and companies:
Defence: After these campaigners get elected they stop criticising NAFTA.

Audio script
Interviewer: What adverse effects has NAFTA had on Mexico and Mexican companies?
Carlos Piñera: Well, opponents of NAFTA will point to the shoe-making industry in Mexico, for example. It has had a lot of problems for a long time, but that's not exactly to do with NAFTA – the competition here is Chinese. They are producing shoes at a really low cost. But when we're talking about industries in Mexico we have to look in detail at the different segments of that industry. For instance, when we are talking about the chemical industry, there are segments of that industry where we are really exporting well, and have really efficient businesses. But there are other segments of this industry where the opposite is true. It's the same for some agro-industries and the textile sector; some of these segments are totally export-orientated, but others are not interested … they are having problems adapting to new technologies, etc. Let me tell you, when you sign up for an opening process, the competition forces companies to be more efficient. Mexican companies now have to deal with this new competition.
When NAFTA was negotiated, not all sectors of the economy were opened up to free trade immediately. Certain industry sectors such as textiles and agriculture were initially protected but then were opened up in stages, allowing them to adapt gradually to the new competitive conditions.
Interviewer: Right.
Carlos Piñera: An important example is in the case of corn. The United States is a big producer of corn, the basic element in the Mexican diet. Politically it was a really sensitive sector and so we established a long period of protection for our farmers that was only phased out in 2008. I can tell you now, with the figures for this industry, that the situation for our farmers is much better than it was before NAFTA.
Interviewer: Right.
Carlos Piñera: So usually when we are talking about the negative effects of NAFTA, it comes mainly from political campaigns. People saying 'NAFTA is a threat to local economies and local companies' – that kind of thing. I have seen a lot of these political campaigns painting NAFTA as the enemy, and once they get elected they forget about this kind of thinking, and they say that NAFTA is exactly the opposite!

Output: Joining an international free trade association

Stage 1

Briefly discuss why learners think the country is keen to sign the agreement. Pair them and refer the As to page 141. In odd-numbered classes, two As could work with one B.

Stage 2

Learners hold a meeting for about 15 minutes. Elicit two or three outcomes as feedback.

12.3 Skills: Managing meetings

Introduction

1 & 2 Pair or group learners to discuss the questions. Re-pair or regroup them to report back and come to a collaborative decision. Elicit one or two of their ideas.

Listening 1: Starting the meeting 2.31

1 Ask learners to predict the answers before listening to check.

Answers
1 False (it is her turn this week)
2 False (at most 45 minutes)
3 True
4 True
5 True

Audio script
Vanessa: OK, so it's my turn to chair this particular meeting with the rotation of the chair. So, we want to try and get through this in at the most forty-five minutes so that we can get to lunch. Is there anything arising from last week's minutes? I think these are OK from my point of view. What about other people?
Jack: Yeah. They look OK to me.
Vanessa: OK. So any matters arising from the Customer First training or is it all on the agenda? Right then. Let's go straight into the first point.

2 Elicit their ideas or pair learners in larger classes to discuss before feedback.

Suggested answers
1 She deals with the start of the meeting in a professional manner and gets to the start of the meeting quickly after checking that everybody is familiar with and happy with the agenda.
2 The chair may have needed to introduce the other members of the meeting and gone over the agenda in more detail before starting with the first point. It is also sometimes necessary to allocate a person to take minutes.

Listening 2: Discussing a problem colleague 2.32

1 Ask learners to predict answers in pairs and then elicit one or two of their ideas. Play 2.32 for them to check.

Answers
1 He thinks that they went very well.
2 She tells her to write down that Jack thinks that he is better than Nick.
3 No
4 that he is very self-important
5 that he only uses PowerPoint and does not provide notes
6 She thinks that participants should be encouraged to fill out evaluation forms of the training sessions.

Audio script
Vanessa: OK, so the next point on the meeting is the business skills course you ran in Brighton. Do you have any feedback on that?
Jack: The afternoon and evening went very well again.
Lucy: Did you get a round of applause again?
Jack: Er, no. I didn't this time. But I got a number of mentions about Nick Hay.
Vanessa: And how much better you are?
Jack: Yes.
Vanessa: Put that down in the minutes, Lucy.
Lucy: I'm not writing that down.
Jack: But seriously, criticism of Nick has come independently from two people over the last couple of days.
Sarah: Are you feeding that back at all to his line manager?
Jack: No.
Sarah: You're not?
Vanessa: I think you shouldn't, we've got to be a bit more proactive with this sort of stuff rather than just complaining to the trainer's manager. What was the nature of the criticism?
Jack: Well, he comes across as very self-important.
Vanessa: Yeah. Well, he did that when I met him. And I don't know how many years ago that was.
Jack: It turns people off. He just gives a PowerPoint presentation. There are no notes.
Stefanie: We're in a meeting. Is it urgent? The staff meeting I mentioned in the morning. I'll call you back.
Vanessa: Well, do they do evaluations on the courses?
Jack: I think that's the next step.
Vanessa: I think people would be prepared to say, you know, 'I don't think the materials are helpful'. There's usually a question on the evaluation form and participants should be receiving these. We have to make sure that people are filling the evaluation forms in before I take this problem with Nick any further.

2 Learners read the questions. Play 2.32 again and then ask them to discuss the questions. Elicit their answers.

Suggested answers
1 It is clear that the group know each other well, so they know when to use humour. It also helps to lighten the mood as it is clear that Jack is going to say something serious. However, using humour can be risky if you don't know the other participants well.
2 The comment is made with good humour, but in general it would be better to hear more of the facts before making a statement.
3 They ignore her. As Stefanie was not warned to turn her phone off at the start of the meeting and finishes the call quickly, this is probably the best tactic.
4 She deals with it well, in that she comes up with a practical solution to get to the bottom of the problem.

Language focus: Negotiating problems in meetings

1 Check learners' understanding of the vocabulary in the problems and solutions, e.g. *off topic*, *come up with*, *clarify*. Then ask learners to match them. Elicit their answers.

> ***Answers***
> 1 e 2 g 3 a 4 d 5 f 6 c 7 b

2 Learners fill in the gaps using the phrases then check in pairs before feedback.

> ***Answers***
> 1 refer back
> 2 absolutely great
> 3 What I'm saying is
> 4 wrap it up
> 5 choices open to us
> 6 Why don't you
> 7 I sometimes feel that

3 Learners match the completed sentences to the solutions (a–g) in exercise 1.

> ***Answers***
> 1 c 2 e 3 a 4 g 5 b 6 f 7 d

4 Pair or group learners to discuss the problems. Elicit two or three of their ideas as feedback.

> ***Suggested answers***
> 1 What I'm saying is that you have a fortnight to complete the work, not a week.
> 2 Can we just refer back to the agenda now? We will have to discuss that another day.
> 3 I think that you all need to sit down together in the next few days and work out what is going on.
> 4 I just think there's an element of not all of the information being disclosed.

Output: Overcoming problems in meetings

Stage 1

Group learners in threes to brainstorm the problems for 5 minutes. If there is an extra one or two people, ask them to use one of the problems brainstormed in stage 1 to design their own role card using one of the team role cards as a model and then join a group.

Stage 2

Assign a role to the three members, and check understanding of the role cards before groups hold a meeting to discuss the issues.

Stage 3

Groups feed back to the chair on the effectiveness of the meeting.

You may want to watch Sequence 6 on the DVD to find out more about Trade, finance and the economy or ask learners to watch it for homework. There is an accompanying worksheet on page 157.

Worksheet 12 (See page 140)

Improve your knowledge of world trade

Level **C1 +**

Time **55–60 minutes**

1 Lead-in (10 minutes)

Pair learners to discuss the questions.

Suggested answers

1 World Trade Organisation
2 The Doha round is the latest trade negotiation at the WTO with the aim of introducing lower trade barriers. It stalled because the less developed nations wanted special protection on some agricultural goods, where a majority of their population work, to prevent an 'import surge'. India, supported by 100 others, argued that the USA was ignoring the interests of the poor in favour of the rich.
3 The World Economic Forum invites CEOs from its 1,000 member companies as well as selected politicians, academics, NGOs, religious leaders and the mass media to Davos at the end of January every year. Some argue it is an arena for world leaders to solve their differences; others argue it serves no purpose and is a modern club for the rich.
4 There are many worldwide. Examples could include EU, EEA, ASEAN, MERCOSUR, GCC. You could write these on the board and ask them what the acronyms stand for (European Union, European Economic Area, Association of South East Asian Nations, Mercado Común del Sur (Common Market of the south), Gulf Cooperation Council).
5 A bilateral agreement is between two countries, a trilateral one is among three and a multilateral agreement is among many countries.

2 Collocations with trade (10 minutes)

Learners match the collocations to their meanings and then compare in pairs.

Answers

Trade	balance*	the difference between money received from exports and spent on imports
	deficit	when the value of imports exceeds that of exports
	mark	name put on a product which cannot be legally used by another producer
	figures	these compare the values of goods bought in and goods sold abroad
	name	a name or a symbol which is put on a product to show who made it
	price	amount at which finished goods are sold to shops by producers
	secret	information about a product known only by the company producing it
	route	a road or sea lane historically used by people buying and selling goods

* also known as balance of payments

3 Negotiate a trade position (20 minutes)

Give each group a set of role cards and tell them they are going to negotiate a trilateral agreement. If your group does not divide by three, two of them could take role A and C to negotiate a bilateral agreement. Monitor and assist with any difficulties as the groups prepare and then select one or two groups to carry out their negotiation. Alternatively, in a larger class you could divide into three large groups so that each country group prepares separately.

4 Describing commodities traded globally (15 minutes)

Divide learners into two groups, A and B. Make copies of the graphs for each learner. Pair learners to describe and roughly sketch the two line graphs. The learner doing the drawing should turn over the worksheet to draw on the back.

Alternatively, in smaller classes, you could ask them to present either one of the graphs outlining the main trends and future predications.

Writing 6: Describing graphs with financial and economic data

Overview of the unit

Financial journalism often uses very specific and dramatic vocabulary (e.g. *soar*, *skyrocket*, *slump*, *plummet*) to capture the reader's attention. Learners need to understand this style of writing, in order to read the financial press.

There are many ways to describe rising, falling, staying the same and wild fluctuations in English, but simpler phrases should be used in formal and official reports. It is important to remember that adverbs follow verbs like *drop* and *increase* and adjectives precede nouns, e.g. *the market dropped dramatically* or *increased dramatically* and *there was a dramatic drop* or *a dramatic increase*.

In visuals, headings must be concise and distinctly describe what the chart or graph represents. Keys should be clear and care must be taken with line or bar colours as some may offend (e.g. choosing colours to match typical skin colour in a country) or not be easy to see. The horizontal and vertical axes in graphs must always clearly tell the audience what the visual is showing and some consideration for the visually impaired in your audience is advisable.

Introduction

Elicit whether any learners regularly look at financial data presented in tables, charts and graphs as part of their work or studies, and what sort of information they get from these. Pair them to discuss the questions and then re-pair them to report back.

Language focus: Describing financial and economic changes

1 Pair learners to mark the headlines and to indicate an increase or decrease. Group them to discuss their ideas before checking answers. You could also elicit which verbs are irregular: *slide–slid*, *shrink–shrank–shrunk*, *dive–dived* (BrE) / *dove* (AmE). Check that learners understand *Q4* in question 12 (final quarter of the financial year).

Answers

2 ☹ ↓
3 ☺ ↑
4 ☺ ↑
5 ☹ ↓
6 ☹ ↓
7 ☹ ↑
8 ☹ ↓
9 ☹ ↓
10 ☺ ↓
11 ☹ ↑
12 ☺ ↑

2 Learners match the underlined words to the definitions, then check their answers.

Answers

a dip
b bounce back, rebound
c plunge, slump, dive
d surge, soar
e edge forward
f slide
g shrink
h wobble

3 Elicit the answers as a whole class and write them on the board.

Answers

1 a slide
2 a plunge
3 a bounce
4 a rebound
5 a wobble
6 a slump
7 a surge

4 Focus learners' attention on the example and elicit the task. Ask them to do it individually before comparing in pairs. Then elicit some answers.

Suggested answers

2 The standard of living is set to plunge as inflation is predicted to rise dramatically.
3 Business confidence has bounced back because business leaders see a sharp rise in new orders.
4 There was a strong rebound in retail figures in January as consumers responded to recent government tax cuts.
5 As a result of a surprising slump in export orders, the German economy has shrunk more than expected.
6 After figures released from the government last week showing unemployment soaring to new highs, there has been a dive in consumer confidence / consumer confidence has taken a dive.

5 Briefly discuss the question as a whole class or group learners in larger classes. Note that headlines 8 and 9 in exercise 1 are covered in exercise 4 (questions 5 and 6).

> ***Suggested answers***
> Headline 5: Stock markets fell briefly due to worries about the immediate political situation in the Middle East.
> Headline 6: The slump in bank shares over the last six months is a result of non-payment of mortgage loan payments.
> Headline 7: The surging household debt in Korea is due to people taking out excessive loans to buy property.
> Headline 10: Jobless figures in the USA dipped by 20,000, showing the first positive effects of the government's economic stimulus package.
> Headline 11: Plummeting consumer spending over the course of the year has led to soaring levels of corporate bankruptcies.
> Headline 12: The strength of the US railroad sector has ensured that FreightCar America's final results have edged forward this year.

Writing skill 1: Describing a single trend line

1 Learners look at the graph for a few seconds. Then elicit the answers.

> ***Answers***
> 1 The graph describes the movement of the NASDAQ 100 index over a three-year period from January 2008 to early 2011.
> 2 in quarters (three-month periods)

2 Pair learners to discuss the questions. Alternatively, elicit the first question and then pair them for questions 2 and 3 before they check their answers in exercise 3. Discuss their reactions.

> ***Answers***
> 1 The audience would probably be extremely bored and frustrated. They would also be no wiser as to the real meaning of the graph, which is described with reference to the <u>main</u> trends.
> 2 See exercise 3.

3 Learners fill in the gaps, and then compare in pairs before feedback.

> ***Answers***
> 1 fluctuated
> 2 plunged
> 3 wobble
> 4 rebounded/recovered
> 5 dipped
> 6 bounced
> 7 soaring/surging

Writing skill 2: Describing multiple trend lines

1 Learners fill in the gaps according to their reading of the graph. Elicit their answers.

> ***Answers***
> 1 changes/movement(s)
> 2 oil
> 3 green
> 4 yellow
> 5 period

2 Learners answer the questions. Then pair them to compare. You may wish to discuss question 2 as a whole class and elicit why they chose the company they did.

> ***Answers***
> 1 The stock with the biggest increase in value over the period was Chevron; the lowest increase was BP and Exxon Mobil.
> 2 BP, because the price was at its lowest then.

3 Discuss the question as a whole class. You could ask learners to do some internet research to discover more about the disaster.

> ***Suggested answer***
> As the price of other oil company stocks followed a different course, the logical conclusion is that it was not a problem affecting the oil industry or the economy as a whole, but negative news affecting BP in particular. What actually happened was a huge oil leak from one of its drilling platforms in the Gulf of Mexico. BP was hit with a clean-up bill of over $20 billion.

4 Learners read the introduction and elicit why they should not describe the lines individually and what they should do instead. Pair them to discuss the questions, then either re-pair or group them to report back.

> ***Answers***
> 1 Shell and Chevron
> 2 Shell, Chevron and Exxon Mobil
> 3 Exxon Mobil and BP
> 4 BP

Output: Write a short report

Ask learners to work alone and write a report of the graph of 150 words in 20 minutes. They could compare and mark their reports in pairs or you could take them in for checking.

13 Sustainable development

Overview of the unit

13.1 Theory: The triple bottom line

> 'What pleases me most is that sustainable development is on almost everybody's agenda now.'
>
> *Maurice Strong*

The term 'triple bottom line', or TBL, was first coined by John Elkington, the founder of a consulting firm called SustainAbility. The term refers to three separate concepts, the first of which is the traditional 'bottom line' of the profit and loss account, i.e. the financial value added after deducting the cost of inputs. The other two concepts in the triple bottom line equation are the 'people account' and the 'planet account'. The idea is also referred to as the economic, social and environmental bottom lines.

The 'people' or 'social' account is a measure of how socially responsible an organisation has been during its operations. That is, how fair and how beneficial have its business practices been towards the communities it operates in, in terms of labour relations and giving something tangible back to the community like health and education programmes?

The 'planet' or 'environmental' account is a measure of the level of a company's environmental responsibility. That is, what steps have been taken to reduce its environmental footprint through energy conservation, waste reduction and disposal policies?

Criticism is based on a number of factors that include the inability to measure the people and planet bottom lines in monetary terms. It can also be argued that TBL is not an efficient market solution such as carbon trading. Critics also claim that it is a public relations stunt for multinational corporations and it is used to weaken social and environmental legislation.

The triple bottom line is likely to be a response to consumer pressure over the use of child labour, minimal wages in outsourced manufacturing bases, rainforest destruction, an over-reliance on fossil fuels and the lack of a measurement for the true cost of manufacturing from the production of raw materials to consumption by the end-user. Only through the use of the 3Ps of profit, people and planet, could a company truly measure its operational impact and be termed socially and environmentally responsible.

13.2 Practice: Masdar – the sustainable city

Profile: Masdar City

Masdar City is a 'cleantech cluster' of five integrated units, including a university and a special economic zone, established in 2006 in Abu Dhabi, one part of the United Arab Emirates. It is a subsidiary of the state-owned Mubadal development company and aims to help the emirate diversify from an over-reliance on hydrocarbon production.

Masdar means 'source' in Arabic and the city aims to be a source of knowledge, and innovation and a place for the development of human talent in the field of cleantech industry and renewable energy or 'green' technology and energy. Masdar seeks to be a model of green urban development coupled with a high quality of life with the lowest environmental footprint in a way that is commercially viable.

The city acts as a real world laboratory for cleantech research and development, and the construction of environmentally friendly buildings, and is a base for the specialisation of labour in the industry. There are no import tariffs and there is no tax on companies, individuals or on the movement of capital.

Through Masdar, the emirate hopes to demonstrate it is a responsible oil producer, by addressing the balance between hydrocarbons and renewables, climate change and energy security.

13.3 Skills: Problem-solving

There are many problems in business, but what is important is to ignore the more immediate 'knee-jerk' reactions which are often inappropriate. Without effective communication, business stops unless everybody communicates convincingly and honestly with each other. Otherwise even everyday challenges and issues can become unmanageable.

Direct and indirect means of communication are powerful tools, but an effective communicator needs to know when to use both of them, as people may respond differently. Direct communication may seem forceful, but it may suit people who prefer a more transactional approach to management. Indirect communication is more subtle, may be easier to accept and may not appear demanding. However, it can be misinterpreted and seem ambiguous.

If people are listening grudgingly, then there is a greater need for indirectness, but in reality it is best to vary your style and remain flexible in order to keep successful work relationships.

13.1 Theory: The triple bottom line

Introduction

1 Pair learners to discuss their choice. You could make a tally on the board to find out where your class stands on the issue of measuring a company's performance. Check that learners understand *metrics* (figures that give information about something and that can be measured).

2 Check understanding of key words in the quote, e.g. *principle*, *ensure*, before re-pairing learners to discuss the question. In smaller classes, hold a whole-class discussion.

3 Group learners to match the stakeholders and business actions. Encourage them to think about what could especially interest the different types of stakeholders.

> ***Answers***
> Making profits: connects to all stakeholders (without profits the company will not be able to pay for things that meet the needs of any stakeholder)
> Educational visits from nearby schools: local community
> Switch to clean energy providers: future generations
> Monitor suppliers: wider community (also consumers if they are concerned about this)
> Run 'stress management' courses for staff: employees
> Ensure honest promotions: consumers
> Provide nursery facilities on premises: employees

4 Discuss the questions as a whole class. Remember that mothers, fathers, grandparents, etc. are often spokespeople for future generations.

> ***Suggested answer***
> Companies can try to engage the different stakeholders in talks about changes to procedures. They can also try to measure the impact that the decisions that they make have on the various stakeholders.

Language focus: Topic verbs linked to sustainability

1 Check understanding of the verbs in the box. You may also wish to check pronunciation of *assign*, *advocate*, *gauge*, etc. Ask learners to work individually and then pair them to check answers before feedback.

> ***Answers***
> 1 incorporated
> 2 accommodate
> 3 gauge
> 4 comprise
> 5 assign
> 6 secure
> 7 eliminate
> 8 advocates/advocated
> 9 driving
> 10 adapt

Reading 1: Defining and calculating the triple bottom line

1 Learners refer to the Introduction to answer question 1, then read 'The Triple Bottom Line Defined'. Elicit their answers.

> ***Answers***
> 1 environmental = planet, social = people, financial = profits
> 2 It measures the impact of an organisation's activities on the world.
> 3 to measure it – you can't put a monetary value on social capital and the environment

2 Elicit the meaning of *monetise*, i.e. give a standard of value to something. Then learners read and then check answers in pairs. You could extend by mentioning the American English use of *-ize* and the British English use of *-ise* or *-ize* to make nouns into verbs.

> ***Answers***
> 1 They do not have a common unit of measure.
> 2 They would all have a common unit (dollars).
> 3 Some critics argue against it on philosophical grounds, while others question the methods needed for finding the right price for non-monetary factors.
> 4 to calculate the TBL in terms of an index

3 Learners discuss the question in pairs and then report back to the whole class.

Reading 2: Creating the index

Ask learners to predict possible answers to the statements before reading the text to check their ideas. They could check in pairs, or you could elicit their answers.

> ***Answers***
> 1 False (There is no universal standard method)
> 2 False (it can be adapted for different entities, projects, policies or geographic boundaries)
> 3 False (the set of measures will ultimately be determined by stakeholders)
> 4 True
> 5 True
> 6 False (For local or community-based projects, the TBL measures … are best determined locally.)

Critical analysis

Group learners to discuss the questions. Re-group them to report back on their discussions.

Output: Using the triple bottom line to discuss impacts on stakeholders

Stage 1

Put learners into small groups to discuss the different stakeholders and the measures.

Stage 2

Re-group learners into threes to discuss the social impact of the changes. It is not necessary for the groups to be exactly of equal size. In one-to-one classes, discuss each impact separately and who has the most to win and lose.

Stage 3

A spokesperson for each group could present their ideas or, alternatively, you could put members of different groups together to discuss their thoughts.

Stage 4

In larger classes, ask learners to discuss this question in small groups and elicit their ideas. In smaller classes, you could discuss this question as a whole group.

13.2 Practice: Masdar – the sustainable city

Profile: Masdar City

Introduction

1 Books closed. Ask if any learner has been to Abu Dhabi and speculate on the realities of desert living, e.g. abundance of sunshine, cheap fuel, water desalination plants which are vital for survival, need for resource-hungry air conditioning systems. Ask learners to read the dictionary definitions of the three phrases, do the exercise, and then check answers.

> ***Answers***
> 1 carbon emissions
> 2 carbon footprint
> 3 greenhouse gas

2 Learners do the quiz. You could elicit why the number of people in the household and eating meat are asterisked before they do it.

3 Pair learners to compare answers. Elicit three or four of their answers as feedback and find out who has the lowest carbon footprint, and the highest.

4 Ask learners to scan the profile and then discuss as a whole class why Abu Dhabi has chosen to build Masdar (as part of its move from an oil-based economy to one based on knowledge, innovation and cutting-edge technologies).

Language focus 1: Green vocabulary

1 Check understanding of possible problematic words such as *emissions* and *carbon* and then ask them to match all the words to *zero*, *green*, *demand* and *waste*. Pair them to check answers and then feed back.

> ***Answers***
> zero waste
> zero carbon
> zero emissions
> green companies
> green knowledge
> green markets
> energy demand
> water demand
> reduce demand
> consumer waste
> waste water

2 Focus learners' attention on the photographs on page 121. Elicit what they can see in them, i.e. solar panels, environmentally friendly buildings and a recycling area. Then discuss the question as a whole group.

> ***Suggested answer***
> The use of renewable energy through solar power and wind towers shows that Masdar City is trying to reduce consumer demand for fossil fuels and may be aiming for zero emissions. It is also trying to reduce waste through its recycling plant.

3 Put learners into pairs or small groups to discuss the question. If the learners are all from the same town, discuss the question as a whole class and ways the town council could improve its green credentials.

Listening 1: Masdar City promotion 2.33

1 Give learners time to read and understand the headings. Play 2.33 and elicit their answers. Alternatively, ask them to predict the headings based on the reading of the section questions before listening. Refer learners to the example in exercise 2.

> ***Answers***
> 1 Welcome to Masdar City
> 2 The Vision
> 3 The Design
> 4 Transport

2 Learners read the questions, then listen again to answer them. Pair them to check answers and then feed back.

> ***Answers***
> 1 They will build the city's most iconic buildings.
> 2 The air is clean.
> 3 The city can be smaller and the streets narrower.
> 4 They will carry people and freight.

3 Discuss the question as a whole class.

> ***Audio script***
> 1 On February the 8th, 2008, the government of Abu Dhabi launched an ambitious plan to create what aims to be the world's first sustainable city, Masdar City. The Arabic word 'masdar' means 'the source'. This is fitting, because the aim is that Masdar City will become home to the world's leading businesses, academics and researchers, involved in the fields of renewable energy and sustainable technologies. Construction is already under way, and the first phase includes some of the city's most iconic buildings.
> 2 This is viewed by many as one of the world's most exciting developments. Seventeen kilometres south-east from the centre of Abu Dhabi in the United Arab Emirates, a vision for all future cities is taking shape. Masdar City aims to be zero waste, zero carbon and a fossil fuel-free city. The elimination of fossil fuel ultimately means that the air is clean, and the pedestrian-only streets provide a level of intimacy and charm for all to enjoy. The ultimate goal of its designers is the highest quality of life, with the lowest environmental impact.
> To realise this vision for a city of the future, the master planners have gone back in time.

3 The city's architects have drawn inspiration from traditional Arabian cities. Every aspect of the city is being designed to reduce energy demand. The city's north-east orientation reduces exposure to the hot desert sun. Parks and green spaces create breezy green oases. Water features evaporate and cool the surrounding air. Without fossil fuel vehicles, Masdar City can be smaller and feature narrow streets. This means more shade and lower temperatures so people can walk, interact and play.

4 It also means Masdar City will feature the first large-scale zero-emission transportation system. A subway of personalised driverless electric vehicles that carry people and freight. In addition, a ground-level light rail system and a subterranean metro high-speed train keep the Masdar citizens well connected. You will never be further than two hundred and fifty metres from public transport.

Listening 2: Masdar city promotion Part 2 2.34

1 Discuss the statements and check understanding of any difficult vocabulary, e.g. *conventional* (ordinary), *solar* (from the sun). Then ask learners to match the statements to one of the section titles from exercise 1.

Answers
Statements 1–5 refer to *Water, Waste* and *Electricity*; statements 6 and 7 refer to *Source of Wisdom*.

2 Ask learners to predict the answers based on what they already know from Part 1. Play 2.34 and elicit their answers.

1 False (80% more water)
2 False (all of it will be)
3 False (it will also come from geo-thermal sources and waste)
4 True
5 True
6 False (it aims to share the knowledge with the rest of the world)
7 True

3 Elicit the types of renewable resources, i.e. biofuel, solar, wind, wave, etc., and discuss their usage in learners' own country. In multilingual classes, you could group them in different nationalities to hold the discussion.

4 Discuss this question as a whole class. Encourage learners to think of well-known university towns in their country and other countries they know of, and what they contribute to the economy.

Audio script
5 The city's design aims to reduce electricity and water demand as much as possible. Smart buildings and appliances will monitor consumption, and reduce demand further still. Masdar City can use around 80% less water than a conventional city. All of the consumer waste is either recycled or turned into energy. Waste water is processed and used to illuminate the city's landscape.
The city will draw one hundred percent of its electricity from renewable sources, such as solar, geo-thermal and even waste. The energy that Masdar City doesn't use gets exported onto the local power grid. But electricity isn't the only thing that will flow from Masdar City.

6 Masdar City is working with the government and schools of Abu Dhabi to raise awareness and engage communities in environmentally friendly behaviour. And soon the knowledge gained here will be shared with the world.
The Masdar Institute has been built as part of phase one: it is the world's first university dedicated to studying sustainability and renewable technologies, and a hub around which green companies can flourish.

Transferable skill: Challenging the consensus

1 Pair learners to read the challenges and discuss if they are logical. Alternatively, ask learners to rewrite the challenges in their own words, elicit a few ideas and then, as a whole class, discuss whether they are valid.

2 & 3 Check understanding of the quote and then pair learners to discuss the questions. Round up by finding out how many of your learners were As, Bs, or Cs for both questions with a show of hands.

4 Put learners into small groups to discuss the question. Encourage them to think of concrete examples of consensus views around them.

Language focus 2: Using the language of contrasts to persuade

1 Pair learners to match the two parts. You could re-pair them to check answers or elicit which words contrast in the sentences, i.e. *highest – lowest*; *future – back in time*; *more – lower*; *here – the world*.

Answers
1 b 2 d 3 a 4 c

2 Pair learners to practise saying the sentences with appropriate emphasis. You could demonstrate what the exercise requires by saying the quote from Neil Armstrong yourself.

Answers
1 The ultimate goal of its designers is the highest quality of life with the lowest environmental impact.
2 To realise this vision for a city of the future, the master planners have gone back in time.
3 This means more shade, and lower temperatures so people can walk, interact and play.
4 The knowledge gained here will be shared with the world.

3 Ask learners to do the exercise individually, and then check their ideas in pairs. Elicit two or three of their ideas for each sentence.

Suggested answers
1 ... the better the air quality.
2 ... more renewable sources.
3 ... the less time we have to find alternatives.
4 ... and less traffic in the city centre.
5 ... the best use of existing resources.

Output: Developing a sustainable city

Stage 1

Put learners into small groups to discuss advantages and disadvantages of the plans. Encourage them to think in terms of the impact on the local population and to use the language of contrast to persuade as appropriate.

Stage 2

Divide the class to read their role cards. Check that they understand the task and then give them 5–10 minutes to prepare for the discussion.

Stage 3

In smaller classes, hold the meeting between the learners. In larger classes, make four groups to hold the meeting. In one-to-one classes you could hold a debate on the issue.

13.3 Skills: Problem-solving

Introduction

1 Learners look at the pictures. Discuss the questions as a whole class. If they have never behaved in the way depicted, ask learners if any of them have seen the things at work or school.

2 Check understanding of words likely to cause comprehension problems, e.g. *stationery*, *gossip*. Pair learners to place the problems on the line and discuss what they would do with the most serious problem. Then put them in groups to compare ideas.

Critical analysis

Group learners to choose two of the problems to discuss the problem of responsibility. You could give an example, e.g. when an employee takes stationery home, the manager is responsible for replacing the lost equipment.

Suggested answer
Problem b could be the institution's fault if the employee is missing deadlines due to being overworked. Problems e and g could be due to the employee not receiving sufficient training.

Listening 1: Problems and causes 2.35

1 Elicit the meaning of working *off-site*, i.e. remotely. Then ask them to predict which reasons could logically go together. Learners then listen, before you elicit their answers.

Answers
a and b

Audio script
Director: How's Magid getting on?
Team leader: Er, well, really slow. I don't know why. I just feel the things that he has to do take too much time. I don't know if he's … if he's lazy, or maybe I pressure him too much or, you know, I'm pushing too much or …
Director: Yeah, well, that's … that's part of it. I mean, there could be a couple of reasons. One is because he's not ready.
Team leader: OK.
Director: Well, he's learning, yeah?
Team leader: Yeah.
Director: One reason could be that he's not doing any work. And we don't know because he's not working in the office.
Team leader: Yeah.
Director: And the third reason and probably the most likely reason is that you're thinking, like any person who's managing would think, 'I could have done that in half a day. Why's it taking him two days?'
Team leader: Uh-huh.
Director: But you know, you have to eventually let the people do it themselves … because if you don't give them a chance, if you do it all yourself, you just end up being really overworked.
Team leader: Yeah, yeah.

2 Ask learners if they would like to listen again to answer the question. Elicit their answer.

Answer
b – The team leader expects too much, too soon.

Listening 2: Deadlines and timescales 2.36

1 Ask learners to predict what they think the director will say. Then play 2.36 for them to check their answers.

Answers
1 c
2 b

2 Discuss the questions as a whole class.

Answers
1 The relationship is a good one: they talk very openly and frankly, and the mood of the conversation is quite calm and friendly.
2 It is important, as otherwise it may be difficult for the team leader to be honest about the problems (because he may worry about the reaction of the boss), and the boss may find it more difficult to offer clear, constructive advice.

Audio script
Team leader: You know, Magid is very helpful and willing. But I'm not happy at the moment with the things that he has done.
Director: Right.
Team leader: Do you know, I think 'Hmm. He's probably not taking the time seriously.'
Director: Right.
Team leader: You know. He has to finish everything on time.
Director: Right. So have you mailed him to say that? Because one thing you could do is say, when you give him work to do, say 'Look, I need this done by this time.' And give him a deadline. Yeah? So instead of saying, you know, 'Can you do this?', say 'Can you do this but have it back by six' or something.
Team leader: What I'm doing is I'm saying 'OK, so I need to do this, this, this and this.'
Director: Yeah.
Team leader: 'When do you think we're going to finish these things?'
Director: Right.
Team leader: He says 'OK, so I think I'll finish on Thursday.'
Director: Well, don't say it like that. Don't let him dictate the timescale to you. You say to him 'I need it done by this date.'

If he can't do it by that time, he should come back to you and say 'I can't do it by then because you've already told me to do this and this and this.' And then you could say 'Well, yes, you're right. You need to do those, so you can do the work I've just given you by next Tuesday.'
Team leader: Right.
Director: OK? So you dictate the timescale to him. When you're managing people, you have to cater for all these sorts of different work styles. And sometimes it's very annoying.

Intercultural analysis

1 & 2 Pair or group learners to discuss the questions. Elicit a few of their ideas for question 1 and then elicit and write on the board the advantages and disadvantages of working in multinational teams. Discuss as a whole class whether they agree with the ideas elicited about multinational teams.

Suggested answers
1 There are many factors that could be relevant here, such as are the local staff willing to be managed by a foreigner (their own prejudices may be relevant here), can the manager communicate effectively in the local language/language used in the workplace, does the manager have negative stereotypes about the local nationality, and, of course, is the manager recognised as having sufficient professional knowledge and experience to do the job?
2 Managers of multinational teams may face challenges related to culture: local vs. company, language, communication styles, different ways of working and dealing with problems. Advantages would include learning about other countries' or cultures' ways of doing things and improving language skills. Disadvantages could include not understanding colleagues (both language and culture).

Language focus: Suggesting solutions and giving advice

1 Ask learners to underline the words or phrases which are examples of direct and indirect suggestions. They could compare their ideas in pairs or you could elicit their answers.

Answer
a is more direct advice, because of the use of *can*; b is more indirect because of the use of *could*.

2 Learners look at the extract. Ask if they think the words underlined are direct or indirect, and why. For example, *Well, don't* is direct because it uses the imperative form.

3 Learners complete the table and then compare their answers in pairs.

Answers
1 direct
2 direct/indirect
3 indirect
4 direct

4 Discuss the question as a whole class. If you have a monolingual class whose first language prefers a more direct style, e.g. German or Russian, discuss whether there are words which can be used to change the language to make giving advice and suggestions less direct and forceful.

Suggested answer
The director is more senior than the team leader and can therefore be more direct. If the team leader wanted to suggest something to the director, he would probably use a more indirect form.

5 Pair learners to change the sentences then re-pair them to compare answers. Elicit their ideas.

Suggested answers
1 Have you thought about doing it this way?
2 It might be a good idea for you to give the terms.
3 You could think about how you could cater for all these different working styles.
4 You might need to give him a bit more time.
5 You could say, 'Your clothes are not really suitable for work.'

6 Refer learners back to the Introduction and pair them to give each other direct and indirect advice on one of the problems. You could re-pair them to discuss another problem from the Introduction.

Output: Discussing solutions to problems

Stage 1

Put learners into small groups of threes or fours to read the notes and discuss the problems in the notes. You might wish to check understanding of *morale*, *fed up with*, *split up*.

Stage 2

Pair learners to have the meeting. You could ask them to role play the meeting twice, so that they both get a chance to give advice and suggestions directly and indirectly. If you have an odd number of learners, make a group with two Student Bs.

Worksheet 13 (See page 142)

Improve your knowledge of incentivising changes in environmental and social behaviour

Level **C1 +**

Time **55–60 minutes**

1 Lead-in (15 minutes)

Pair learners to discuss the questions. Before the discussion, you may wish to check understanding of *pie in the sky*, i.e. unrealistic expectations, and *actions speak louder than words*, which is a proverb that means 'doing something about an issue is more effective than merely talking about it'.

Answers

1 The roots of the green movement lie in the 19th century, with the attempts to solve problems caused by polluted air and open sewers. After 1945, the movement focused on the proliferation of nuclear power and weapons. In 1972, the UN Conference on the Human Environment discussed the global environment and led to the creation of the UN Environment Programme. In recent years, the movement has focused on global warming. The ongoing UN Earth Summits are global conferences on environmental issues.

2 Depends on the learners. Examples of international pressure groups include Greenpeace and Worldwide Wildlife Fund. National or local pressure groups tend to focus on single issues ranging from road safety for cyclists to the protection of rural areas. Most countries have a Green party, but policies may vary.

3, 4 & 5 Learners' own opinions. Check understanding of *pie in the sky* (something you want but which is unlikely to happen) and *actions speak louder than words* (what you do is more important than what you say).

2 Contrasting and persuasive language (10 minutes)

Pair or put learners into small groups to fill in the gaps. Re-pair or regroup them to discuss their answers. If they are finding the exercise too difficult, you can give them an extra letter for each word.

You could follow up by asking them to say the sentences with the correct stress and pausing appropriately.

Answers

1 practical
2 risky
3 dictatorial
4 collaborative
5 consensus

3 Radical policies (15 minutes)

Pair learners to discuss the policies. Encourage them to think how people would react to being told that the policies were to happen in their local area. Elicit which one they think would encounter the most resistance. In smaller classes, you could ask learners to rank the policies in order of those they think would encounter resistance and then justify their opinion.

4 Planning for a sustainable new town (25 minutes)

1 Ensure that the learners understand what a 'new' town is, i.e. a town built completely from scratch. British examples include: Milton Keynes, Redditch and Welwyn Garden City. Discuss what a planning committee is, and then group them to plan the new town.

2 Regroup learners with members of other groups, to compare their plans, and decide if they are sustainable developments or not. Alternatively, you could ask the groups to present their ideas to the class and then take a vote on what would be the best place to live and bring up a family.

14 Social enterprise

Overview of the unit

14.1 Theory: Perspectives on social enterprise

> 'The old ways of getting things done – public services versus charities versus private enterprise – are starting to merge and the future is hybrid.'
>
> *Peter Holbrook*

A social enterprise applies business strategies to achieve philanthropic goals rather than a rate of return for investors. They make and do things that earn money, but reinvest their profits in public goods, an area notoriously neglected by the free market, i.e. they invest in local community projects, environmental protection schemes, and creating jobs for those people who feel left out and are at the 'bottom of the pile' or 'on the scrapheap'.

Social enterprises are all sizes from small neighbourhood cafés to clothes recycling and redesign firms to national newspapers, e.g. *The Big Issue*. They are usually started by a person or a group that has a passion for social and environmental issues and a resolute business idea.

Social enterprises act like private enterprises in that they make money from trading, cover operating costs and pay salaries, but they are social, because they plough back their profits 'to make a difference', rather than make profits for shareholders, and they rely on volunteers, donations and grants from government.

Interest in this form of business organisation has grown in recent years and it stems from various charities' wish to trade more and be more sustainable. There has also been a growing awareness from consumers about how their spending decisions affect other people worldwide and the global environment. Similarly, multinational companies, through the concept of Corporate Social Responsibility, are well aware of the impact of the business on social and environmental conditions.

Social enterprises may well be the future where business operates for people and the environment rather than just for profit. However, if the business plan of the enterprise does not set profitability as the ultimate goal, then investors who do not share the commitment to the public good are more than likely to see the enterprise as philanthropy and not an investment.

14.2 Practice: Trashy Bags – a social enterprise in action

Profile: Social enterprise – Trashy Bags

Trashy Bags is a social enterprise in Accra, Ghana, that makes recycled eco-friendly bags and other gift items from used plastic. The company was founded by Stuart Gold in 2007 and employs over sixty local people to collect, clean, and stitch together plastic litter in the form of drinks and ice-cream sachets into useful bags and gifts such as laptop bags, purses and vanity cases. It also employs in-house designers to make these products more fashionable and uses designer labels such as Moonlight and Fish Bag.

The company hopes to demonstrate the usefulness of plastic trash and wants to educate people about the seriousness of land pollution in Africa by encouraging the responsible disposal of waste. It would also like to reduce the need for new single-use plastic bags to be given away at supermarkets and other retail outlets in Accra and other areas of Ghana.

Trashy Bags, in conjunction with other organisations, works with Ghanaian elementary schools and aims to bring art and environmental education in areas of Accra. The company sews the students' artwork into change purses, which are then sold to benefit the schools involved in the project.

14.3 Skills: Conference calls

A conference call is a telephone call among three or more people and is a very useful tool when employees are scattered across many locations and client sites. In the case of a large number of participants, some of them may just listen in. Some participants can join the conversation if the organiser phones them. Other participants can also join the conference call by dialling a number or pin code that connects them to a 'conference bridge', which is a piece of equipment that links telephone lines. Digital call conferencing uses voice routes rather than these analogue, static-prone bridges.

A lot of communication that is not done by email happens via conference calls. Well-managed conference calls should be treated similarly to meetings in structure. That is, a good conference call has an objective, a list of participants, an agenda with time allotted for each task, and a summary; and it starts and ends on time.

Of course, conference calls are not meetings in that non-verbal communication such as facial expressions is not present, unless it is a video conference call. There may also be technical glitches and background noise. It is always a good idea to check your equipment first and try to minimise background noise before embarking on a conference call.

14.1 Theory: Perspectives on social enterprise

Introduction

1 Elicit the meaning of *tackle these problems*, i.e. address or attend to these problems. Then pair students to discuss the question. Elicit two or three of their ideas.

2 Learners read the quote. Elicit what a *social enterprise* is and then discuss the questions as a whole class.

> ***Suggested answer***
> Social enterprises blur the boundaries between the private and public sector by operating in the same way as a private business, but provide the services and have aims that are more traditionally connected with the public sector.

Language focus: Common word partnerships linking business and social issues

1 Ask learners to fill in the gaps with the word combinations with *social*, and then check their answers in pairs. Explain that Joseph Wharton was a 19th-century American industrialist and philanthropist who founded the world's first business school.

> ***Answers***
> 2 social entrepreneurs
> 3 social entrepreneurship
> 4 social responsibility
> 5 social housing
> 6 social need
> 7 social change
> 8 social problems

2 Pair or group learners to discuss the questions and then elicit one or two of their ideas for each one. In larger groups, you could re-pair them to report back.

> ***Suggested answers***
> 1 Companies now pay more attention to these issues because society as a whole cares more about social responsibility – and society includes customers.
> 2 CSR of a private company is one aspect of the company's activities, whereas for a social enterprise the social or environmental dimension is central.

3 Ensure learners understand they can choose more than one word to fill the gap. Then, ask them to do the exercise and check their answers in pairs.

> ***Answers***
> 1 a, b, c
> 2 b, c
> 3 a, d, e
> 4 a, b

Reading: Comparing social enterprises to profit-making companies

1 Ask learners to skim read the texts from Professor Jane Wei-Skillern and Dr Helen Haugh to answer the question, and then check their answers. Alternatively, divide the class in two, ask one group to skim read the first and the other to skim read the second and then pair learners from each group to check answers.

> ***Answers***
> A Dr Helen Haugh
> B Professor Jane Wei-Skillern

2 Pair learners to categorise the statements. Re-pair them to check answers before feedback.

> ***Answers***
> 1 N
> 2 HH
> 3 N
> 4 B
> 5 JWS
> 6 JWS

3 Remind learners of the meaning of *metrics* (see 13.1) and check that they understand it in this context (measurable figures that give information about how successful an activity is). Refer learners to the photos at the beginning of the unit. As a whole class discuss possible metrics of success. Alternatively, group students and assign each group a picture to discuss and present some of their ideas to the rest of the class.

> ***Suggested answers***
> To judge whether a social enterprise is successful we must measure its impact on people within the scheme or what it is doing to halt a negative trend. For example, in an organisation dealing with a lack of adequate housing we can look at how much more housing is provided over a period of time and how many people have benefited from it. Similarly, the success of an organisation dealing with a lack of convenient and reliable energy can be judged by how many peoples' lives are improved. For an organisation aiming to alleviate poverty, how peoples' lives are improved economically would be the metric of success. The success of an organisation trying to stop deforestation may be measured firstly by a slowing down of the process and a lower impact on the environment. It may be a long time before they will be able to stop the process completely.

Listening 1: Social entrepreneurs 2.37

1 Ask learners to predict the answer and then listen to check.

> ***Answer***
> No – she says that the typical characteristics of an entrepreneur do not transfer well to the social enterprise sector.

> ***Audio script***
> **Professor Jane Wei-Skillern:** I think society's view of an entrepreneur is as a charismatic, hard-driving, celebrity type, and this way of thinking has been transferred to the social sector, sometimes at the cost of mission impact. For-profit entrepreneurs look to advance their organisations and build shareholder value.
> In the social sector, we need people who are committed to working towards the mission – in many cases, even at the cost of advancing their own organisations or their own individual interests toward the larger cause. In the business world, being more organisational or ego-focused is acceptable, and we

admire those types of leaders. These norms have also influenced current views of leadership in the social sector. However, to achieve large-scale and sustainable social impact, I believe that we need leaders that are less focused on individual and organisational-level success and instead work with and through others toward system, not just organisational-level, change.

2 Give learners time to quickly read the questions and then ask them to listen again to answer the questions. Elicit their answers.

Answers
1 charismatic, hard-driving, ego-focused, celebrity-type
2 advancing their organisation and building shareholder value
3 people who are committed to working towards the social mission even at the cost of advancing their own organisation or their own individual interests

Listening 2: Social enterprise goals 2.38

1 Ask learners to predict the answer and then listen to check

Answer
No – she says that social and economic goals should be treated equally.

Audio script
Dr Helen Haugh: What we really want within a social enterprise is to treat the social goals as equally important as the economic and environmental goals. And one of the dangers is to sort of get what you might call 'mission drift'. This is when the economic goals become more important than the social goals. And if that happens then you are losing what is distinctive about social enterprises, which is about using your tried and tested techniques from the private sector to improve the performance of the social enterprise, but not losing sight of the social purpose of the organisation.

2 Ask learners what they think *mission drift* and *lose sight of* mean. Then they listen again to answer the questions. Elicit their answers.

Answers
1 'Mission drifts' is where 'economic goals gradually become more important than the social goals'.
2 It's important not to lose sight of the 'social purpose of the organisation'.

Critical analysis

Pair or group learners to discuss the question. Elicit which academic they agree with, if any. In smaller classes, discuss the question as a whole class.

Output: Crisis meeting

Stage 1

Ask learners to read the profile of Centro and the summary of its projected income and discuss any problematic vocabulary, e.g. *severe*, *pitch*, *nursery*, *admin*.

Stage 2

Divide the class in two and direct the groups to the relevant pages. In larger classes, you could have two A and two B groups. In one-to-one classes, read both role cards and discuss a possible solution to the problem. Ask the learners to read the role cards and elicit the task, i.e. a meeting to balance the books of Centro. Check that learners understand *balance the books*, i.e. ensure that you do not spend more than you receive.

Stage 3

In their groups, learners discuss the problem and then get together with members of the other group to come to a decision. Alternatively, you could pair members of each group.

14.2 Practice: Trashy Bags – a social enterprise in action

Profile: Social enterprise

Introduction

1, 2 & 3 Pair learners to discuss the three questions. You could re-pair them to report back or elicit two or three of their ideas for each.

Suggested answer
On a personal level, you would learn to cope in an environment and culture different from your own and make new personal contacts and friendships. On a professional level, you would develop the skills to develop an understanding and respect for a different culture and different ways of working which are fundamental skills for any future international assignment. Depending on the job assignment in Trashy Bags, you could also expect to learn a whole range of skills such as marketing, staff management, team working, operations management, etc.

Transferable skill: Using a dictionary to decode a brand name

1 Learners read the dictionary definitions. Elicit other possible synonyms for *trash* (e.g. *garbage*, *litter*, *waste*), trash bag (e.g. *rubbish bag*, *garbage bag*) and *trashy* (e.g. *inferior quality*, *cheesy*, *flash*, *flashy*, *garish*, *tacky*). Discuss as a whole class how good they think the brand name is.

Suggested answer
'Trashy Bags' combines both the product they sell (the bags) with the material used to make the bags (trash) and at the same time has a connotation with a provocative style of fashion (trashy style). The word *trash* is very high-impact and gets media attention. It sends out a very clear environmental message of recycling that communicates clearly to customers in many international markets, who respond to this message and buy the product.

2 Check understanding of the words and then pair students to discuss the question. Re-pair them to report back or elicit their ideas. You could ask learners to divide the adjectives into positive (*appropriate*, *eye-catching*, *honest*, *ingenious*, *creative*, *relevant*), negative (*shocking*, *inappropriate*, *disrespectful*, *offensive*) and neutral (*forceful*, *provocative*, *direct*, *extreme*).

3 Discuss the question as a whole class. As an extension, write the following list of companies on the board. Using dictionaries to help them, learners discuss their possible meanings and how they link to the company's area of business. Elicit answers and discuss how effective learners think this type of branding is (for example, in 1 and 4 you need to understand the play on words).

1 Tiecoon (a play on the word *tycoon*) – a tie retailer
2 Brain Thaw – a marketing agency
3 Retriever – a GPS for pets
4 Alexander the Grate (a play on the word *great*) – a fireplace retailer

Suggested answers
1 A *tycoon* is a very rich and successful business person. The playful suggestion here is that these ties will bring you business success.
2 *Thaw* means to change from a frozen state to liquid or soft one. Here it refers to a process of moving from a state of being mentally blocked to being fluid again, suggesting a freer flow of thoughts and ideas.
3 *Retriever* refers both to a type of dog and to someone or something that goes and fetches something to bring it back to its rightful place. Here it associates with the GPS technology which allows you to find your pet and bring it back home should it get lost.
4 *Alexander the Grate* refers to Alexander the Great, a famous emperor of Ancient Greece. It also refers to *grate* which is the part of a fireplace that holds the coal or wood.

Reading: About Trashy Bags

1 Ask learners to predict the content of the text using the photos and the questions. Elicit two or three of their ideas for each question.

2 Learners read the text to check their predictions. Give feedback.

Answers
1 *Life after death* refers to plastic sachets/packaging coming 'back to life' as a fashionable Trashy Bag product after being discarded on the street.
2 *The Problem* refers to the environmental damage caused by discarded plastic litter.
3 *The Solution* refers to increasing the lifespan of plastic packaging by collecting it and turning it into Trashy Bags, thus helping solve the environmental problem.

3 Ask learners to read the text to answer the questions. Check their answers.

Answers
1 packaging from drinking water, plastic drinking sachets, ice-cream sachets
2 The 22,000 tons of plastic litter per year has risen by 70% in the last 10 years.
3 It blocks drains, causing flooding and disease.
4 It is very environmentally friendly as little energy is used and there is no reprocessing apart from washing the sachets.

4 Pair or group learners to discuss the question. Elicit two or three of learners' views.

Language focus: Using referencing to build cohesion

1 Write *referencing in texts* and *cohesion* on the board and elicit what learners understand by the concepts. Cohesion in a text is essential to an individual's comprehension of a passage. Referencing can be within the text or to something outside the text. This, along with substitution, is a grammatical way of improving cohesion and adding extra information for the reader. Pair learners to complete the first column of the table, before re-pairing them to check answers and then report back.

Answers
2 plastic packaging
3 plastic drinks sachets
4 the sachets
5 waste plastic
6 people in Africa
7 sachets
8 people in Ghana
9 waste produced from plastic packaging
10 waste from plastic packaging
11 streets in West African countries
12 discarded plastic
13 incorporating complete sachets into products

2 Ask learners to complete the third column individually. Then elicit their answers.

Answers
2 referring back
3 adding information
4 adding information
5 referring back
6 referring back
7 referring back
8 outside reference
9 referring back
10 referring back
11 referring back
12 referring back
13 referring back

3 Discuss the question as a whole class. In larger groups, learners discuss the question and elect a spokesperson for each group to summarise the discussion for the class. Learners then rewrite the text. Give them a time limit of 10–15 minutes.

4 Refer learners to the model answer on page 190 and then they compare their answers in pairs. Discuss any major differences between what the learners wrote and the model.

Answer
Trashy Briefcase & Laptop Bag
The Trashy Briefcase or Laptop Bag will really turn heads when you arrive at a business meeting. The difference between the products is that the Laptop Bag has padding stitched between the outer layer and the lining that serves to protect your valuable laptop computer. Inside there are two divisions leaving the central compartment for easy extraction of your laptop; especially useful at airport security! Both products come in two sizes and have a removable shoulder strap and two fixed handles.

Output: Competing for a work placement opportunity

Stage 1

Ask learners to read the profile and elicit the kinds of work placement schemes Trashy Bags runs.

Put learners into small groups and assign either an A role or a B role to them. In smaller classes, you could have more Group As than Bs and put two As with a B in stage 2. Check understanding of the task and ask them to discuss and fill in the table accordingly.

Stage 2

Put a Group A and a Group B together and ask the members of Group A to make a short presentation on why their team is the best candidate for the work placement. Group B tick the criteria that Group A's presentation meets.

Stage 3

Ask the Group As to move to another Group B to make another short presentation. This could continue depending on the number of groups you have. At the end of the round of Group A presentations, ask the Group Bs to present and explain their choice of Group A to get the work placement place.

14.3 Skills: Conference calls

Introduction

1 Ask if any of the learners have used any of the equipment depicted in the photos and then discuss the question as a whole class. In larger classes, pair learners and elicit a few of their ideas.

> ***Suggested answer***
> When you speak to a person face-to-face you have the benefit of reading gestures and facial expressions. Speaking to someone over the web or by phone can make it harder to judge emotions and know when to interrupt. One advantage of using web-based conferencing is that you can instantly share information and visuals that you have on your computer with the people you are communicating with.

2 Discuss the second question and elicit a few ideas.

> ***Suggested answer***
> When communicating with one person it is easier to hold their attention and to know when it is your turn to speak. In group discussions it is important to make sure that everybody is engaged and has a chance to get their point of view across.

3 Pair learners to discuss the tips and then elicit which tip each pair thinks is most important. Alternatively, pair learners to rank the tips in order of the three most important and then re-pair them to compare their rankings.

> ***Suggested answer***
> All of the tips are important for teleconferences. 4, 5, 7 and 9 are more important for the web and phone-based meetings. 4, 6 and 10 are important because the other participants can't see you. 7 is often a temptation as you can't be seen. 9 is only relevant to this type of meeting.

Listening 1: Opening the call (2.39)

1 Learners predict possible answers to both questions. Play 2.39, ask them if they want to listen again and then check answers.

> ***Answers***
> 1 a
> 2 a

> ***Audio script***
> **Operator:** Welcome to today's RESNA conference call. As a reminder, today's conference will be open and interactive and all lines will be open for the duration. We ask that you use a mute button when not speaking to cut down on the background noise. Also if you need to step away from today's call, please do not place your line on hold as doing so may feed music into the conference. At this time, I would like to turn the conference over to Ms Nancy Meidenbauer. Please go ahead, ma'am.
> **Nancy Meidenbauer:** Thank you so much, and welcome everyone to the RESNA conference on creating a brand for our financial loan programmes. We're lucky to have with us again Mary Virtue of Cornerstone Consultants and she's going to be working with us on our branding of our loan programme, the benefits of the brand, how to create one and also how to protect a brand. Before we begin, what we'd like to do is have a ... to find out who's all on the call. We'd like to have a roll call, so I'd like people to identify themselves and what state they're from.
> **Jane Fortune:** Jane Fortune from Arizona.
> **Marion Black:** Marion Black from Michigan.
> **Justin Corey:** Justin Corey, Pennsylvania.

2 Elicit which of the tips from the Introduction were covered.

> ***Answer***
> tips 4 and 5

Listening 2: The reputation of the brand (2.40)

1 Ask learners to think of possible answers and then play 2.40. Learners listen again if necessary before comparing answers in pairs and feeding back.

> ***Answers***
> 1 three
> 2 She suggests they should *call on* people (go around and ask them individually).
> 3 She was on another call.
> 4 She's not sure, but she also says *I think it's positive*.

> ***Audio script***
> **Mary Virtue:** So, I'm now going to open this up a little bit to get some sense from all of you. What do you know about your reputation, your brand? But I think it's helpful to start with a baseline of where we are, so the question is – what do you know about what your reputation is right now?
> **Nancy Meidenbauer:** I think maybe we have to call on these people. We'll start right at the beginning. Jane from Arizona.
> **Jane Fortune:** Yes. Actually, I apologise. I got distracted by a different phone call so why don't you just go on to the next person.
> **Nancy Meidenbauer:** Marion in Michigan.
> **Marion Black:** Could you repeat the question?

Mary Virtue: Sure, sure. What I'm trying to find out is what do you know about your reputation right now? Is it positive? Are there places where it's negative? What is your sense of that?
Marion Black: I really don't have a sense of it. I think it's positive because we get a lot of applications and people seem to hear about us from friends or family or people that they know, so I guess it's positive since people spread the word for us.
Mary Virtue: Yeah.
Marion Black: But I don't know how to track it actually. I wouldn't know how to ... how to get a sense of it ...
Mary Virtue: Yes.

2 Pair learners to discuss the questions. Elicit an answer for each question.

Answers
1 Mary ignores tip 10.
2 Jane ignores tip 7.

Language focus 1: Managing a conference call

1 Ask learners to find the phrases to correspond to the function before they compare in pairs and give feedback. You could either refer them to the audio script to underline the phrases or they could listen to both extracts again.

Answers
1 We ask that you use a mute button ... may feed music into the conference.
2 At this time, I would like to turn the conference over to Ms Nancy Meidenbauer.
3 Thank you so much, and welcome everyone to the RESNA conference on creating a brand for our financial loan programmes.
4 We'd like to have a roll call, so I'd like people to identify themselves and what state ... they're from.
5 ... why don't you just go on to the next person.

2 Learners practise saying the phrases in a friendly fashion as a whole class. To extend the exercise you could ask them to say the phrases in what they consider an unfriendly fashion.

3 Ask learners to visualise a conference call they may make in the future and refer them to page 165 of the audio script to practise opening it in pairs.

Language focus 2: Interrupting

2.41

1 Learners read through the short extracts and then listen to fill in the gaps. Learners compare their answers in pairs, listening again if necessary. Elicit their answers.

Answers
1 B: Can I interrupt you?
2 B: Just let me stop you there
3 B: You might want to shut up

Audio script
1
A: Yes. Well, we've all ...
B: Can I interrupt you? So, what I need to see ...
2
A: Patrick was leaving in January and ...
B: Just let me stop you there – he paid you the ...
3
A: Well, I think the best thing is ...
B: You might want to shut up, Henry, because we've accepted ...

2 Discuss the questions as a whole class.

Answers
The intonation used in example 2 is aggressive. The language used in example 3 appears aggressive when read, but the intonation makes it clear that this is being said in a friendly manner.

3 Elicit a few topics on the board that learners could talk about and then pair them to practise interrupting while talking on the topics elicited.

Intercultural analysis

Pair learners in different nationalities if possible to discuss the question. Elicit two or three examples of where interrupting is unacceptable. In monolingual classes, discuss the question as a whole class and elicit a few examples.

Output: Conference calls to discuss branding

Stage 1

Ask learners to read the profile and elicit what they will be expected to do in the task. Set the situation up with conference call equipment if possible.

Stage 2

Put learners into groups of three and refer the CEO to page 141 and the External Marketing Consultant to page 145. The Sales Director's instructions are on page 133. In one-to-one classes, you could use the CEO and the Sales Director roles only.

Stage 3

Learners hold the meeting for 10–15 minutes. As a round-up, elicit what the groups decide to do.

You may want to watch Sequence 7 on the DVD to find out more about 21st century enterprise or ask learners to watch it for homework. There is an accompanying worksheet on page 159.

Worksheet 14 (See page 143)

Improve your knowledge of work placement schemes

Level **C1 +**

Time **55–60 minutes**

1 Lead-in (10 minutes)

Pair learners to discuss the questions.

Suggested answers

1 A work placement is a temporary position or job someone has in an organisation.

2 Internship has two meanings:
- a period of training in a hospital after graduation (AmE)
- a period of training spent in a variety of organisations (BrE).

Internships are often part-time for three months either during the regular school year or during the summer. They can be either paid or unpaid.

3 An apprenticeship is where a person works for a skilled person for a particular period of time and often for low minimal payment, in order to learn that person's skills.

4 & 5 Answers will depend on learners' ages and experience.

2 Word partnerships with *work* (15 minutes)

1 Learners match words and parts of words in bold to work to make word partnerships. Ask them to check their answers in pairs.

Answers

work ethic	a moral belief that work is fundamentally a good thing
work permit	an official document that allows you to work in a foreign country
work–life balance	time spent at work versus time spent with family or on hobbies
work-to-rule	industrial action where employees strictly follow contractual terms
work experience	a period of time spent with an employer to gain knowledge
workmanlike	skilful
workaday	something ordinary and not unusual
workable	describes a system or plan that can be used effectively
workaholic	a person who works constantly and finds it difficult not to work
workload	the amount of work required during a particular period
work station	a place in an office, especially a desk with a computer terminal
workshy	describes a person who is disinclined to work

2 & 3 Pair learners to discuss the questions. Elicit their answers.

Answers

2 an activity you do not want to do because of the amount of effort involved

3 There is no point in doing shoddy work

3 Statements from organisers of and participants in work schemes (15 minutes)

1 Students work in pairs to carry out the activity, then form new pairs to report back. In smaller classes, elicit their ideas.

Suggested answers

1 Trainee (positive): a reference is very useful when looking for a job, although *at least* indicates that the speaker did not enjoy the experience.

2 Trainee (negative): *dogsbody* is a derogatory term for someone doing worthless tasks.

3 Company (positive): the employer was able to develop their full-time staff members.

4 Trainee (negative): there was not any structure to the scheme set out at the beginning.

5 Trainee (positive): the intern built up their self-confidence.

6 Trainee (negative): the intern did not feel that the experience was worth the effort.

7 Company (positive): the employer is able to fill gaps in the workforce without using an agency.

8 Trainee (positive): the intern enjoyed a return to stability in their life.

2 Discuss the question as a whole class. In smaller classes, pair learners to discuss it and elicit a few of their ideas.

4 Choose an internship (20 minutes)

Put learners into small groups to discuss the pros and cons of each internship and decide on an internship either for themselves or a friend or relative who is near to graduation. Regroup them to report back on their discussions. Elicit which one is the most popular.

Alternatively, you could divide learners into groups of three and give each learner one of the internship cards. The group members then argue the case for their internship.

As a follow-up, you could ask learners to write a covering letter for the internship they like best.

Writing 7: Writing a covering letter for a CV

Overview of the unit

A covering letter normally accompanies a CV and can make the difference between getting a job interview and your CV being ignored. It is often the first written contact with a potential employer and, therefore, creates that crucial first impression. It should complement and not duplicate a CV and be written in a more personal style.

A covering letter should include a contact information section, a salutation, information on why you are qualified for, interested in and suitable for the position available, a closing and a signature.

As a covering letter is a first contact, it should be reviewed carefully before it is sent. It is always worthwhile to run a spellcheck and proofread for punctuation errors. It is also best to avoid contractions and colloquial expressions. By ensuring that you appear as professional and as proactive as possible, you give yourself a better chance of securing that all important face-to-face interview, where you will have another opportunity to impress your potential future employer.

Introduction

1 Ask learners to work individually and match the sentence beginnings with the endings. Pair them to compare answers and then elicit their answers.

> ***Answers***
> 1 d 2 a 3 b 4 c 5 f 6 h 7 e 8 g

2 & 3 Pair or group learners to answer the questions. Elicit two or three of their ideas after 5 minutes.

Language focus 1: Correcting common misspellings

1 Discuss the difference as a whole class. Some learners may have not heard of *typo*, so you might want to give a few examples that you commonly make when using a keyboard. Point out that whether the mistake is conscious or not, it will be equally unacceptable on a CV.

> ***Answers***
> A *misspelling* is a spelling mistake where it is clear that the writer is unaware of the correct spelling. A *typo* is where the writer has pressed the wrong keys on the keyboard and made a mistake – for example, *follwoing* instead of *following*.

2 Ask learners to find the mistakes and then compare their answers in pairs. You could ask a learner to come to the board to write the correct spelling to check their answers.

Answers

1 accommodation	7 liaise
2 acknowledge	8 occasion (correct)
3 definite	9 achieve
4 responsibility	10 completely (correct)
5 disappoint	11 environment
6 separate	12 truly

Reading: Interpreting the job advertisement and planning the response

1 Pair learners to read the advertisement and find the qualities needed for the job. Re-pair them to report back and then elicit a few of their ideas.

2 Learners highlight the lines in the advertisement. Pair them to compare and then check their answers.

> ***Answers***
> 1 devise, develop and deliver new customer relationship strategies
> 2 your knowledge of call centre technology and industry developments is in-depth and up to the minute
> 3 constantly improving our customer satisfaction ratings
> 4 you'll ensure the smooth running of customer service centre operations at either our Nottingham or Derby sites
> 5 championing exceptional customer service

3 Learners check the advertisement again to find the missing key point. Ask learners to write the missing note.

> ***Answer***
> Missed point: practical experience (the ad says *Experience in a similar role is essential*)
> Accompanying note: I have hands-on experience of doing this kind of job.

Writing skill: Content, structure, format and style of a covering letter

1 Learners read the sample cover letter to find and underline examples that address the points in the notes. Pair them and refer them to the answer key to check their answers. Tell learners they will choose the correct words and phrases in italics in a later section.

> ***Answers***
> She does include all the points.
> **Example of points 1, 2, 5**
> Championed implementation … has increased productivity by 2%.
> **Example of point 3**
> Decreased customer waiting times by 4% … waiting times.
> **Examples of point 4**
> I have three … Endsleigh.
> Cross-trained … training cover.

2 Ask learners to match the relevant section to the question. Then elicit their answers.

> *Answers*
> 1 section 2 2 section 1 3 section 3

Language focus 2: Correcting errors and writing with confidence

1 Learners read the covering letter again to choose the correct word or phrase in italics. Elicit their answers.

> *Answers*
> 1 I'm keen
> 2 as seen
> 3 managing
> 4 incentivising
> 5 team members
> 6 which
> 7 are
> 8 would
> 9 commitment
> 10 assure
> 11 find
> 12 look
> 13 kind regards

2 Ask learners to find and underline the three phrases and then elicit them.

> *Answers*
> *I'm keen to ... , Championed ... , I would relish ...*

3 Discuss possible synonyms for *overselling yourself*, e.g. *showing off*, *aggressively self-promoting*. Ask learners to rewrite the examples in the tables and pair them to check answers. Do the same for *underselling yourself* in the second table. Possible synonyms could be *moderately self-promoting*, *lacking confidence in ability*. Ask learners to rewrite the examples in the tables and then check answers.

> *Answers*
> 1 I have the right skills, experience and educational qualifications that make me a strong candidate for the job.
> 2 I am available for an interview at any time convenient to you over the coming weeks.
> 3 As part of a team project, I conducted market research to find out customers' perceptions of the brand.
> 4 I reviewed our contracts with suppliers and managed to save the company over $120,000 last year.

Intercultural analysis

Pair or group learners to discuss the question and then elicit their ideas. You may wish to highlight the appropriate closing phrase for *Dear Sir/Madam*, i.e. *Yours faithfully* and *Dear Ms Smith*, i.e. *Yours sincerely*.

> *Answers*
> Unless you are sure that the convention in your particular field is to use first names, it is probably wise to avoid them.

3 Discuss the question as a whole class. You could extend by discussing what learners consider is the difference between overconfidence and selling yourself appropriately.

Output: Write a CV covering letter

Find and give students some job advertisements, or ask them to find one before you do this exercise. You could take them to a computer room, if you have access to one, to search for a suitable job advertisement.

Stage 1

Ask them to highlight key words in the advertisement, before they compare their ideas in pairs.

Stage 2

Students work alone to write a covering letter for their job advertisement and the reread it to check spelling, punctuation, etc. Ask them to give it to a partner to proofread and comment upon with reference to the job applied for.

Progress test 3 (See page 124)

> *Answers*
>
> **Grammar 1**
> 1 Absolutely fantastic! Our sales *have risen* by over 20% since the beginning of the year.
> 2 The number of people claiming welfare payments *has been impacted* by the lack of growth.
> 3 Inflation *is going to rise* faster than we had first thought.
> 4 Many social problems *could disappear* with targeted government expenditure.
> 5 A further need for the company to borrow *will arise* sometime in the future.
>
> **Grammar 2**
> 1 Such was the collapse in the housing market we had to increase investment in tourism.
> 2 Had the shop not had a poor 4th quarter, it wouldn't be struggling to pay costs.
> 3 Not only do some nations want to keep agricultural subsidies, they also want to protect infant industries.
> 4 Under no circumstances will the total harmonisation of tax law within the European Trade Area be allowed to happen.
> 5 Only by countries working together can a future financial crisis be avoided.
> 6 At no time did I advise him to tell lies on his job application.
> 7 Were we to lower trade barriers, there would be an import surge.
> 8 Not until the bridge linking Spain and Morocco is built will there be free movement of goods between Africa and Europe.
> 9 So successful was the business (that) we were able to diversify.
> 10 Such is the seriousness of the disputes surrounding agricultural subsidies in different countries, an agreement on international trade is impossible.
>
> **Vocabulary 1**
> 1 sector 2 return 3 recovery 4 intervention 5 Interest rates
>
> **Vocabulary 2**
> 1 growing polarisation 2 bilateral trade 3 inward investment
> 4 income disparity 5 export-orientated
> 6 removing trade barriers 7 duty-free trade
> 8 economic integration 9 compliance with
> 10 Protectionist trade policies
>
> **Vocabulary 3**
> 1 change 2 problems 3 housing 4 enterprise 5 need
> 6 good 7 value 8 mission 9 entrepreneurs
> 10 responsibility
>
> **Writing**
> Allow 2 marks each for task achievement, organisation, grammar, vocabulary and coherence.

Photocopiable materials

Progress tests

Progress test 1 (Units 1–5)
Progress test 2 (Units 6–10)
Progress test 3 (Units 11–14)

The role of the Progress tests

The Progress tests aim to show what business knowledge, vocabulary and aspects of language learners have acquired over the period of study. They will motivate learners and will allow them to assess how successful their learning strategies are. The tests will also help both you and the student to identify areas of difficulty and weakness which need further work, within the broad umbrella of the skills that the course seeks to develop.

Worksheets

1 Improve your knowledge of aspects of pronunciation
2 Improve your knowledge of brand strategy
3 Improve your knowledge of prepositions
4 Improve your knowledge of risk-taking behaviour
5 Improve your knowledge of fundraising
6 Improve your knowledge of leading and managing
7 Improve your knowledge of intercultural competence
8 Improve your knowledge of regional development policies
9 Improve your knowledge of employee appraisal
10 Improve your knowledge of new business models in newspaper publishing
11 Improve your knowledge of taxation
12 Improve your knowledge of world trade
13 Improve your knowledge of incentivising changes in environmental and social behaviour
14 Improve your knowledge of work placement schemes

The role of the Worksheets

The Worksheets are designed to be used in conjunction with their respective units and are intended to build on the knowledge learners gain by working through the Student's Book. They aim to stretch learners' understanding and use of both the business concepts and the aspects of the language being studied. They will work best if they are used during a unit or after it has been completed.

DVD worksheets

Introduction
1 International marketing
2 Competition and entrepreneurship
3 Management and leadership
4 Globalisation
5 Design, technology and innovation
6 Trade, finance and the economy
7 21st-century enterprise

The role of the DVD worksheets

The DVD worksheets have been developed to use in conjunction with the DVD that is packaged with the Student's Book. After completing every two units of the Student's Book, learners can watch the DVD in class or in their own time at home. The activities included in the worksheets will enable students to discuss the themes that they have studied and watched, further develop vocabulary, check comprehension skills and raise awareness of key business themes. The DVD scripts are on the website: www.cambridge.org/elt/businessadvantage.

Progress test 1

Units 1–5

Grammar 1: Dependent prepositions

(10 marks)

Put the correct preposition (*to*, *of*, *on*, *in*, *at*) into the following sentences.

1 The intensity ______ competition has led to a number of mergers in the industry.
2 Our survival strategy depends ______ a range of factors.
3 We do not have the resources to compete ______ the same level as other companies.
4 The company has invested a lot of time and money ______ research and development.
5 We should not underestimate the bargaining power ______ the industry buyers.
6 The 'Five Forces' model gives firms a good understanding ______ their own competencies.
7 SWOT analysis is also available ______ a company to analyse their external environment.
8 There is extreme pressure ______ companies to compete more effectively.
9 The company failed to recognise the threat ______ the digital revolution to its survival.
10 There have been many changes ______ the industry as a whole over the last 20 years.

Grammar 2: Expressions to quantify data

(5 marks)

Put the following expressions to quantify data, so that they fit into the sentence logically.

a fair amount of	a great number of	a limited quantity of	billions of	few

1 __________ people want to travel to Australia by ocean liner. Most people prefer to fly.
2 We have __________ fresh water to drink at sea. We have to dock every six weeks.
3 The massive global advertising campaign has cost the parent company __________ euros.
4 There is __________ cash in the bank, enough to keep us afloat for some time.
5 __________ people prefer to shop online nowadays. The market is booming.

Vocabulary 1: Marketing and international marketing terms

(5 marks)

Match the following terms with their definitions.

1 Economies of scale	a decision where to place a product or service
2 Branding strategy	b generally accepted behaviour
3 Market positioning	c recognition of the diversity of beliefs and behaviours
4 Cultural norms	d lower unit costs as a result of producing more
5 Cultural sensitivity	e creating positive associations for a product or service

Vocabulary 2: Verb, adjective and noun forms

(10 marks)

Write in the missing forms for the following words.

Verb	Adjective	Noun
adapt		
		differentiation
	minimal	
	global	
standardise		

Vocabulary 3: Strategy and tactics

(10 marks)

Put these words in the following sentences.

broad	common	coherent	delaying	effective
illegal	integrated	long-term	strong-arm	underhand

1 It's not unusual, it's just a ______ tactic that shops use to get you to buy impulsively.

2 Overall, the ______ strategy is not to replace workers at the plant when they retire.

3 The management team decided to use ______ tactics to force the unions to negotiate.

4 We are not being consistent. We need a ______ strategy in order to compete effectively.

5 Mel is extremely adept at using ______ tactics to take credit for ideas not her own.

6 The shareholders are being short-sighted. The ______ strategy is to extend the brand.

7 Our ______ strategy consists of three strands: brand recognition, increasing production, and expanding overseas.

8 Oil companies are often accused of using ______ tactics to keep prices artificially high.

9 Two of our debtors are using ______ tactics again. They won't pay in full until March.

10 ______ tactics are vital for dealing with the constantly changing economic climate.

Writing

(10 marks)

Write an executive summary for an invented business or a business you know well.

Write about 120 words and include the following points.

- target market
- how the market is growing and other key financial performance information
- your relevant experience and skills
- the competition
- your contacts and the support they give
- how much you want to borrow
- any financial investments already made by you

Progress test 2

Units 6–10

Grammar 1: Linking ideas in spoken and written English

(10 marks)

Complete the sentences with the expressions in the box.

adding that	although	and thus	as	but
by	of whom	saying	whether	while

1 ________ introducing these new health and safety rules, we should see a decrease in fatalities.
2 We employ 27 software engineers, some ________ are also responsible for development.
3 The company's sales are falling, ________ critics are blaming the CEO's strategy.
4 All meetings will start on time ________ all participants are in the room or not.
5 'Sales are stable,' Simon said, ________ he expected to see a small increase in the 4th quarter.
6 Jane agreed to take the minutes ________ you were going to be late to the meeting.
7 It's a centre of excellence for innovation, ________ also being a great place to live.
8 Notes are a personal record of meetings, ________ minutes are important legal documents.
9 Investors are not sure if it will be successful, ________ it depends on economic conditions.
10 Management and leadership are different, ________ there may be an overlap.

Grammar 2: Multiple adjectives

(5 marks)

Put the following statements into the correct order.

1 supermarket / of / range / local / a / produce / wide / that / stocks / fresh
2 box / hand-painted / wooden / beautiful / a
3 lovely / some / colourful / cosmetics / sweet-smelling
4 and / paperback / compact / indestructible / the / almost / portable / is
5 revolutionary / invention / the / is / printer / 3D / a / fantastic

Vocabulary 1: Collocations with *design*

(5 marks)

Write the correct form of *design* in the gaps.

1 We employed an interior ________ to give our offices a new look.
2 ________ clothes are so expensive; they are only made for celebrities in my opinion.
3 At the recent motor show we unveiled our newly ________ concept car for the future.
4 My partner and I established our ________ company a few years ago.
5 I love my new tablet device. It's so well ________ and easy to use on the move.

Vocabulary 2: The language of leadership

(10 marks)

Choose the correct alternative in the following sentences.

1 Good leaders have confidence and *passion* / *motivation* / *self-belief* in their ability.

2 Exceptional leaders can *energise* / *inspire* / *persuade* their followers by example.

3 It's important to be *charismatic* / *dictatorial* / *passionate* about work or you could lose interest.

4 Good leaders are always active and have high levels of *consistency* / *energy* / *persuasion* to use up when pursuing the achievement of their dream.

5 Good leaders should avoid a(n) *dictatorial* / *inspirational* / *motivational* approach towards colleagues.

6 The ability to influence and infuse others through the use of *charisma* / *dictatorship* / *energy* is often cited as an important quality of leadership.

7 Weak leaders lack the powers of *motivation* / *persuasion* / *vision* to win people over to their ideas.

8 A successful leader has to be a *self-believer* / *dictator* / *visionary* and put their ideas across imaginatively.

9 Weak leaders are indecisive and generally lack *consistency* / *inspiration* / *motivation*.

10 A good leader is not *inspired* / *motivated* / *persuaded* by greed alone.

Vocabulary 3: Language of outsourcing

(10 marks)

Use the following key words and phrases to complete the sentences.

back office	core business	downsizing	just-in-time	logistics	provider
reintegrate activities	renegotiate	shortfall in inventory	switch providers		

1 When we look for an outsourcing ________________ in new countries, the cost and the level of English language skills are the most important factors.

2 Outsourcing can result in ________________ and internal redundancies.

3 We need to ________________ and take back control of the technical planning.

4 ________________ is the process of minimising stock levels to save on storage costs.

5 We have a ________________ and cannot meet our delivery commitments this month.

6 The level of service provided is poor, so we'll have to ________________ .

7 We must ________________ the contract to improve our terms and conditions.

8 We need to concentrate on our ________________ in order to maintain our competitive advantage in the coming few years.

9 ________________ is ensuring raw materials are in the right place at the right time.

10 The ________________ staff don't have any direct contact with any of the clients.

Writing

(10 marks)

You recently gave a sales presentation for an office equipment supplier called *WEquip* to a prospective client. Write a follow-up email of about 120 words. Include the following points.

- Remind them of the meeting and of *WEquip's* business activity.
- Remind them of their interest in your products.
- Tell them you are attaching a brochure containing details of *WEquip's* product range.
- Tell them you have some special discounts up to 25% on selected items.
- Tell them to feel free to ask any questions of *WEquip*.
- Thank them for coming to the original presentation.

Progress test 3

Units 11–14

Grammar 1: Transitive and intransitive verbs

(5 marks)

Correct the mistakes in the verb forms in the following sentences.

1 Absolutely fantastic! Our sales have raised by over 20% since the beginning of the year.

____

2 The number of people claiming welfare payments has impacted by the lack of growth.

____

3 Inflation is going to be raised faster than we had first thought.

____

4 Many social problems could be disappeared with targeted government expenditure.

____

5 A further need for the company to borrow will be arisen sometime in the future.

____

Grammar 2: Inversion

(10 marks)

Invert and rewrite the following sentences using the phrases given in brackets.

1 We had to increase investment in tourism, because the housing market collapsed. (such was)

____

2 The shop had a poor 4th quarter and it is struggling to pay costs. (had the shop not)

____

3 Some nations want to keep agricultural subsidies and they also want to protect infant industries. (not only)

____

4 The total harmonisation of tax law within the European Trade Area won't be allowed to happen. (under no circumstances)

____

5 If countries work together, a future financial crisis can be avoided. (only by)

____

6 I didn't advise him to tell lies on his job application. (at no time)

____

7 If we lowered trade barriers, there would be an import surge. (were we to)

____

8 There will be free movement of goods between Africa and Europe when the bridge linking Spain and Morocco is built. (not until)

____

9 The business was successful and we were able to diversify. (so)

____

10 An agreement on international trade is impossible because of the seriousness of the disputes surrounding agricultural subsidies in different countries. (such is)

____

Vocabulary 1: Financial and economic word partnerships

(5 marks)

Choose the correct word in the following sentences.

1 The financial *sector / markets / crisis* is worth trillions of pounds to the British economy.
2 You have to fill in your tax *collection / return / planning* form once every year.
3 An economic *recovery / downturn / activity* should follow a period of recession.
4 Agriculture is a market subject to government *policy / intervention / funding* in Europe.
5 *Outlook / Interest rates / Currency* have been kept stable to help the credit market.

Vocabulary 2: Economic convergence and divergence

(10 marks)

Put the correct terms into the appropriate gap in each sentence.

bilateral trade	compliance with	duty-free trade	economic integration
export-orientated	growing polarisation	income disparity	inward investment
protectionist trade policies	removing trade barriers		

1 The UN General Assembly is meeting today to discuss the ______________________ between rich and poor nations worldwide and why the gap is widening.
2 The president's visit to Saudi Arabia was aimed at increasing ______________________ between the kingdom and France.
3 India is extremely successful at attracting ______________________ because of its low labour costs.
4 Since the 1980s, ______________________ has widened dramatically in the USA.
5 China, Germany and Japan are all very much ______________________ economies and their goods can be found almost everywhere in the world.
6 The UK and the Commonwealth have agreed on the general benefits of ______________________, but the Commonwealth tries to reduce exposure to trade competition from larger countries.
7 The principle of free circulation allows ______________________ on the movement of goods produced within the EU.
8 Russia is seeking much closer ______________________ and greater political ties with some other former Soviet Republics.
9 All goods which enter the USA must be in ______________________ all US laws and regulations.
10 ______________________, such as import tariffs, effectively raise the cost of goods and inflate their price.

Vocabulary 3: Business and social issues

(10 marks)

Put the following words into the correct gaps.

change	enterprise	entrepreneurs	good	housing
mission	need	problems	responsibility	value

1 The swift urbanisation of the developing world is producing rapid social __________ .

2 It's the government's job to address social __________ such as crime and unemployment.

3 A former steelworks has been demolished to create space for some new social __________ .

4 A social __________ is a business that is for people and the environment as well as for profit.

5 Many governments subsidise the price of basic foods because it meets a social __________ .

6 In addition to creating economic opportunities, business leaders should also take into account the social __________ .

7 Social __________ creation is the fundamental purpose, not giving dividends to shareholders.

8 The company's social __________ is to improve the quality of life of the people in the countries it operates within.

9 Social __________ are game changers who are radically changing existing business models.

10 Corporate social __________ makes clear a company's ethics, principles and values.

Writing

(10 marks)

The following graph shows sales for digital and film cameras at Galaxy Electronics. Write a description, grouping similar information together appropriately and noting the major trends and any possible predictions for the future.

Write about 120 words.

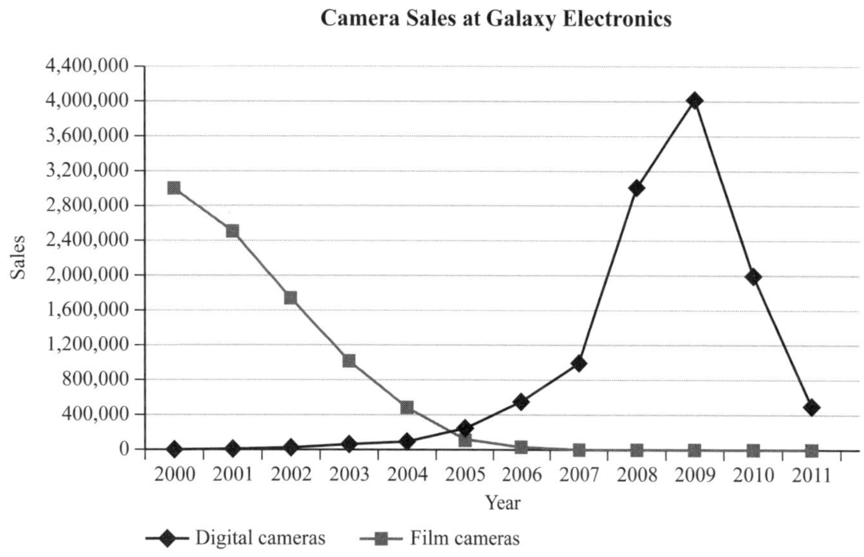

Worksheet 1

Improve your knowledge of aspects of pronunciation

Aims
- Improve knowledge of certain sounds.
- Raise awareness of stress and tone of voice.
- Revise some brainstorming techniques and increase learner autonomy.

Tasks
- Eliminate the wrong word by sound.
- Identify linking and correct word stress.
- Brainstorm a pronunciation website.

1 Lead-in

Discuss the following questions with a partner.

1 Do you think native speakers speak too quickly? Why/Why not?
2 What is word stress?
3 What is intonation?
4 When is word stress and intonation changed in your first language?
5 Look at the phonemic chart below. Which sounds do you have problems producing and hearing?

	Monophthongs				**Diphthongs**			
Vowels	iː	ɪ	ʊ	uː	ɪə	eɪ	**voiced** unvoiced	
	e	ə	ɜː	ɔː	ʊə	ɔɪ	əʊ	
	æ	ʌ	ɑː	ɒ	eə	aɪ	aʊ	
Consonants	p	b	t	d	tʃ	dʒ	k	g
	f	v	θ	ð	s	z	ʃ	ʒ
	m	n	ŋ	h	l	r	w	j

2 Odd word out

Cross out the word which doesn't have the sound illustrated.

e.g. /θ/ strengthen – threat, ~~these~~, theory, thrive, throughout

/ʌ/ company	budget, bullet, substitute, judge, production
/tʃ/ launch	pitch, switch, structure, characteristic, chain
/æ/ shadow	horizontal, massive, analyse, tablet, lack
/ə/ dependant	entrant, conspicuous, rival, ferocious, franchising
/iː/ team	boutique, technique, bean, resort, piece

3 Connected speech

1 **Say these expressions very slowly to start off and then gradually build up speed. Mark the links between the words as if spoken and the word stress.**
  1 Let's start with an ice-breaker before getting into groups to generate ideas.
  2 What a brilliant idea! We should implement it immediately!
  3 I believe that it is quantity that breeds quality.
  4 We tend to think our target profile group are successful in their own right.
  5 What about franchising as an option?
2 **Practise changing the stress on words in the sentences. Is there a change in meaning?**

4 Setting up a website role play

1 **You are going to create a website called *Pronunciation help!* Form two groups to brainstorm ideas for its content according to the type of brainstorming technique.**
  Group 1: Lateral association
  Group 2: Provocation
2 **Present your idea to the class.**

Worksheet 2

Improve your knowledge of brand strategy

Aims

- Review types of brands.
- Identify some adjectives to describe brands.
- Distinguish between brand awareness and loyalty.

Tasks

- Match common adjectives to types of brand.
- Match marketing questions to branding concepts.
- Branding strategy role play.

1 Lead-in

Discuss the following questions with a partner.

1 What is the difference between brand positioning and brand strategy?
2 Which well-known brands do you like and dislike? Why?
3 Which type of consumers are own-brand products aimed at?
4 Which company do you think is the leading brand in consumer electronics? Why?
5 How do brands of similar products (e.g. Coca-Cola and Pepsi Cola) compete?

2 Describing types of brands

1 **Match the adjectives to the types of brand. Discuss why you think they match.**

Type of brand	Adjective
Premium	affordable authentic chief comfortable confident economical famous foremost inexpensive inferior mysterious primary principal rare recognisable reliable reputable sensual superior thrifty
Well-known	
Leading	
Own	

2 **Which adjectives do you associate with brands from your country of origin? Why?**

3 Building brand loyalty and awareness

1 **Match these branding concepts to their definitions (1–8).**

brand experience   brand extension   brand management
brand recall   brand recognition   dominant brand
first-thought-of brand   iconic brand

1 An existing brand name is used for new or modified products. ___________
2 The creation and maintenance of a brand. ___________
3 Most consumers believe the brand outperforms all others. ___________
4 The aggregate of all points of contact with the brand. ___________
5 Contributes to consumer's self-expression and personal identity. ___________
6 A brand name is acknowledged for its benefits. ___________
7 A brand name brings to mind a product or service. ___________
8 The name of a product or service prompts a brand name. ___________

2 **Marketers use questions based on a type of product and its usage to find out how aware and loyal consumers are to a brand.**

1 In pairs, ask a few questions to your partner about their attitudes to different consumer products and their buying habits, e.g. *Which brand do you associate toothpaste with? Which toothpaste brand do you habitually buy? Do you leave the outlet if your toothpaste brand is unavailable? Are you indifferent when buying a toothpaste brand? When you hear the word 'toothpaste', which brand springs to mind?*
2 Use the list of branding concepts above to help you think of more questions.

4 Brand strategy for 'QT cola' role play

1 **QT cola is an affordable alternative brand to the world's leading cola brands in the country of Qistan, and the company now wishes to expand its presence in Eurasia. In pairs, agree on what you think would be the best brand strategy to achieve this aim.**

Student A

You believe the strategy for QT should:

- emphasise country of origin
- place product in local films
- sponsor local sports events
- utilise merchandise for cafés
- market QT as a 'stand-alone' drink.

Student B

You believe the strategy for QT should:

- emphasise the region of origin
- place product in international films
- sponsor visiting international DJs
- have a clothing and accessory range
- market QT as a drinks complement.

2 **Present what you agree on and write a slide giving reasons for your brand strategy to the class.**

Worksheet 3

Improve your knowledge of prepositions

Aims
- Classify different types of prepositions.
- Raise awareness of prepositions that collocate with *time*.
- Revise common dependent prepositions.

Tasks
- Illustrate and give examples of usage of common prepositions of place.
- Match the correct preposition to a phrase with *time*.
- Match the dependent preposition to a list of verbs.

1 Lead-in

Discuss the following questions with a partner.

1 Where do prepositions typically come in a sentence?
2 What is a preposition of time? Can you give any examples?
3 What is a preposition of movement? Can you give any examples?
4 What is a compound/complex preposition? Can you give any examples?
5 Do you find prepositions difficult to learn? What advice would you give for learning them?

2 Visualising prepositions of place

1 Visualise the following prepositions of place using a combination of brackets, dots and dashes, as in the example.

IN [.]	BETWEEN	ACROSS
AT	ABOVE	BELOW
THROUGH	ON	BEHIND
NEAR	AMONG	AGAINST
OUTSIDE	INSIDE	OPPOSITE

2 In pairs, nominate a preposition to elicit a business-related example sentence from your partner.

3 Prepositions that collate with *time*

Put the following prepositions into the correct example sentences.

at by for in until

1 The materials were produced to a strict deadline, and were given just ___________ time.
2 A lot of hotels were run independently ___________ the time budget chains entered the market.
3 We cannot continue working on the project ___________ the time being.
4 ___________ the time Jack started working, it was already 10 o'clock in the morning.
5 The budget forecast is correct ___________ the time of writing.

4 Dependent prepositions

1 Match the verb lists to their dependent prepositions.

TO	accuse, approve, consist, know, think
FOR	concentrate, depend, focus, rely, insist
FROM	consent, contribute, introduce, refer, respond
IN	aim, apologise, apply, ask, prepare
OF	prevent, protect, recover, suffer, save
ON	agree, argue, deal, interfere, provide
WITH	believe, invest, specialise, succeed

2 Which of the verbs above can match with other prepositions?

5 Dependent prepositions dialogue

Create a dialogue with five verbs and their dependent prepositions. Then read your dialogue aloud for your class to guess the correct missing preposition.

Worksheet 4

Improve your knowledge of risk-taking behaviour

Aims
- Review some adjectives to describe character.
- Raise awareness of how supermarkets place products to influence buying behaviour.
- Review the components of an executive summary.

Tasks
- Decide on the characteristics of a successful/unsuccessful entrepreneur.
- Organise a supermarket floor plan to optimise impulse buying.
- Write an executive summary for a new business.

1 Lead-in

Discuss the following questions with a partner.

1 What do you understand by 'you have to speculate to accumulate'?
2 What are the major risks in life? How can you spread them?
3 What are the major risks in opening a business? How can you spread them?
4 What advice would you give to a risk-averse person?
5 Are there any risks when buying products from supermarkets?

2 Risky behaviour

In pairs, discuss and mark the typical characteristics of a successful (S) and an unsuccessful entrepreneur (U).

- thinks and acts on their feet
- ignores their own intuition
- can think 'outside the box'
- feels embarrassed to 'sing their own praises'
- is motivated by fear rather than optimism
- stands their ground with aggressive behaviour
- has a highly competitive spirit
- has a strong work ethic
- can deal with failure
- procrastinates until the 'time is right'

3 Impulsive behaviour

In pairs, place the following product categories in the supermarket plan below in a way to encourage impulsive buying.

drinks batteries bread products condiments confectionery dairy products fresh vegetables meat products products on special offer soft drinks tinned products toiletries

4 Executive summary

You would like to set up a supermarket in a small town, but need a bank loan to achieve it. In groups, write an executive summary for a bank in order to get the loan. Use these ideas to help you.

- target market
- own-brand products
- range of products
- luxury-brand products
- type of shop
- location of shop
- loyalty card
- goals for the first year
- loss leaders?
- company/team history

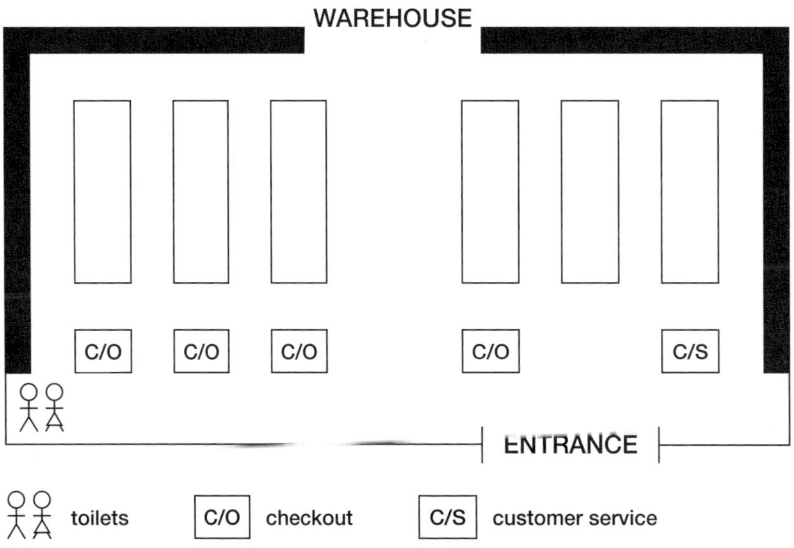

Worksheet 5

Improve your knowledge of fundraising

Aims
- Review common collocations with money.
- Analyse public and private sector funding.
- Illustrate different fundraising possibilities.

Tasks
- Match frequent verbs to money and preposition to create a phrase.
- Discuss similarities and differences between public and private sector funding.
- Role play a fundraising course of action.

1 Lead-in

Discuss the following questions in pairs.

1 Which of the following can't you *raise*? *capital*, *shares*, *equity*, *funds*, *stake*
2 What is the difference between *funds* and *capital*?
3 What do you think is the role of a *fundraiser*?
4 Which of the following can't be *issued*? *shares*, *funds*, *bonds*, *Treasury bills*, *gilts*
5 What is the difference between a *non-profit organisation*, a *non-government organisation* and a *charity*?

2 Verbs, prepositions and *money*

1 Match the verbs that collocate with *money* to their dependent prepositions in the third column to create phrases.

borrow save invest raise spend waste put	money	on for in on in for from	underperforming shares a charitable good cause the kitty an unscrupulous loan shark a new outfit for an office party a rainy day a second home to let to tenants

2 Can you think of any other verbs that collocate with *money*? What are their dependent prepositions? Can you give an example phrase?

3 Private and public sector funding

1 In pairs, discuss the similarities and differences between the two sectors using these prompts.

• bankruptcy • donations • fundraising events • government grants	• internal market • outsourcing • profit dividends • reclaiming taxation	• renting buildings • restructuring loans • selling shares • selling assets

2 Is a large public sector or is a large private sector good for growth in an economy? Why?

4 Fundraising role play

1 You are a large educational charity that wishes to organise six fundraising activities and events. In pairs, come to a decision on what to do and why you think it is the best course of action.

Student A

Prefer a New Year show – well attended.

Hire out minibus in summer – not used.

Sell investments – not making money.

Pay back bank loan – interest rate is high.

Create an internal market – other parts of the organisation can do things more cheaply.

Fancy dress street collection – passers-by can donate more.

Student B

Prefer a summer fête – old and new faces.

Look for savings – energy costs are high.

Restructure bank loan – interest rate is high.

Employ street canvassers – students are free.

Organise a sponsored parachute jump – staff would be very interested.

Hold a raffle at the local café – people will know about the charity and its work.

2 Re-pair with another student and compare your decisions and reasoning.

Worksheet 6

Improve your knowledge of leading and managing

Aims
- Learn some words and phrases to describe leadership and management.
- Review ways of dealing with dissatisfied employees.
- Raise awareness of the content of Business Studies courses.

Tasks
- Match adjectives to describe traditional leadership and management styles.
- Discuss job satisfaction and dissatisfaction.
- Present an overview of a curriculum for an ideal Business Studies course.

1 Lead-in

Discuss the following questions with a partner.

1 What is the difference between a coach and a manager?
2 Can you train to be a coach and a manager?
3 Which subjects would you include on a 'preparing for leadership' course?
4 What do you understand by the 'carrot and stick approach' to management?
5 Why do you think Business and Management Studies courses are so popular?

2 Describing a manager's and a leader's points of view

1 **With a partner, decide which word or phrase traditionally describes a leader's or a manager's point of view. Mark each word (L) or (M) depending on your choice.**

Points of view		
Relationship with co-workers	followers	subordinates
Organisational culture	represents	shapes
Risk	minimises	takes
Rules and regulations	breaks	makes
Outlook for the future	long-term	short-term
Persuasive technique	sells	tells
Source of power	authority	charisma
Strives for	achievement of objectives	vision
Dynamism	proactive	reactive
Zeal	control	passion

2 **Do you think it is now possible to describe a modern manager using some of the 'L' words from the table?**

3 Satisfaction & dissatisfaction with management

1 **Read the statements and decide if the employee is satisfied or dissatisfied and why.**
   1 'It doesn't say that in my job description.'
   2 'Management can't be learned from books; it takes years of real-world experience.'
   3 'My manager's office door is always open for discussion.'
   4 'We've always done things this way; I say you don't fix things unless they are broken.'
   5 'Our manager lets us get on with it if she is sure of our capability to do the task.'

2 **What could you do to motivate the employees above who are dissatisfied?**

4 Ideal Business Studies course

1 **Discuss the list of possible components for a Business Studies course and decide which six would be included in an *ideal* course for you.**
- Basic accounting
- Business objectives
- Business structure
- Cash flow management
- Entrepreneurship
- Globalisation
- Human resource management
- Inventory management
- Management and leadership
- Marketing mix
- Motivation
- Project management
- Quality management
- Stakeholders in business
- Sources of finance

(Source: *Cambridge A & AS Level Business Studies*)

2 **Present an overview of your curriculum for your ideal Business Studies course including what you would expect to study under each heading.**

Worksheet 7

Improve your knowledge of intercultural competence

Aims
- Discover different cultural expectations in meetings.
- Discover different cultural expectations of management style.
- Raise awareness of aspects of cultural competence.

Tasks
- Match nationality to behaviour in meetings.
- Match nationality to management style.
- Agree on the content of a cultural competence programme.

1 Lead-in

Discuss the following questions in pairs.

1. Have you ever experienced any cultural misunderstanding? If so, what happened?
2. Does *culture* refer to age and gender? If so, how do these issues affect international business?
3. Do you think stereotyping makes it easier to anticipate others' cultural behaviour?
4. What cultural similarities do you think all people share?
5. Do you think culture is embedded in language? Why/Why not?

2 Cultural expectations in meetings

1. **Discuss and match the following quotes about behaviours with the correct nationality.**

Nationality	Meeting behaviour
Argentinian	'There's polite conversation about mutual contacts and good small talk.'
Nigerian	'Meetings are directed with attendees speaking one at a time.'
Japanese	'Things are slower here. It is vital to get to know your hosts.'
Polish	'Punctuality is better than in other places in Latin America.'

2. **Which quotes do you think can be used to describe other nationalities' attitudes to meetings?**

3 Attitudes to management styles

In pairs, discuss and match the quotes about preferred management style with the correct nationality.

Nationality	Preferred management style
Indian	'My managers are transformational. They act as facilitators and include everybody in the decision-making processes.'
Taiwanese	'Our manager values interpersonal skills and a *hands-on* approach. She prefers to request assistance rather than being direct.'
Swedish	'Seniority and the managerial position command respect. My manager gives instructions to us and we obey.'
British	'My manager is the boss: he gives explicit directions which must be followed fully, even if everybody disagrees.'

4 Improving cultural competence

In groups, discuss what you would ideally study before doing business with members of the following nationalities.

- American
- Brazilian
- Chinese
- Kenyan
- Qatari
- Russian

5 Cultural competence programme

1. **Your company wants to improve cultural competence in order to facilitate overseas sales and has requested a cross-cultural communication consultant to give three presentations. In groups, discuss which three of the following modules that they offer are most important to study. Give reasons for your answers.**
   - Building multi-national teams
   - Managing international mergers and acquisitions
   - Developing relationships with global clients
   - Successful staff relocation
   - Clarifying non-verbal communications across cultures
   - Attitudes towards time, timing and timeliness
   - Speaking and writing using an interpreter/translator
   - Overcoming culture shock
   - Managing face-to-face meetings across borders
   - Gift-giving and business entertainment across cultures
2. **Decide on a secretary to present your ideas to the class as a whole. Then come to a decision on the three presentations you will ask the consultant to give.**

Worksheet 8

Improve your knowledge of regional development policies

Aims
- Raise awareness of international and regional development policies.
- Discuss the purpose of the European Union's regional policy.
- Raise awareness of development policies to promote employment and economic growth in deprived areas.

Tasks
- Match the European Union's pillars of regional policy to their purpose.
- Match policy objectives with a selection of policy tools.
- Design a regional development policy and present it to investors.

1 Lead-in

Discuss these questions in pairs.

1 How would you define regional development?
2 Can regional development be urban, rural and international?
3 What can a national or regional government do to promote regional development?
4 What does your home region do to promote development?
5 What is the role of transnational development organisations? e.g. European Regional Development Fund, Organisation for Economic Cooperation and Development, International Labour Organisation.

2 Regional development policy of the European Union

1 **In pairs, match the pillars of the European Union's regional development policy to their purpose.**

Pillar	Purpose
Convergence	improving territorial cohesion
Regional Competitiveness and Employment	reducing regional disparities
Cross-region/country cooperation	making regions more alluring to investors

2 **What do you think is the overall aim of the European Union's regional policy?**

3 **What fraction of the European Union's budget do you think is allocated to regional policy?**

3 Regional development policy objectives and tools

1 **Match the policy objectives to the tools for achieving them, and then compare with a partner.**

Policy objective	Policy tools
Create sustainable jobs	networking and exchange of experience events
Stimulate economic growth	shared economic, social and environmental programmes
Ensure environment and risk prevention	direct aid and investments in small/medium businesses
Improve transport and telecommunications	opportunities for R&D and entrepreneurship
Special assistance for remote areas	added capacity, reduced bottlenecks, improved efficiency
Promote innovation and knowledge	free trade, tax policy, infrastructure investment
Enhance cross-border cooperation	integrated conservation strategies in land use
Advance interregional cooperation	education, social stability, incentivised risk taking

2 **Which policy objectives would be appropriate to your region? Why/Why not?**

4 Regional development policy role play

You are managers of regional development policy in an area of a country that has over 40% unemployment among its working population. In groups of three, discuss which *five* policies would be best to attract both foreign and domestic investment into the area and present them to the rest of the class.

Manager A

Emphasise:

- Manufacturing skills base
- Numeracy skills of workforce
- A rent-free period for existing buildings
- Vast experience of re-training people of all ages
- Waste and water management policies

Manager B

Emphasise:

- Ease of hire and fire of labour
- The lack of unionisation of workforce
- Availability of a tax break for new buildings
- Computer skills of workforce
- Cultural affinity with target investor(s)

Manager C

Emphasise:

- Level of English language skills
- Excellent industrial relations record
- Road, rail and air transport links
- Reduction of local tax on existing buildings
- Sponsorship of staff development courses

Worksheet 9

Improve your knowledge of employee appraisal

Aims
- Become familiar with content of employee appraisals.
- Raise awareness of aspects of positive and negative language.
- Appraise an employee appropriately.

Tasks
- Make word transformations with *critic.*
- Match category and content of employee appraisals.
- Role play an employee appraisal.

1 Lead-in

Discuss the following questions with a partner.

1 Do you find criticism easy to give or difficult to receive?
2 What is the role of a film or theatre critic?
3 How does the use of language affect the tone of criticism?
4 How do you respond to overtly negative criticism?
5 Do you think *feedback* is synonymous with *constructive criticism*?

2 Forms of *critic*

Fill in the gaps with the correct form of *critic*.

1 The emagazine's business writer has been ____________ acclaimed by some CEOs and academics.
2 Our financial situation will become ____________ if we do not do something about the debt burden.
3 I read the restaurant ____________ on *findameal.com.* It was excellent, so I took the participants there.
4 My supervisor was ____________ and praised our team's performance during the last project.
5 Simone Valquez is a freelance writer and ____________ who often writes for our free local newspaper.
6 All of this negative ____________ that is around the office at the moment is extremely depressing.
7 Although Jake was unsure if his boss's judgement was sound, he fulfilled the task ____________ .
8 Why do you always have to ____________ me? I am not the one to blame for your problems!

3 Linguistic reactions

How would you react to being told the following?

1 'I can easily find someone else to do the job tomorrow, if you don't want to.'
2 'We value your enthusiasm, but this job is just not up to standard.'
3 'Who gave you permission to leave early yesterday?'
4 'Your customer service skills are improving. How do you visualise continuing this improvement?'
5 'Social media has no place in this office.'

4 Employee appraisal competencies

1 **Appraisal interviews often focus on lists of competencies like those in the table below. Match the appraisal categories to their content.**

Competency	Content
Team working	advising and monitoring colleagues to realise their full potential
Customer service	ability to prioritise and achieve deadlines
Flexibility	achievement of expected monetary targets
Self-awareness	rating of the employee's work as a whole
Organisational skills	ability to adapt to a changing working environment
Financial compliance	understanding of one's emotions and their impact on others
Overall performance	identifying or creating opportunities and maximising them
Intercultural competence	cooperation across departments to achieve shared goals
Mentoring	delivery of appropriate and high-quality services
Entrepreneurship	consideration for a variety of beliefs and traditions

2 **Would you include all of these categories in an employee appraisal? Why/Why not?**

5 Employee appraisal role play

The following notes have been made on an employee's performance.

- is slightly offhand with customers
- does not prioritise adequately
- thinks laterally and creatively to find solutions
- makes false assumptions about other people
- encourages team members to think on their feet
- loses temper easily
- weighs up pros and cons of actions sufficiently
- provides clear feedback to team members

Role play the following situation with a partner.

Line manager

Decide which are positive and negative aspects of behaviour and either praise or attempt to remedy the situation accordingly, using appropriate language.

Employee

Decide which are positive and negative aspects of your behaviour, accept any criticism gracefully and offer reasons for the underperforming behaviour. You have criticisms of your own: you would prefer more direction in tasks; you feel the line manager does little to motivate the team; and you are not sure of the best time to approach him/her.

Worksheet 10

Improve your knowledge of new business models in newspaper publishing

Aims
- Raise awareness of changes in a business model.
- Review collocations with *printed*, *media* and *computer*.
- Role play a meeting to decide on a business model to adapt.

Tasks
- Create some collocations with *printed*, *media* and *computer*.
- Match a newspaper business model to its positive and negative characteristics.
- Discuss a new business model for a failing newspaper.

1 Lead-in

Discuss these questions in pairs.

1 How often do you buy a newspaper?
2 Do you think the existing print model of newspaper publishing is failing?
3 Why do you think people subscribe to an online newspaper?
4 Do you think the general population has developed a 'snack information' culture?
5 Do you think pictures are more important than the printed word in attracting attention?

2 Word collocations with *printed, media* and *computer*

Match the following. The words can go before or after the main word.

Printed	animated based copy designed edition generated graphics hype mass matter mogul multi new version word
Media	
Computer	

4 Declining revenue problem

The printed copy circulation and advertising revenue of *The Global Informer* has been falling steadily due to increased competition for readers from the Internet.

You have noticed that a specialist newspaper *The Money Educator* has maintained its revenue stream, despite selling fewer printed copies, through a monthly metered pay wall subscription service on its online edition. Hold a meeting and discuss the following points in small groups and innovate a new business model to increase revenue for your newspaper.

- Content strategy
- Local coverage
- Use of bloggers and freelance staff
- Ownership of the customer relationship
- Online payment systems
- New sources of advertising revenue
- Staff retraining in a basic knowledge of HTML and CSS
- Exploiting brand name through conferences, bookshops, sponsorship, etc.

3 Newspaper business models

1 **What do you think the names of the types of business models in the table below mean?**
2 **Match each type of business model to its positive and negative characteristics.**

Model	Positive characteristics	Negative characteristics
Traditional	casual reader is not deterred, a limited number of stories are free	app market is not developed enough to replace print revenue as yet
Pay wall	not dependent on print advertising or physical printing press	people will take more time to move away from printed copy to new media
Metered pay wall	readers may be more prepared to pay for content on smart devices	younger readers and advertisers have shifted to a new media
Mobile services	subscribers get access to all digital content, allows reader to choose	most customers are unwilling to pay for general news content
Joint digital/ print	access is restricted, advertising is more targeted and valuable	reliant on donations, grants and corporate sponsorship of specific issues
Online not-for-profit	audience easy to reach, they employ professionals, cheap to produce	some people will read what is allowed and will not visit again

Worksheet 11

Improve your knowledge of taxation

Aims
- Raise awareness of collocations with *tax.*
- Raise awareness of different types of taxes.
- Review presenting comparative information.

Tasks
- Match collocations with *tax* to their definitions.
- Match types of tax to when they are levied.
- Discuss and present some tax statistics.

1 Lead-in

Discuss the following questions with a partner.

1 What is the difference between *direct* and *indirect* taxation?
2 What is an *excise duty*?
3 What are *tax-exempt* goods and services? Can you name any in your country?
4 Do you think tax cuts result in a *trickle-down* effect for the general population?
5 How is local government funded in your country?

2 Collocations with *tax*

1 Match the words that collocate with *tax* and their definitions.

TAX	loophole	can be subtracted from the total taxable amount
	haven	money returned after an overpayment of tax is calculated
	avoidance	a person who moves to a place where taxes are lower
	evasion	an amount of tax that a person or business must pay
	deductible	the percentage of an amount or value that has to be paid in tax
	office	the income information that is given to the tax authorities each year
	liability	the national authority to make and deal with tax decisions
	exile	illegal ways of paying less tax than you should
	rate	reduction, by legal methods, of the amount of tax paid
	declaration	a system that allows a person not to pay tax on some of their income
	relief	a mistake in the law which allows the chance to avoid tax
	refund	a place where people pay less tax than their own country

2 Do you know of any other words that collocate with *tax*?

3 Types of tax

Match the types of tax to when they are levied.

Income tax	is levied	by government on businesses' profits
Sales tax		on profits made from selling something you own
Inheritance tax		on personal property and financial assets above a particular level
Wealth tax		when people buy goods or services
Corporation tax		at each stage of production on the worth of the product at that stage
Road tax		on money or property received from a relative who has died
Capital gains tax		on people's earnings, salary or wages
Value added tax		on a vehicle before being allowed to drive it legally

4 Limiting tax liabilities

1 Below is a table showing the tax rates for Corporation and Value Added Tax across eight countries in the world. With a partner, decide how the information could be presented more clearly on a slide to enable a better comparison.

Country	Corporation Tax	Value Added Tax
Argentina	35%	21%
Russia	20%	18%
Philippines	30%	12%
Saudi Arabia	20%	0%
Cyprus	10%	15%
South Africa	28%	14%
Bulgaria	10%	20%
Canada	15%	5%

2 In small groups, compare how you have decided to present the statistical information and then present your best idea to the rest of the class using a rough sketch of the visual.

Worksheet 12

Improve your knowledge of world trade

Aims
- Exemplify some collocations with *trade.*
- Describe trends in commodities traded globally.
- Raise awareness of the difficulties in reaching trade agreements.

Tasks
- Match collocations with *trade* to their meaning.
- Describe a graph.
- Negotiate a trading position.

1 Lead-in

Discuss the following questions with a partner.

1. What does the acronym *WTO* stand for?
2. What is the 'Doha round' of negotiations at the WTO? Why did the negotiations stall in 2008?
3. What is the World Economic Forum? What is the purpose of its meeting in Davos every year?
4. Can you think of any acronyms for groups of countries that trade together with few restrictions?
5. What is the difference between a bilateral, a trilateral and a multilateral trade agreement?

2 Collocations with *trade*

Match the following collocations with *trade* to their meaning.

Trade	balance	a name or a symbol which is put on a product to show who made it
	deficit	amount at which finished goods are sold to shops by producers
	mark	the difference between money received from exports and spent on imports
	figures	information about a product known only by the company producing it
	name	a road or sea lane historically used by people buying and selling goods
	price	these compare the values of goods brought in and goods sold abroad
	secret	name put on a product which cannot be legally used by another producer
	route	when the value of imports exceeds that of exports

✂- -

Country A
- protect developing IT and medical industries
- guarantee intellectual property rights
- improve government transparency
- keep all agricultural subsidies
- reduce waste discharge at sea

✂- -

Country B
- allow access to markets for rice, cotton & soya
- ensure supply chain security on land / at sea
- minimise customs procedure for imports
- recognise bureaucratic inefficiency in regions
- ensure conformity of product labelling

✂- -

Country C
- license medication for consumer protection
- lower import taxes on textiles
- policing anti-piracy laws is impossible
- simplify visa procedure for professionals
- reduce agricultural export subsidies

✂- -

3 Negotiate a trade position

In groups of three, negotiate a trilateral trade agreement between three nations. Each nation has a list of objectives depending on its level of development outlined below.

4 Describing commodities traded globally

In pairs, describe the graphs for your partner to make a rough sketch.

Student A

Price of fossil fuels and metals

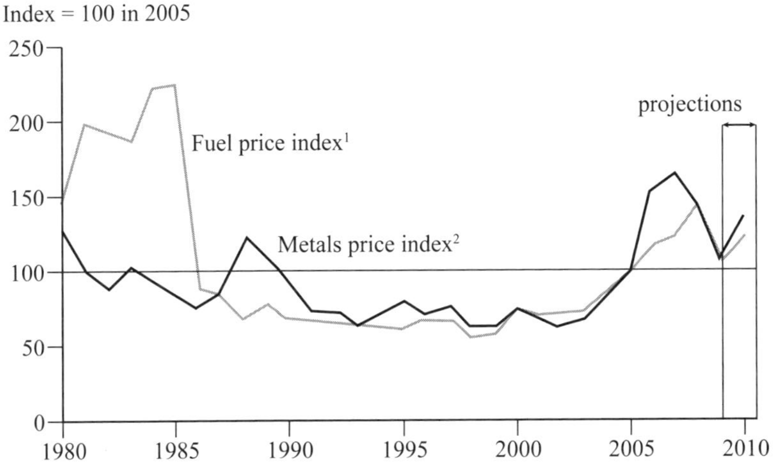

1 - Including crude oil (petroleum), natural gas and coal.
2 - Including copper, aluminum, iron ore, tin, nickel, zinc, lead and uranium.
Source: IMF, World Economic Outlook Database, October 2010.

Student B

Price of recyclable materials

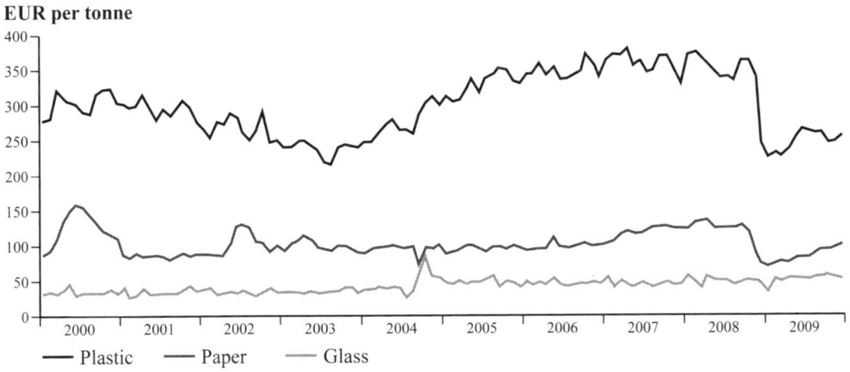

Source: Eurostat

Worksheet 13

Improve your knowledge of incentivising changes in environmental and social behaviour

Aims
- Develop an understanding of the pros and cons of green arguments.
- Use of language for contrast and persuasion.
- Raise awareness of town planning issues.

Tasks
- Find a word that contrasts with the word given.
- Discuss radical ways to influence and change environmental and social behaviour.
- Role play a government planning committee meeting to build a new town.

1 Lead-in

Discuss the following questions with a partner.

1 What are the origins of the green movement?
2 How widespread are green pressure groups and political parties in your country?
3 Barack Obama said 'the transition to clean energy has the potential to grow our economy and create millions of jobs – but only if we accelerate that transition'. Do you agree or disagree?
4 Is the idea of a sustainable solution to the world's environmental problems *pie in the sky*?
5 Do *actions speak louder than words* in encouraging a change in environmental behaviour?

2 Contrasting and persuasive language

Fill the gaps with an appropriate contrasting word. The first letter has been given to help you.

1 We are not dealing with a theory here; the ideas are entirely p_ _ _ _ _ _ _ _.
2 It is not safe to continue as we are; in fact it is extremely r_ _ _ _ for future generations.
3 I do not find green people democratic at all; they are all quite d_ _ _ _ _ _ _ _ _ _ in my opinion.
4 The decision was made by one person alone; it was not a c_ _ _ _ _ _ _ _ _ _ _ _ one.
5 No one can agree on the future; it is always extremely difficult to get c_ _ _ _ _ _ _ _.

3 Radical policies

With a partner, discuss which of the following green policies would be too radical to implement and why you think the policy's introduction would encounter resistance. All of these radical policies have been proposed or implemented in different countries.

- Use waste cooking oil to fuel vehicles.
- Have an electric vehicle only policy.
- Put solar panels on every house.
- Meter water and penalise for overuse.
- Introduce non-flush or 'dry' toilets.
- Encourage remote working from home.
- Have an individual bin for recyclable waste.
- Introduce parking charges near schools.
- Have bicycles which people hire instead of using public transport.

4 Planning for a sustainable new town

The population of your country is expected to grow by 20% within the next few years. You have decided to build a sustainable new town, in an area that is presently countryside, to meet this growth prediction.

1 **In small groups, role play a government planning committee meeting to discuss the following ideas. Come to a collaborative agreement on how to build the town at minimal cost to the treasury, and take into account environmental and social issues according to your view on the issue.**
   - **Housing:** affordable? environmentally friendly? private firms? smaller and larger homes?
   - **Transport:** build air links and road links? or rail links and tram links with fewer roads?
   - **Power generation:** a coal/gas fired or a nuclear power station? a plant to burn recycled material? a wind farm?
   - **Public services:** a park? schools? library? hospital? leisure centre? or private provision of these services?
   - **Waste disposal:** recycling? an incinerator? a land-fill rubbish dump?
   - **Employment:** sustainable small businesses? private retail or business parks? government building in the town?
   - **Internet access:** free Wi-Fi network across town? or private provision?
   - **Funding:** tax breaks? tax funded? joint public/private venture?

2 **Get together with learners from other groups and compare your plans for the new town. Do you think your plans are good examples of sustainable development?**

Worksheet 14

Improve your knowledge of work placement schemes

Aims
- Raise awareness of different types of work placement schemes.
- Exemplify some word partnerships with *work*.
- Raise awareness of the benefits and problems associated with work placement schemes.

Tasks
- Match words and phrases with *work* to their definitions.
- Discuss statements on the pros and cons of work placement schemes.
- Decide on a work placement scheme for yourself or a younger relative.

1 Lead-in

Discuss in pairs.

1 What is a work placement?
2 What is an internship? Do you get paid as an intern?
3 What is an apprenticeship? Do you get paid as an apprentice?
4 Have you ever participated in a work placement scheme?
5 Would you advise young people to take part in a work placement scheme?

2 Word partnerships with *work*

1 Match the following words and parts of words in the table with *work* to their definitions.

work ethic	skilful
work permit	something ordinary and not unusual
work–life balance	a person who works constantly and finds it difficult not to work
work-to-rule	the amount of work required during a particular period
work experience	an official document that allows you to work in a foreign country
workmanlike	industrial action where employees strictly follow contractual terms
workaday	describes a person who is disinclined to work
workable	a period of time spent with an employer to gain knowledge
workaholic	a moral belief that work is fundamentally a good thing
workload	a place in an office, especially a desk with a computer terminal
work station	describes a system or plan that can be used effectively
workshy	time spent at work versus time spent with family or on hobbies

2 What is *too much like hard work* used to describe?

3 What does the proverb *if a thing is worth doing, it is worth doing well* mean?

3 Statements from organisers of and participants in work schemes

1 The following statements are from former trainees, and companies who participated in work schemes. Decide who said them and whether they are positive or negative. Why/Why not?

1 'I at least got a reference, something that was previously lacking on my CV.'
2 'I was a general dogsbody and I was better off on welfare benefits.'
3 'The scheme gave our staff the chance to develop their mentoring and supervisory skills.'
4 'We did not discuss a personal development plan when we started.'
5 'My input was recognised and valued.'
6 'I felt I was still doing voluntary work even though I was paid travel and subsistence costs.'
7 'The scheme has allowed us to fill gaps in our staff profile.'
8 'I was able to get back into a structured routine, after being underemployed for so long.'

2 Are you in favour of work schemes? What advice would you give to people applying for a work scheme?

4 Choose an internship

The following are all examples of internships. In pairs, discuss the pros and cons of each and decide which one you would choose for yourself, a friend or a younger relative who was about to graduate from university and why.

Digital Marketing & Communications Assistant Internship

Location: Manchester, England

Salary: Travel and subsistence

Commitment: 3 days per week

Context: This role will focus on the charity's fundraising events that include giant cake-making events, fun runs, sponsored walks and many others. The aim of this role is to inspire people to fundraise for the charity using all digital channels available: our website, social networks, email, etc.

Retail Internship

Location: Nairobi, Kenya

Salary: Shared accommodation is provided, self-funded

Commitment: From 2 to 3 days a week for 3 months or more

Context: Internee(s) will take role of assistant to the shop manager and learn how to manage a shop, taking on responsibility for the shop's banking duties and understanding its finances.

Live, Work and Study in New York – 12-month internship scheme

Location: New York City, USA

Salary: Participants receive an allowance of $600 a month plus accommodation and medical insurance. Internee pays for a US work permit.

Commitment: Full-time

Sector(s): Accountancy, Banking, Investment, and Financial services

Context: Work placements are intensive and pressurised. Interns hit the ground running from day one and gain invaluable exposure to management practices and an insight into the financial sector.

DVD worksheets

How to use the *Business Advantage* DVD

In the Student's Book you will find a DVD. It is intended for viewing after every two units of the book. You can use the DVD in class in conjunction with the worksheets which follow or students can simply watch the different films in their own free time.

How to use the worksheets

The worksheets have been written by Jeremy Day and are designed to be used in class. Each worksheet includes pre-watching activities that help to check learners' understanding of the main ideas and prepare them for the topic.

While watching, students are asked to complete comprehension questions, which are then followed up by further vocabulary development and discussions that are designed to raise awareness, develop understanding and stimulate conversation around the key issues.

The format of each film

Each film consists of a documentary following a case study approach and focusing on a real company with interviews with key decision makers and employees of the organisation. The interviews are broken up into sections to give students the opportunity to reflect on what they have seen. At the end of each film there is also a brief discussion with students from the Cambridge Judge Business School looking at some of the key points that were focused on in the documentary.

The choice of organisations

All of the organisations featured on the DVD were chosen in order to complement the topics covered in the book. The use of an authentic case study approach was decided upon in order to expand on the theories covered in the book and to have a familiar format to the practice lessons.

The role of Cambridge Judge Business School

The students that you will see speaking at the end of each case study are all MBA students from the Cambridge Judge Business School. They come from a wide range of business and national backgrounds and their discussions will help your students see the perspectives of people from different cultural backgrounds and in turn this will help stimulate further discussion around the topics they have seen developed.

DVD contents

Student's Book	Section title	DVD title	Information on the organisation	Sections on the DVD
Units 1 and 2	International marketing	Market entry strategies with Broadcom	Broadcom is a global communications company focused on hardware and software to enable communications in handheld devices.	The challenges of entering new markets [0.00] What is 'near field communication' (NFC)? [1.12] Using NFC for 'mobile wallets' [2.01] Differentiating the product for different regions [2.56] Who does Broadcom target in order to establish NFC in new markets? [3.50] The challenges of entering new and unique regional markets [5.27] How does Broadcom set about expanding into a new region? [6.39] How typical are Broadcom's market entry strategies? [10.04]
Units 3 and 4	Competition and entrepreneurship	Entrepreneurship with the Old London Underground Company	The Old London Underground Company takes disused underground stations in London and makes them into venues, tourist attractions, and spaces for different businesses.	Transforming disused underground stations into profitable businesses [0.00] The plan [1.49] The finance [2.28] The people and the politics [3.09] Risk and planning [4.11] The team [5.49] The public reaction [6.43] The learning curve [7.07] What qualities do you think Ajit Chambers has that will make this business work? [7.54]
Units 5 and 6	Management and leadership	Crisis management with the Institute of Travel & Meetings	ITM is a group of buyers and suppliers from the travel industry who work together to influence and get the best out of the travel industry.	The role of the ITM [0.00] The ash cloud [2.25] ITM Phoenix – a crisis management support tool [5.24] How important is an organisation like the ITM, especially in a crisis? [7.46]
Units 7 and 8	Globalisation	International communication with the OECD	The OECD's mission is to promote policies that will improve the economic and social well-being of people around the world. It provides a forum in which governments can work together to share experiences and seek solutions to common problems.	Working in an international language [0.00] The languages of the OECD [1.13] The advantages for an organisation of using an international language [3.20] Miscommunication between speakers of an international language [4.15] The rise of a global language in business [5.27] Advice for organisations adopting an international language [6.54] The HR perspective on English as an international language [7.57] What do you think are the pros and cons of an international organisation using one language for its communication? [9.37]
Units 9 and 10	Design, technology and innovation	Design and innovation with Williams F1	Williams F1 is one of the world's leading Formula One motor racing teams and has a strong culture of technological innovation, particularly in aerodynamics and lightweight materials.	Technological innovation at Williams F1 [0.00] Hybrid systems technologies in Williams F1 cars [1.02] Where did the idea to develop hybrid systems come from? [2.25] Some elements of successful innovation [3.35] Applications of the technology outside of F1 [5.23] The Williams Technology Centre in Doha, Qatar [6.39] Some difficulties in technological innovation [8.11] Doing exceptional things all of the time [9.34] What can a company do to encourage innovation and foster a culture of 'doing exceptional things all of the time'? [10.49]
Units 11 and 12	Trade, finance and the economy	The economic environment with Gleadell Agriculture Ltd	Gleadell Agriculture is an international grain trading business and a large seller of seed and fertiliser to UK farmers.	What does Gleadell Agriculture Ltd do? [0.00] The effect of exchange rates [1.52] The effect of interest rates [3.04] The effect of taxation [4.41] Market influences [5.31] An unexpected cost [7.05] The future of the cereal production industry [8.30] What tools can a company use to deal with external factors that affect it financially? [9.14]
Units 13 and 14	21st-century enterprise	Focus on Cambridge Programme for Sustainability Leadership	CPSL is an organisation that focuses on helping businesses and governments worldwide to respond to the challenges of sustainability.	What the CPSL does [0.00] How do organisations benefit from being sustainable? [1.48] The role of the CPSL [2.44] What kind of organisations can make an impact? [3.57] Why participants came to the Climate Leadership Programme [5.04] Where are the best examples of sustainability in practice? [6.14] The role of the individual [7.18] What future challenges do business leaders face? [9.03] How important do you think sustainability is to companies and is this changing? [10.27]

DVD Worksheet 1: International marketing

Market entry strategies with Broadcom

Discuss

1 **You are going to watch an interview with Craig Ochikubo, Vice President and General Manager of Broadcom's Wireless and Personal Networking business. Before you watch, look at this list of words and phrases that Craig Ochikubo uses in the interview. What do you think Broadcom does? Discuss in small groups.**

the cloud	NFC (near field communications)
handset	Oyster card
hardware and software	passive credit cards
mass transit system	store convenience cards
mobile phones/cellphones	transportation ticketing
mobile wallet	

Part 1 (0.00–2.55): The challenges of entering new markets; What is 'near field communication' (NFC)?; Using NFC for 'mobile wallets'

2 **Watch Part 1 of the interview to check your predictions.**

3 **Are these statements true or false? Watch Part 1 again to check. Correct the false statements.**

1 Broadcom makes handheld devices such as mobile phones.
2 Broadcom focuses on infrastructure to connect people with 'the cloud', no matter where they are.
3 NFC is fairly new technology, but it is becoming much more important.
4 Broadcom developed the Oyster card system of credit cards.
5 A mobile wallet application can replace credit cards, store cards and tickets.
6 The biggest problem with mobile wallets is security.

Part 2 (2.56–6.38): Differentiating the product for different regions; Who does Broadcom target in order to establish NFC in new markets?; The challenges of entering new and unique regional markets

4 **Watch Part 2 to answer these questions. Make notes for each question.**

1 What example does Craig Ochikubo give of differentiating a product in different markets? What is not differentiated?
2 What three groups of people does Broadcom target? How does it try to appeal to each group?
3 What challenges does Craig Ochikubo mention?

Connecting everything®

5 **Make collocations by taking a word from the left and word from the right. Watch Part 2 again. What does Craig Ochikubo say about each phrase?**

to adhere broader continuous differentiated global revenue security	credentials ecosystem features standards stream support to a standard

Part 3 (6.39–10.03): How does Broadcom set about expanding into a new region?

6 **Watch Part 3. In what order does he mention the following topics?**

- Broadcom's functions in China
- Broadcom's marketing strategy
- Learning from customers
- Expanding the website
- Two types of translation
- Hiring people from the target country

7 **Watch Part 3 again. Make notes on what he says about each topic.**

Part 4 (10.04–11.29): How typical are Broadcom's market entry strategies?

8 **Discuss the question in groups. Then watch Andrey and Alejandra, two Judge students, discussing the question. Compare their ideas with yours. What three types of translation does Andrey mention? What does Alejandra mean by 'making that double pitch'?**

DVD Worksheet 1: International marketing

Market entry strategies with Broadcom

Background reading

Broadcom's website is www.broadcom.com. For an introduction to Near Field Communication (NFC), see www.nfc-forum.org/aboutnfc. It is also worth reading about contactless smart cards here: en.wikipedia.org/wiki/Contactless_smart_card.

1 Tell learners that all the words and phrases are used in the first part of the interview, and therefore that their guesses about Broadcom's work should include all of the words and phrases. Learners discuss the question in small groups and then share their ideas with the class. Avoid confirming or rejecting their ideas at this stage.

Answers

The cloud refers to cloud computing, i.e. the principle that computing is a service, not a product. Instead of buying software or memory storage, users access these through the Internet.
A *handset* is the part of a telephone that you hold.
Hardware refers to physical objects, especially in the context of IT (e.g. computers, monitors). Software refers to programs.
Mass transit systems include rail, bus and underground (metro/subway) networks.
A *mobile wallet* is an electronic device (or software program on a device such as a mobile phone) which replaces traditional items in a physical wallet such as cash, credit cards and tickets.
NFC (Near Field Communication) is a technology for smartphones, etc., which enables them to communicate with each other (and other devices) and share information over short distances. The technology has some similarities to systems such as Bluetooth and WiFi.
Oyster cards are e-ticketing cards used in London, for use on various forms of public transport.
A *passive credit card* is one that can be used simply by holding it near to an electronic reader. In the DVD, Craig Ochikubo refers to Oyster cards as a type of passive credit card. In fact, they are not credit cards, but credit-card sized contactless smart cards, which can be pre-loaded with payments.
A *store convenience card* is a card for use in a specific shop (or chain of shops), which can be pre-loaded with payments.

2 Play Part 1 for learners to find out what Broadcom does. They discuss their answers in pairs, using as many of the phrases from exercise 1 as possible. Discuss answers with the class.

Suggested answer

Broadcom focuses on hardware and software to enable communications between handheld devices (e.g. mobile phones, smartphones), home devices (e.g. digital television, set-top boxes) and the cloud. Broadcom uses NFC, which is used for mobile payment (e.g. the Oyster card system, which is like a passive credit card to do transportation ticketing) and mobile wallet type applications (replacing tickets for mass transit systems, store convenience cards, etc.) on handsets.

3 Learners discuss the statements in pairs and then watch Part 1 again to check. When you check the answers with the class, discuss the reasons for their answers.

Answers

1 False (It focuses on hardware and software inside mobile phones, but doesn't actually make the phones.)
2 True (*... from the cloud ... whether he's at home or moving around ...*)
3 True (*it's been around for about a half a dozen years, but it's really starting to gain a lot of traction ...*)
4 False (This is just an example of NFC technology – there is no suggestion that Broadcom developed it.)
5 True (*... combining all the functions that you have in your wallet ...*)
6 False (*It's much more secure than a traditional wallet.*)

4 Go through the questions with the class. Then play Part 2 for learners to make notes. They compare their notes in pairs and watch again if necessary before feeding back to the class.

Answers

1 Sometimes the transaction takes place *in a device that's removable from the phone*; other times the device is *permanently part of the phone*. The standard is not differentiated (*They'll adhere to the standard*) from one country to another.
2 Handset makers (so that they can make differentiated products); carriers (so they are financially motivated to include the technology onto as many devices as possible in order to make them attractive to customers); and consumers/users of the technology (so the devices work as part of a broader ecosystem and are compatible with each other).
3 Regionality/uniqueness of the different market segments: time zones, continuous support, and communication.

5 Learners work alone to make phrases and then watch again to make notes for each phrase. Discuss the answers with the class.

Answers

Different countries **adhere to the standard;** You can remove your **security credentials** from the phone; Broadcom drives **differentiated features** in order to appeal to the handset makers; When customers use the device, the carriers have a **revenue stream;** Broadcom creates a **broader ecosystem,** by putting NFC in handsets, digital TVs, etc.; There's a challenge of **continuous support;** Broadcom has tended to focus on **global standards** with the focus on making products that become regionalised.

6, 7 Play Part 3 for learners to put the topics in order and then again to make notes. They compare their notes in pairs and watch a second time if necessary before sharing their ideas with the class.

Answers

Learning from customers: spending time with that customer, being empathetic, understanding that culture.
Hiring staff from the target country: they hired Chinese national people in China, because they understood the customers, they had past business experience, and so were senior and very experienced.
Two types of translation: from a language perspective (what they're literally asking for), and translating the cultural innuendo (what their true needs are).
Broadcom's functions in China: engineering; sales and support; design centre
Expanding the website: now includes multiple languages, not just English, and regional web pages. They are continually refining communication and marketing of new products.
Broadcom's marketing strategy: understanding where the technology is (i.e. where it's going to go from a volume perspective); developing the features to add value to the end customer; customising for each region.

8 Put learners in small groups to discuss the question (*How typical are Broadcom's market entry strategies?*), using their own experiences, and then share their ideas with the class. Then play Part 4 for learners to compare it with their ideas and answer the two additional questions. Finally, discuss the additional questions with the class.

Answers

Andrey mentions translating the language, the customer needs and the business model. For Broadcom, the double pitch involves selling to the cellphone companies as well as the end user.

Entrepreneurship with the Old London Underground Company

Discuss

1 **Look at this extract from an interview with Ajit Chambers, the Founder and CEO of the Old London Underground Company. Then discuss the questions in small groups.**

I started this company two years ago to make use of the underground portfolio of space in London, specifically using the disused underground stations as flagship sites.

1. How do you think he plans to use the underground spaces?
2. How much progress do you think he made in two years?

Part 1 (0.00–2.27): Transforming disused underground stations into profitable businesses; The plan

2 **Watch Part 1 of the interview to check your predictions.**

3 **Watch Part 1 again to answer these questions.**

1. What is Ajit Chambers' background?
2. How did he come up with the idea?
3. How will the site survive its first years?
4. How is a *proof of concept* different from a *pilot*?

Part 2 (2.28–5.48): The finance; The people and the politics; Risk and planning

4 **Each of the walls in Ajit Chambers' office has a different theme. In pairs, discuss what you think he puts on the following walls:**

- the financial wall
- the political wall
- the inspirational wall
- the card wall
- the quote wall.

Then watch Part 2 to check your ideas and make notes about the five walls.

5 **Match these words and phrases from the interview to the different walls. Write F (financial wall), P (political wall), I (inspirational wall), C (card wall) or Q (quote wall) for each word or phrase. Then watch again to check.**

delivering revenue ______	plan, prepare and research ______
to fund something ______	a pledge ______
luck and fate ______	push yourself ______
magical ______	risk ______
objectives ______	stakeholders ______
paperwork ______	time lines of discussions ______
personal relationships ______	wins and successes ______
projects and new businesses ______	

6 **In pairs, discuss these quotes from Part 2. Do you agree with them?**

- *Don't let risk stop you doing things. Risk is why it's a winner.*
- *I change fear into excitement.*
- *As much as you push yourself, the world around you will be able to cope with it.*
- *It would be more of a risk if we didn't do this kind of stuff.*
- *Things happen because you've prepared yourself to be in the right place at the right time.*

Part 3 (5.49–7.53): The team; The public reaction; The learning curve

7 **Predict whether these statements are true or false. Then watch Part 3 to check.**

1. Ajit Chambers believes his team should be much better than other teams.
2. He believes it is important to have a range of different mindsets in the team.
3. He has borrowed money from many small investors.
4. His team is quick because they don't waste time writing and waiting for emails.
5. The public reaction was very positive from the beginning of the project.
6. Ajit Chambers regrets that the project has taken so long.
7. He learned a lot by starting with a very large project.

Part 4 (7.54–9.08): What qualities do you think Ajit Chambers has that will make this business work?

8 **Discuss the question in groups. What is the most important skill he needs? What adjectives would you use to describe his character? Then watch Alejandra and Warren discussing the question. Compare their ideas with yours.**

DVD Worksheet 2: Competition and entrepreneurship

Entrepreneurship with the Old London Underground Company

Background reading

The website of the Old London Underground Company (www.theoldlondonundergroundcompany.com) includes an interesting blog about the company's progress and a virtual tour of one of the company's venues. There are also some good background videos at www.youtube.com/oldunderground.

1 Discuss with the class what they know (or can guess) about what is below the ground in London (e.g. the oldest underground railway in the world; the second largest underground network in the world). Discuss also why some stations might be disused (**Answer:** some were closed because they were making significant losses). Learners then discuss the quote and the questions in small groups. Check with the class, but avoid confirming or rejecting their suggestions at this stage.

2 Play Part 1 for learners to check their answers. They discuss in pairs before feeding back to the class. You could discuss what learners think Ajit Chambers means by *venues* (i.e. places to watch concerts and other live events) and *tourist adventures* (i.e. places to explore and experience, to keep the historic value of these sites alive).

Answers
1 The disused stations will be used as venues (e.g. for concerts) or tourist adventures. There will also be restaurants and bars.
2 The first site opened in May. There are plans for the next six stations, and 26 more underground spaces have been identified.

3 Learners discuss the questions in pairs and then watch Part 1 again to check. Then discuss the answers with the class.

Answers
1 He worked in banking, from the trade floor to looking after the chief executives of some of the biggest banks in the world.
2 He was looking for more adventurous things to do in London rather than visiting the same places.
3 He has built the business around an equity fund. Each site has three different businesses that go into the sites (restaurants and bars, venues and tourist attractions). The first and second of these should generate income streams to fund development of the third.
4 A pilot is about checking if something will work. Ajit Chambers claims that they don't need to see whether the proof of concept can work; they're going to make it work.

4 Learners discuss their predictions in pairs and share their ideas with the class. Point out that Ajit Chambers doesn't give each wall a name, but refers to what it does. Then play Part 2 for learners to make notes on the five walls. They compare notes in pairs and then feed back to the class.

Suggested answer
The financial wall shows the methodology. It includes a £10 million pledge from their first investor after four days, and the structure of three businesses that will support each other.
The political wall includes all the political stakeholders in the UK that are of benefit to projects and new business.
The inspirational wall shows time lines of discussions, showing how long it takes for different people to respond and whether two people know each other; some objectives; some wins and successes.
The card wall is *very magical and strange*. The cards are useful when he's talking on the phone; they show the meetings and personal relationships that he has built up and has spent time finding out what they can deliver to the project.
The quote wall contains quotes from MPs and politicians on the state of the UK economy and the financial times.

5 Learners work in pairs to try to remember the context of each phrase. You may need to check the meaning of some of the words (e.g. *fate* = the idea that our lives are subject to powers beyond our control; *a pledge* = a promise, usually to give money). Then play Part 2 for learners to complete the task. They check in pairs and feed back to the class.

Answers
F: to fund something; paperwork; a pledge
P: projects and new businesses; stakeholders
I: objectives; time lines of discussions; wins and successes
C: delivering revenue; magical; personal relationships
Q: luck and fate; risk; plan, prepare and research; push yourself

6 Learners discuss the quotes in pairs, and then share their ideas with the class. You may need to check some words (e.g. *to cope*).

7 Learners work in pairs to predict whether the statements are true or false. Play Part 3 for them to check. They compare their answers in pairs and watch a second time if necessary. When you check with the class, discuss the reasons for their answers.

Answers
1 True (He wants them to be not just the best, but significantly better than the rest.)
2 False (Everyone must have the same mindset.)
3 False (He has tried to fund it completely himself until he can find a *proper investor*, i.e. one that can invest a large amount in the project.)
4 True (*... we do it in minutes, hours and days, not emails, and weeks and months ...*)
5 False (People thought it was a *crazy* idea.)
6 False (It has taken longer than necessary, but he doesn't regret it because it has been a good learning experience.)
7 True (*... I couldn't have without the experience that I've got from this one. That is why it is very important to have done a huge project first ...*)

8 Learners work in small groups to discuss the question (*What qualities do you think Ajit Chambers has that will make this business work?*) plus the two supplementary questions. Play Part 4 once or twice for learners to answer the questions. They discuss their answers in pairs before feeding back to the class.

Suggested answer
Warren suggests that Ajit Chambers' banking background means that he's used to working very long hours and getting a deal done; his job is not to build the bars and restaurants but purely to find the financing.
Warren says that the primary skill he needs is selling.
Warren describes Ajit Chambers as extremely *confident*, *enthusiastic*, *pumped* and *ready* to go.

Crisis management with the Institute of Travel & Meetings

ITM

INSTITUTE OF TRAVEL & MEETINGS

Discuss

1 **The Institute of Travel & Meetings (ITM) is a group of buyers and suppliers from the travel industry. You are going to watch an interview with Jamie Hindhaugh (ITM Chairman) and Paul Tilstone (CEO). Before you watch, work in groups to discuss these questions.**

1 Is there a person or team in your organisation who is responsible for business travel?
2 What do you think this role involves (either in your own organisation or other organisations)?
3 Why is business travel an important consideration for many large companies?
4 What are some examples of buyers and suppliers from the travel industry?
5 How do you think the ITM helps these people?

Part 1 (0.00–2.24): The role of the ITM

2 **Watch Part 1 of the interview and make notes about what Jamie Hindhaugh and Paul Tilstone say about questions 2–5 above.**

3 **Watch Part 1 again and answer the following questions.**

1 What is the relationship between the chairman, the board, the secretariat and the members?
2 What, according to Paul Tilstone, are the biggest expenses of a business? Do you think this is an accurate analysis?
3 What example of a *white paper* does Paul Tilstone give?
4 How much has the organisation grown?

Part 2 (2.25–5.23): The ash cloud

4 **Look at the map. It shows the extent of the ash cloud that resulted from eruptions of Eyjafjallajökull, a volcano in Iceland, in April 2010. Discuss these questions in groups. Then watch Part 2 of the interview to check your predictions.**

1 Do you remember the disruption to air traffic that followed these eruptions? If not, what do you think was the effect on international travel?
2 Paul Tilstone thinks this was a *useful* crisis for the ITM. What do you think he means?
3 What three roles do you think the ITM played during this crisis?

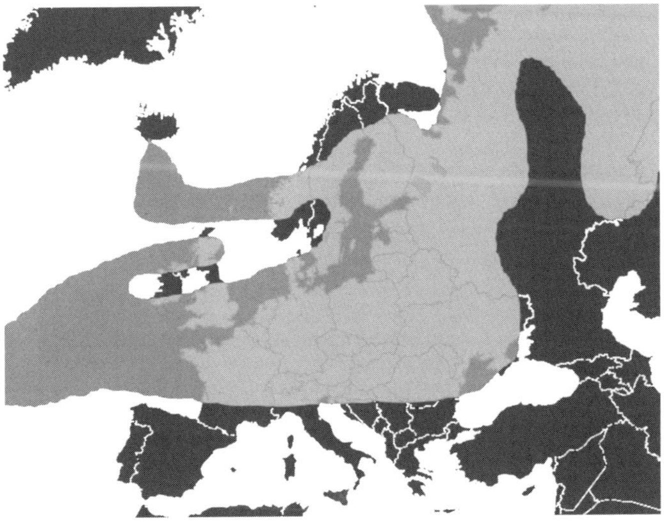

5 **Watch Part 2 again. Summarise what Paul Tilstone and Jamie Hindhaugh say about the ash cloud and its consequences, using the following words and phrases.**

fatalities	to cripple something
to track something	to conflict with
to rip something apart	denied passenger boarding
corporates	to get something sorted
down	to charter a flight
to stay put	lines of communication

Part 3 (5.24–7.45): ITM Phoenix – a crisis management support tool

6 **Watch Part 3 of the interview and answer these questions.**

1 In what ways is ITM Phoenix like a hub and a filter?
2 How did the ash cloud crisis influence ITM Phoenix?
3 How do buyers and suppliers interact with ITM Phoenix?
4 Why don't companies tend to focus much on business continuity?
5 How does ITM Phoenix enable people to influence their CEOs and their boards?

Part 4 (7.46–9.54): How important is an organisation like the ITM, especially in a crisis?

7 **Discuss the question in groups. Focus first on the general importance of organisations like the ITM, and then on their value during a crisis. Then watch Kira and Kate, two Judge students, discussing the question. Compare their ideas with yours.**

DVD Worksheet 3: Management and leadership

Crisis management with the Institute of Travel & Meetings

Background reading

The ITM website (http://www.itm.org.uk/) contains a useful 'About us' section. The ITM Phoenix service is for members only, but you can still find out about it on the website (phoenix.itm.org.uk/).

1 Learners discuss the questions in groups. After a few minutes, open up the discussion to include the whole class.

2 Play Part 1 for learners to make notes on the four questions. They compare their notes in pairs before feeding back to the class.

Answers

2 People in this role manage business travel on behalf of their organisations, ensure that travellers know how to behave, and facilitate their travel experience. They make sure that all of the business executives within the company travel safely, effectively, and at the lowest cost on behalf of their businesses.
3 Business travel is somewhere between the second and fourth biggest expense of a business, and it has massive implications for businesses because there are so many people on the road who are seen as ambassadors of their company.
4 **Buyers:** Somebody from AstraZeneca or PricewaterhouseCoopers (either somebody in procurement or a dedicated travel manager). **Suppliers:** British Airways, Virgin Atlantic or Hilton hotel group.
5 ITM's members work together to get the best out of the travel industry and to influence the travel industry. The ITM provides guidance in the form of white papers on industry issues.

3 Learners discuss the questions in pairs to see how much they remember. You may need to check they understand the words from the Background notes below. Play Part 1 again for them to check, and then discuss the answers with the class, especially the second part of question 2 which will depend on learners' own experience.

Background notes

A *secretariat* is the group of people responsible for the management of an organisation, typically an international or political one.
A *white paper* is a formal report. Governments use white papers to present and discuss a planned new law. Companies and other organisations also use white papers to present their own research and analyses, often as a form of marketing.

Answers

1 The **chairman** manages a **board**, which sets the strategy for ITM and empowers the **secretariat** to deliver what the **members** need.
2 Facilities and land rental, staffing and business travel
3 How to balance the reduction in cost and carbon emissions from a traveller's journey with the requirement to provide duty of care, etc.
4 It grew from three people in 1956 to 1,500 people in 2011.

4 Discuss the map briefly with the class to make sure everyone understands what 'the ash cloud' was. Refer learners to the photos of the cloud in Part 2, from 2.30–2.52, and the meteorological path of the cloud from 2.50–2.60. If learners don't know anything about the story, you could discuss question 1 with the whole class. Learners then discuss the questions in pairs to predict the answers. Play Part 2 again for them to check and then discuss the answers with the class.

Answers

1 Many flights were cancelled, so people were stranded away from home. There was not enough information. Paul Tilstone suggests that the phone lines and the mobile phone systems were also *down* (out of service).
2 It caused no fatalities, so the industry could digest and analyse what was happening within companies without worrying about people in danger.
3 They tried to filter conflicting information into what was actually valid for their members; they spoke to government to demand guidance on denied passenger boarding legislation; they tried to help *corporates* (businesspeople) to work together to share information and transportation.

5 Go through the list of words and phrases to check everyone understands them. Learners then work in pairs to remember what was said using each word or phrase. Play Part 2 again for them to check and to take notes. They discuss again in pairs before feeding back to the class.

Suggested answers

The crisis caused no **fatalities.** Companies were trying to **track** their travellers. The ITM could **rip apart** all of the processes and the traveller tracking systems to help **corporates** to do their job better in the future. An ash cloud causes serious problems when the phone lines and the mobile phone systems are **down.** The best course of action may be to **stay put.** The volcanic ash cloud **crippled** everybody. The guidance given by airlines was **conflicting** with government, agencies and news channels. **Denied passenger boarding** means if you turn up for a flight and it's cancelled, you are entitled to some compensation. Paul Tilstone told the Department for Transport to **get** the problem **sorted.** If a company has people stranded in Guatemala, they may need to **charter a flight.** The ITM are encouraging members to open up their **lines of communication** with each other.

6 Go through the questions with the class to make sure everyone understands words like *hub*, *filter* and *business continuity*. Then play Part 3 for learners to answer the questions. They discuss their answers in pairs and watch a second time if necessary before checking with the class.

Answers

1 It's a central hub because information comes in from many sources (airlines, hotel groups, car companies, etc.). The information is then filtered to one place (so that users need only access one source for all their information).
2 The idea came while they were trying to deal with that crisis and particularly the lack of information about what was going on.
3 Suppliers update it; there are forums for buyers to talk to each other.
4 Business continuity is often managed in separate departments from safety and security, and it's not an exciting subject.
5 They can show their CEOs what other organisations are doing, how their policies are structured and what they are learning from intelligence.

7 Learners work in pairs to discuss the question (*How important is an organisation like the ITM, especially in a crisis?*), including both the general importance of organisations like the ITM, and then on their value during a crisis. After a few minutes, open up the discussion to include the whole class. Then play Part 4 for learners to compare what Kira and Kate say with their own ideas. Discuss the Judge students' ideas with the class.

Suggested answers

General importance: Provide the best deal for travel and hotels very quickly and efficiently. Companies can *leave things up to the expert* and get the best deal.
Value during a crisis: You can find out what's going on, which airports can be used, etc.; you can share information and gain knowledge of best practices to make better decisions.

International communication with the OECD

Discuss

1 **In small groups, discuss what you know (or can guess) about the OECD. Think about the following.**

- its purpose
- its members
- its headquarters
- its official language(s)

Part 1 (0.00–3.19): Working in an international language; The languages of the OECD

2 **Watch Part 1 of an interview with Makoto Miyasako, the Head of Strategy and Business Analysis Group at the OECD. Answer these questions.**

1 How did he learn English?
2 What does he say about communicating in his own first language, Japanese?
3 Where does the OECD have its offices? How is the work divided between these locations?
4 Which organisation uses more English, the UN (with its six official languages) or the OECD (with two)? Why?
5 How is French used in the OECD?

3 **Look back at the answers to exercise 2. In pairs, discuss which answers you find surprising.**

Part 2 (3.20–6.53): The advantages for an organisation of using an international language; Miscommunication between speakers of an international language; The rise of a global language in business

4 **Watch Part 2 of the interview and answer the questions.**

1 What does Makoto Miyasako say about the main advantage of using an international language? What does he say about the transaction cost?
2 Does he believe language proficiency is the main cause of miscommunications?
3 How do OECD employees minimise the risk of misunderstandings?
4 Why are some Japanese companies choosing English as the office language?

5 **Discuss these questions in pairs.**

1 Could your organisation use English as an office language? Should it?
2 What do you think Makoto Miyasako means by the phrase *implicit mutual understanding*?
3 Could you have a formal/informal policy to try to minimise miscommunication? Should you?

Part 3 (6.54–9.36): Advice for organisations adopting an international language; The HR perspective on English as an international language

6 **Watch Part 3 and make notes on the following topics.**

1 Two key things to consider before adopting an international language
2 The benefits of learning English and French for potential OECD employees
3 The need to have advanced language skills

Part 4 (9.37–11.05): What do you think are the pros and cons of an international organisation using one language for its communication?

7 **Discuss the question in groups. Think about the pros and cons for both the organisation as a whole and for individual employees. Then watch Andrey, a Judge student, discussing the same question. Compare his ideas with yours.**

8 **Discuss these questions in groups, using examples from your own experience.**

1 Andrey mentions the problem with relying on translators. What would you say are the advantages and disadvantages of using translators?
2 Andrey suggests there is a problem of an unfair advantage for native English speakers. Do you agree that this is (a) a problem and (b) unfair? Are there any situations when being a native English speaker can be a disadvantage?

DVD Worksheet 4: Globalisation

International communication with the OECD

Background reading

The OECD's website (www.oecd.org) contains a very useful 'About' section, including a video explaining its purpose and history. The 'Careers' page, which you can navigate to from the home page, also contains information relevant to this DVD lesson.

1 Check briefly with the class if they have heard of the OECD. If not, it is better to run the discussion activity as a whole class. If learners are able to discuss in groups, go through the answers with the class at the end. Discuss any surprises with the class.

Answers

The OECD's stated purpose (its mission) is to promote policies that will improve the economic and social well-being of people around the world. The OECD provides a forum in which governments can work together to share experiences and seek solutions to common problems.

It has 34 members, mainly from western and central Europe but also including other rich countries such as the USA, Japan and Australia (see the OECD website for a list of members).

Its headquarters is in Paris, France.

There are two official languages: English and French.

2 Go through the questions with the class. Then play Part 1 for learners to answer the questions. They discuss their answers in pairs before feeding back to the class.

Answers

1 He didn't speak any English until age 22, and then moved to the USA to learn at graduate school.
2 He would find it difficult to work in Japan using Japanese as a means of communication in a business setting.
3 Around 98% of the employees are located at the headquarters in Paris, where almost all of the work takes place. They also have very small offices in Washington, Mexico, Berlin and Tokyo.
4 The UN, where English is predominant. In the OECD, there is more of a balance between English and French.
5 Mainly for internal communications. Only about 10% of the OECD's output (e.g. policy analysis or recommendations) is produced in French.

3 Learners discuss the answers in pairs, bringing in their own experiences (for questions 1 and 2) and those of their organisations (questions 3, 4 and 5).

4 Go through the questions with the class. Check everyone understands the meaning of *transaction cost* (see Background note below) and elicit what the transaction cost of using an international language might be. Play Part 2 for learners to answer the questions. Learners discuss the answers in pairs and watch again if necessary before feeding back to the class.

Background note

A ***transaction cost*** is the cost you must pay in order to participate in a market. For example, you often have to pay a broker's fee if you want to buy and sell shares. Makoto Miyasako uses the phrase (in fact he says *transactional cost*) in a more abstract way, to refer to the cost (in time, effort and money) of enabling multinational groups to communicate in English. This cost might be borne mainly by the organisation (e.g. by employing translators or providing language classes) or the employees (e.g. if the employer insists upon a certain language level for all new recruits).

Answers

1 It is a cost saving. The transaction(al) cost is shifted to each individual employee, who has the responsibility to master the language.
2 No. He believes it is sometimes a cause, but sometimes not. For example, native speakers also have misunderstandings when communicating with each other.
3 They need to be a bit more flexible and make sure there is no misunderstanding.
4 The companies are trying to go beyond (i.e. to expand beyond their current focus/markets) and need to do as the international players are doing, which means working in English. They also want to send a clear message to its employees about the company's changing direction.

5 Learners discuss the questions in pairs. After a few minutes, open up the discussion to include the whole class.

Suggested answer

Implicit mutual understanding is when people understand each other by 'reading between the lines' and working out what the other person means from context, body language, tone of voice, etc.

6 Learners watch Part 3 to make notes. They compare their notes in pairs and watch a second time if necessary. Then discuss the answers with the class.

Suggested answers

1 It needs to align with the strategic direction; the organisation needs to spend enough resource and time to make the transition successful.
2 English is really essential to work at the OECD. French is useful, especially for living in France.
3 The majority of the OECD's work requires a high language level (e.g. publishing papers and books, coordinating and leading discussions at government committee level).

7 Learners work in groups to discuss the question (*What do you think are the pros and cons of an international organisation using one language for its communication?*). Make sure they consider the pros and cons for both the organisation and for employees. Then play Part 4 for learners to compare their ideas with those of Andrey. Finally, discuss the question with the class.

8 Learners discuss the questions in groups. After a few minutes, open up the discussion to include the whole class.

Suggested answers

1 Advantages: no need to learn foreign languages; reduced risk of miscommunications. Disadvantages: expensive and difficult to organise (especially for less common languages); sometimes causes miscommunication due to the translator's overconfidence or lack of subject knowledge; inconvenient for speakers – breaks the flow of fluent speech; possible issues of confidentiality.
2 Native English speakers often find it difficult to grade their language, i.e. speak simply, slowly and clearly enough to be understood, a skill which non-native speakers may find easier. Being a native English speaker may be a disadvantage if working in a company where the majority have a different first language because of the risk of making assumptions that turn out not to be correct.

Design and innovation with Williams F1

Discuss

1 What do you think the following words and phrases mean in the context of designing a Formula 1 (F1) car?

acceleration	kinetic energy
aerodynamics	hybrid system
battery management systems	lightweight materials
to brake	lithium-ion cells
to corner	power-to-weight ratio
down force	to spin
drag	storage device
to exit a corner	vacuum
flywheel	

Part 1 (0.00–2.24): Technological innovation at Williams F1; Hybrid systems technologies in Williams F1 cars

2 **Watch Part 1 of an interview with Alex Burns, the CEO of Williams F1, to answer these questions. The words and phrases in exercise 1 will help you.**

1 What are Williams F1's two core engineering capabilities? Why are they important?

2 What two storage technologies does Alex Burns describe? What does he say about them?

3 How is Williams F1 different from other teams, in terms of technological innovation?

Part 2 (2.25–5.22): Where did the idea to develop hybrid systems come from?; Some elements of successful innovation

3 **Watch Part 2 of the interview. In what order does Alex Burns explain the following? What does he say about each?**

a a can-do mentality
b changes to the regulations
c creative engineers
d developing the flywheel in-house

4 **Match the beginnings on the left with the endings on the right to make phrases from Part 2.**

it was deemed …	… do with that
we took …	… equity in the company
its sole …	… of creativity
you have to make …	… of possibilities
how are we going to rise …	… to be giving an advantage
there's a whole world …	… to this challenge
we need a spark …	… purpose

Part 3 (5.23–8.10): Applications of the technology outside of F1; The Williams Technology Centre in Doha, Qatar

5 **Watch Part 3 and answer these questions.**

1 In what two ways is a Formula 1 car like a city bus?

2 What two key areas are being developed in the technology centre in Qatar? In what fields outside of F1 will they be useful?

Part 4 (8.11–10.48): Some difficulties in technological innovation; Doing exceptional things all of the time

6 **Predict the answers to these questions. Then watch Part 4 to check your predictions.**

1 Why is it difficult to recruit good engineers for Formula 1 racing? Think of at least two reasons.

2 What are the main sources of income for Williams F1 and other F1 teams like Ferrari?

3 Why can't Williams F1 afford to stand still? Think of at least two reasons.

Part 5 (10.49–12.46): What can a company do to encourage innovation and foster a culture of 'doing exceptional things all of the time'?

7 **Discuss the question in groups. Then watch Roberto and Warren, two Judge students, discussing the same question. Compare their ideas with yours.**

8 **Discuss these questions in groups, using examples from your own experience.**

1 What do you think of Roberto's idea of tolerating or even rewarding failure?

2 Do you agree with Warren that banks and governments can't, and shouldn't, be especially innovative?

Design and innovation with Williams F1

Background reading

The Williams F1 website (www.williamsf1.com) contains an interesting history of the company (www.williamsf1.com/team) and an interactive virtual tour of the headquarters (www.williamsf1.com/team/hq-tour). The section on CSR (www.williamsf1.com/spark) is most relevant to this DVD lesson.

1 Learners discuss the question in small groups. Tell them that the words and phrases all appear in the DVD. Encourage them to guess the meaning of any words and phrases they don't know. With weaker classes, go through the list with the class first to elicit their meanings before the group discussions. After the discussions, discuss the question and any remaining vocabulary problems with the class, as this will help them to understand the DVD. However, avoid explaining how a *flywheel* works as a storage device until after exercise 2.

Suggested answers

Acceleration **means increasing speed. The opposite is** ***braking*****.**
Aerodynamics **is the study of the motion of air, typically over a moving object (e.g. a plane, a car). Engineers study aerodynamics in order to reduce** ***drag*****, i.e. the force that slows the moving object down as a result of friction between the surface and the air. They also aim to increase** ***down force*****, i.e. the opposite of the force that causes aeroplane wings to lift.**
A ***battery management system*** **(BMS) is an electronic device that monitors and modifies the performance of a battery.**
A major challenge for F1 cars is to ***corner*** **(go round a corner), without losing too much speed or stability. They then accelerate rapidly when they exit (leave) a corner.**
A ***hybrid system*** **uses a combination of two or more systems. For example, some hybrid cars are powered by both a petrol engine and an electric motor.**
A ***flywheel*** **is a type of** ***storage device*** **which is used to store energy. In F1 cars, applying the brakes causes the wheel to** ***spin*** **(go round) faster. The flywheel is in a** ***vacuum*****, i.e. there is no air around it to slow it down. This spinning wheel can then be used to help the car accelerate.**
Kinetic energy **is the energy of an object because of its motion. This is what makes a vehicle travel forwards even after the brakes are applied.**
The ***lightweight materials*** **used for F1 cars are mainly carbon-fibre composites.**
Lithium-ion cells **are commonly used as rechargeable batteries in consumer devices such as mobile phones.**
A car's ***power-to-weight*** **ratio is calculated by dividing its horsepower by its weight.**

2 Go through the questions with the class to elicit some possible answers. Then play Part 1. Learners compare their answers in pairs and watch again if necessary before checking with the class. You could use this opportunity to go through the list of words and phrases in exercise 1 again, to discuss what Alex Burns said about each of them.

Answers

1 Aerodynamics: the cars need high down force and low drag, so they can corner very quickly, brake very suddenly and achieve high top speeds with a low drag.
Lightweight materials: they need a good power-to-weight ratio to get the maximum acceleration.
2 A flywheel: it converts electrical energy into kinetic energy, which can be reused by slowing the flywheel down and generating electricity from it.
Battery technology: advanced lithium-ion cells, put together into complex battery systems. They have developed battery management systems to keep the battery in good condition. The battery stores electrical energy between braking and accelerating.
3 They have done the most to develop hybrid systems in-house.

3 Elicit what a *can-do mentality* is (a desire to overcome problems rather than admit defeat). Then play Part 2 twice for learners to put the headings in order and make notes. They compare their answers in pairs before feeding back to the class.

Answers

The order is b, d, a, c
b Formula 1 needed to be more relevant to the challenges that people face, so they phrased regulations that would allow the storage and re-use of energy on the cars for the first time.
d They couldn't find an electric motor that was small enough, or light enough for their requirements, so they developed their own. They identified the flywheel technology called 'Magnetic loaded composite flywheel technology'. They took equity in the company that was developing it.
a Whatever the problem, they can find a solution. When they are at a race track on the other side of the world with a small group of people, they have to make do with what they've got.
c In some areas, e.g. safety, they want engineers who are not especially creative. But they need creative engineers in areas like aerodynamics or where there are new regulations. The spark of creativity is difficult to identify during the recruitment phase.

4 Learners work alone to make phrases. Play Part 2 again to check. Make sure everyone understands the meaning of each phrase and discuss what was said about each one.

Answers

It was deemed to be giving an advantage; we took equity in the company; its sole purpose; you have to make do with that; how are we going to rise to this challenge; there's a whole world of possibilities; we need a spark of creativity

5 Elicit possible answers to the questions. Then play Part 3 once or twice. Learners discuss their answers in pairs. Then go through the answers with the class. You may need to check everyone understands the meaning of *CSR* (Corporate Social Responsibility).

Answers

1 They both stop and start frequently. A bus at relatively low speeds has the same kinetic energy as a Formula 1 car at high speed.
2 The large flywheel (to be used in metro systems to capture and reuse the energy of the metro trains) and simulator technology (to train the drivers in taxi fleets or bus fleets to be safer on the roads).

6 Learners work in pairs to predict answers to the questions. Elicit some ideas from the class and write them on the board. Then play Part 4 for learners to compare the answers with the answers on the board. Discuss the answers with the class.

Answers

1 There is a skill shortage in the UK market at the moment; they task their engineers with doing what others would think is impossible.
2 They sell sponsorship on the cars and get money from the centre of the sport (e.g. from the TV rights for the sport).
3 In terms of engineering (because of the intensity of the competition – any team that stops developing will slip backwards through the grid) and as a business (because they must keep looking for new challenges and new markets).

7 Learners work in small groups to discuss the question (*What can a company do to encourage innovation and foster a culture of 'doing exceptional things all of the time'?*). After a few minutes, open up the discussion to include the whole class. Then play Part 5 for learners to compare the Judge students' ideas with their own. Finally, discuss any differences with the class.

8 Learners discuss the questions in small groups and then feed back to the class.

DVD Worksheet 6: Trade, finance and the economy

The economic environment with Gleadell Agriculture Ltd

Discuss

1 Gleadell Agriculture is an international grain trading business. You are going to watch an interview with David Sheppard, Gleadell Agriculture's Managing Director. Before you watch, try to match the products on the left with the purposes/customers on the right.

1 They sell seed and fertiliser ...	**a** ... for beer production.
2 They sell wheat ...	**b** ... to UK farmers.
3 They sell malting barley ...	**c** ... for human consumption and for feed.
4 They sell oil-seed rape ...	**d** ... for feed production, biscuit manufacture and flour milling.
5 They sell pulses ...	**e** ... for use in vegetable oils and biodiesel production.

Part 1 (0.00–1.51): What does Gleadell Agriculture Ltd do?

2 Watch Part 1 of the interview (0.00–1.51) to check your answers to exercise 1. Where does it sell the products from exercise 1? What else does Gleadell Agriculture sell?

Part 2 (1.52–5.30): The effect of exchange rates; The effect of interest rates; The effect of taxation

3 Check that you understand all the words and phrases in bold. Then watch Part 2 to correct the factual mistake in each sentence.

1. There are two important **spreads** and exchange rates for Gleadell Agriculture's day-to-day business.
2. Gleadell Agriculture **moves its whole position into** euros every night, however **far forward** the exchange rate is.
3. Gleadell Agriculture sometimes has problems with access to cash, but only when the company makes a loss.
4. Gleadell Agriculture's share price **fluctuates enormously**.
5. They sometimes ask the bank to put pressure on difficult shareholders.
6. They lend money to farmers at an **exorbitant** interest rate.
7. They **lobby** their shareholders for cash inputs for investment in **infrastructure and plant**.

Part 3 (5.31–9.13): Market influences; An unexpected cost; The future of the cereal production industry

4 In Part 3, David Sheppard tells four stories: Story A (*A falling-out with a supermarket*); Story B (*A new loaf*); Story C (*Mycotoxin testing*); and Story D (*World population growth*). Watch Part 3. For questions 1–5 below, write A, B, C or D.

1. Which stories involve a positive impact on Gleadell Agriculture? ______ ______
2. Which stories involve trying to persuade farmers? ______ ______
3. Which stories demonstrate changes in customer demands? ______ ______
4. Which stories involve a lot of investment for Gleadell Agriculture? ______ ______
5. Which stories represent a serious risk for Gleadell Agriculture? ______ ______

5 Discuss these questions in small groups. Describe any similar stories from your own experiences.

1. Why do you think the bread manufacturer fell out with the supermarket? What does this story tell you about the relationship between supermarkets and suppliers?
2. Why do you think it was so important to have 100% British wheat, even though it produced low yields? What does this story tell you about the role of marketing?
3. How does David Sheppard feel about the new mycotoxin tests? Why do you think they were introduced?
4. Why do you think demand is growing exponentially? What do you think is fuelling this growth?

Part 4 (9.14–9.58): What tools can a company use to deal with external factors that affect it financially?

6 Discuss the question in groups. Then watch Andrey S and Andrey T, two Judge students, discussing the question. Compare their ideas with yours.

7 The Judge students mention the possible use of *options*, *futures* and *credit default swaps* (CDSs). How suitable would these be for Gleadell Agriculture's day-to-day business?

DVD Worksheet 6: Trade, finance and the economy

The economic environment with Gleadell Agriculture Ltd

Background reading

Gleadell Agriculture's website (www.gleadell.co.uk) contains useful information on the company's products.

1 Discuss with the class what they think a grain trading business is. You could check they understand the agriculture words in the table (*seed, fertiliser, wheat, malting barley, pulse, feed, oil-seed rape, milling, biodiesel*). Learners then work in pairs to try to match the products with the purposes/customers. Discuss the answers with the class, but avoid confirming or rejecting their suggestions.

2 Play Part 1 for learners to check the answers and answer the two additional questions. They check quickly in pairs before feeding back to the class.

Answers

1 b 2 d 3 a 4 e 5 c

They sell the products throughout the EU and into the Mediterranean and occasionally further afield. They also sell advisory services to farmers.

3 Go through the sentences with the class to elicit the meanings of the words and phrases in bold. Then play Part 2 for learners to identify the factual mistakes. They discuss their answers in pairs and watch a second time if necessary before feeding back to the class.

Background notes

A *spread* is the difference between the exchange rates for buying a currency and the rate for selling the same currency.

David Sheppard says they *move their whole position into pounds every night, however far forward the exchange rate*. He means the company transfers all of its money into pounds, no matter how expensive the pound is at the time.

If something such as a price *fluctuates enormously*, it goes up and down a lot quickly and frequently.

If a price is *exorbitant*, it is unreasonably expensive.

If you *lobby* somebody, you try hard to build a relationship with them in order to influence them. Many businesses try to lobby politicians.

In this context, *plant* means buildings, especially factories and warehouses, and the machines, etc., inside those buildings; *infrastructure* means other things which are constructed to support those buildings and connect them with the outside world, e.g. internal roads, electricity lines, water supply, etc.

Answers

1 **There are <u>three</u> important rates and spreads (sterling/euro, sterling/dollar and euro/dollar).**
2 **It moves its position into <u>pounds</u>.**
3 **The company doesn't make losses. Its problems with access to cash are connected with <u>movements of grain stocks</u>.**
4 **The <u>amount of physical stock</u> (i.e. grain) they hold fluctuates. (The word *stock* can also be used to refer to shares, but this is not what David Sheppard means.)**
5 **They ask <u>shareholders</u> to put pressure on their <u>bank</u>.**
6 **It's a <u>competitive</u> rate, but not exorbitant.**
7 **They lobby <u>the government</u> for <u>changes in corporation tax levels</u>. They never ask their shareholders for money for investment.**

4 Discuss the titles of the four stories with the class to elicit what they might involve. Then play Part 3 once or twice for learners to answer the questions. They discuss their answers in pairs before feeding back.

Background note

A *mycotoxin* is a poisonous substance (a toxin) produced by a mould (a type of fungus). The term usually refers to toxins from moulds on crops, which can enter the food chain. See http://www.knowmycotoxins.com for background on mycotoxin regulations.

Answers

1 B, D 2 B, C 3 B, D 4 B, C 5 A, C

5 Learners discuss the questions in small groups. You may need to check they understand the meaning of *yield*. After a few minutes, open up the discussion to include the whole class.

Background notes

In agriculture, *yield* is a measure of productivity: the amount of crop harvested relative to either the land area or the number of seeds planted. Yield is also used in finance, as a measure of the return from a security (e.g. a share).

Suggested answers

1 **Perhaps the supermarket demanded a lower price, and the bread manufacturer refused. It suggests that supermarkets have enormous power over suppliers, especially if the number of supermarket chains is small.**
2 **Hovis is an old British company, and uses its heritage as part of its marketing. Many people prefer to buy products from their own countries, in order to support employment, etc. The story shows how marketing can drive new product development. It also shows how a more expensive, lower quality product can still be preferable.**
3 **He hints that they were unnecessary (*the wheat was the same as we'd been eating and using for the last 25 years, and the UK is a low risk area anyway, and we have had no reports of any illness outbreaks or anything caused by this*). The introduction of this test may have resulted from a media-driven health scare. Alternatively, there may have been an international commitment to introduce such a test (e.g. an EU-wide directive).**
4 **The population is growing, and it is getting richer. These changes are accelerating because increased demand fuels new supply (e.g. more supermarkets), which in turn fuels more demand.**

6 Learners work in small groups to discuss the question (*What tools can a company use to deal with external factors that affect it financially?*). Discuss the answers with the class and then play Part 4 for learners to check what the Judge students suggested.

Background notes

***Options* and *futures* are financial instruments that allow the buyer to engage in a future financial transaction for a pre-arranged price. With *options*, the buyer has the choice as to whether to engage in the transaction. With *futures*, both parties are obliged to engage in the transaction. They are both used to manage risk by transferring that risk to the other party.**

***Credit default swaps* (CDSs) are agreements to pay the holder of the CDS if there is a default on a specific loan. They work in much the same way as insurance policies, in that they act as a third party protection for someone buying bonds in the company.**

7 Discuss the question with the class, making sure everyone understands the three terms. Note that in the DVD, Andrey uses a shorter form, *credit swaps*.

Suggested answer

These would make Gleadell Agriculture's currency trading more sophisticated, but also much more complicated. It would need to employ specialists to conduct this new type of trading. These tools are useful for managing risk of wild currency fluctuations, but the currencies that Gleadell uses are relatively stable, so perhaps the benefits would be limited.

Focus on CPSL

UNIVERSITY OF CAMBRIDGE
PROGRAMME FOR
SUSTAINABILITY LEADERSHIP

Discuss

1 Discuss these questions in small groups.

1 Polly Courtice is Director of the University of Cambridge Programme for Sustainability Leadership. What do you think the programme involves?
2 What sort of person would attend such a programme? Why do participants enjoy the programme?

Part 1 (0.00–1.47): What the CPSL does

2 Watch Part 1 of an interview with Polly Courtice and Aris Vrettos, the CPSL's Programme Development Director. What do they say about the questions in exercise 1?

3 What do Polly Courtice and Aris Vrettos mean by the phrases in bold?

1 **senior practitioners** from business and the policy community
2 the solutions that we can **bring to bear**
3 to talk very **compellingly**
4 the highlight of the programme is **the journey**
5 a great **faculty**
6 it is something that **stays with them** forever

Part 2 (1.48–5.03): How do organisations benefit from being sustainable?; The role of the CPSL; What kind of organisations can make an impact?

4 Watch Part 2 and answer these questions.

1 What are the barriers that stop companies from 'doing the right thing'?
2 What is the tension that many companies are wrestling with?
3 What two systems does the programme look at?
4 What examples does Polly Courtice give of what is happening in societies around the world?
5 What three examples of companies does she mention? What do they have in common?
6 What does Polly Courtice mean by a *collaboratory* process?
7 Why doesn't the programme focus on persuading companies that there is a problem?
8 What does Polly Courtice say about processes and activities that are *inherently unsustainable*?

Part 3 (5.04–7.17): Why participants came to the Climate Leadership Programme; Where are the best examples of sustainability in practice?

5 Watch Part 3. Match the eight people with their opinions, based on what they say in Part 3.

1 Tanya Spencer 2 Daniela Torres 3 Paul Crewe 4 Wing Hong Chan 5 Richard Pamenter 6 Polly Courtice 7 Paul Polman 8 Jeff Immelt	**a** It's interesting to discuss what's the same and what's not. **b** We are going to make more money but do less damage. **c** We're all wrestling with the same problems. **d** We can discuss our experiences and ideas freely. **e** I wanted to take away some good, practical advice. **f** Environmentally friendly products can be good for business. **g** It is easier to identify sustainable actions rather than sustainable companies. **h** I was keen to meet people and build relationships.

Part 4 (7.18–10.26): The role of the individual; What future challenges do business leaders face?

6 Predict what Polly Courtice will say about the following topics. Then watch Part 4 to check your predictions. Take notes for each topic.

1 the relative impact on the environment of individuals and companies
2 paradoxes and trade-offs
3 'choice editing'
4 'the three pillars of sustainability'
5 technological solutions

Part 5 (10.27–11.53): How important do you think sustainability is to companies and is this changing?

7 Discuss the questions in groups. Then watch Kate and Roberto, two Judge students, discussing the questions. Compare their ideas with yours. What do they say about consumers and shareholders?

DVD Worksheet 7 21st-century enterprise

Focus on CPSL

Background reading
The CPSL website (www.cpsl.cam.ac.uk/) includes an introduction to the topic of sustainability leadership (www.cpsl.cam.ac.uk/Resources/What-is-Sustainability-Leadership.aspx). There is also a detailed report on the state of sustainability leadership available at www.cpsl.cam.ac.uk/Resources/State-of-Sustainability-Leadership.aspx.

1 Learners discuss the questions in small groups. You may need to check they understand the meaning of *sustainability* (the situation where your actions cause little or no damage to the environment and therefore can continue for a long time). Discuss the questions with the class, but avoid confirming or rejecting their ideas.

2 Play Part 1 for learners to make notes on the questions in exercise 1. They check in pairs before feeding back to the class.

Answers
1 The programme lasts three and a half days and focuses on helping leaders in business and government all around the world understand the challenges of sustainability and work out how to respond to them. They look at the practical challenges and the solutions through interactive games, iPads, climate change games and debates.
2 Senior practitioners from business and the policy community. They love it because it's very challenging and the experience stays with them forever.

3 Learners discuss the phrases in pairs. You could play Part 1 a second time if necessary. Then discuss the answers with the class.

Answers
1 Important people; governments and organisations which influence government policies
2 apply influence to achieve a particular result
3 persuasively, in a way that makes people listen and believe them
4 the learning process
5 group of academic staff (e.g. lecturers) specialising in a particular subject
6 they will never forget it

4 Learners discuss the questions in pairs to predict possible answers. You may need to check the meaning of *inherently unsustainable* in question 8 (i.e. their nature means they cannot be sustained). Then play Part 2 for learners to check their predictions. They discuss their answers in pairs and watch a second time if necessary before feeding back to the class.

Answers
1 Doing the right thing may not increase their access to capital, because the investment community don't always appreciate what the companies are trying to do.
2 The tension between long-term value creation and short-term profit.
3 social and ecological
4 She refers to the employment and well-being of young people, women or communities whose land is seen by more developed economies as a natural resource rather than where they make their living.
5 GE, Unilever and Wal-Mart which are among the largest companies in the world.
6 Helping companies to engage with the other players in their supply chain and other stakeholders to think about really what changes are realistic.
7 Most of the companies already know there is a problem.
8 They need to change.

5 Before learners do the exercise, point out that some of the eight people appear in the DVD, while others' opinions are simply mentioned by Polly Courtice. Make sure learners understand that sentences a–h are not spoken by the people but sum up the opinions they hold. Play Part 3 for learners to complete the task and then feed back to the class. You could discuss the opinions of Paul Polman and Jeff Immelt with the class, to find out whether learners think they are realistic.

Background note
If you *bounce ideas around*, you discuss them freely, as in a brainstorming meeting. The idea is that even bad ideas may help someone come up with a good idea.

Answers
1 e 2 c 3 h 4 a 5 d 6 g 7 b 8 f

6 Learners work in pairs to predict what Polly Courtice will say. Then play the clip for them to take notes. They compare notes in pairs and watch a second time if necessary before feeding back to the class.

Suggested answers
1 Companies can help to scale up individual actions either by engaging with their consumers or simply by providing products and services which allow individuals to live in a more environmentally friendly way.
2 As individuals, we are compromised all the time through our actions. For example, flying is bad for the environment, but by flying, Polly Courtice can talk to people to help them live more sustainably.
3 Not offering things to customers that are inherently damaging.
4 They are not equivalents. The economy is a subset of human society, and human society a subset of the biosphere.
5 Technology is part of the solution but not the whole solution.

7 Learners work in groups to discuss the two-part question (*How important do you think sustainability is to companies and is this changing?*). Then play Part 5 for learners to compare the Judge students' ideas with their own and to answer the additional question (*What do they say about consumers and shareholders?*). Discuss the additional question with the class, including whether learners agree with the opinions.

Answer
In the future, shareholders and customers will demand sustainability.